A S

New Guinea

John Dademo Waiko

Melbourne

OXFORD UNIVERSITY PRESS

OXFORD UNIVERSITY PRESS AUSTRALIA

Oxford   New York   Toronto
Delhi   Bombay   Calcutta   Madras   Karachi
Kuala Lumpur   Singapore   Hong Kong   Tokyo
Nairobi   Dar es Salaam   Cape Town
Melbourne   Auckland   Madrid
and associated companies in
Berlin   Ibadan

OXFORD is a trade mark of Oxford University Press

National Library of Australia
Cataloguing-in-Publication data:

Waiko, John.
  A short history of Papua New Guinea.

  Bibliography.
  Includes index.
  ISBN 0 19 553164 7.

  1. Papua New Guinea — History. I. Title.

995.3

Edited by Kerry Herbstreit
Designed by Sarn Potter
Typeset by Syarikat Seng Teik Sdn. Bhd., Malaysia.
Printed by Kyodo Printing Co (S'pore) Pte Ltd.
Published by Oxford University Press,
253 Normanby Road, South Melbourne, Australia

Contents

List of illustrations and sources

List of tables

List of maps

Preface

How can I put fifty thousand years of my people's history into fifty thousand words? Such a task is, of course, not possible and I have not attempted to do so in this *Short History of Papua New Guinea*. One reason why it is difficult is that, for almost all of this time, there is so little evidence upon which to base our history. All Melanesian societies prior to the nineteenth century were pre-literate and there was only sporadic European and Asian contact prior to the colonisation of the region by the British and the German colonial powers in the late nineteenth century.

Relatively little but very important archaeological work has been done in northern Melanesia. It is from the archaeological record that we know that people were living in Papua New Guinea fifty thousand years ago and that evidence of cultivation in the highlands nine thousand years ago means that our ancestors were probably amongst the earliest gardeners in the world. There has also been very little but important work done in recording the oral tradition of our people. Important as this is, people's memories of times past are limited to approximately ten generations. Thus, we must depend upon limited archeological and oral history sources to try to reconstruct all but the very recent past. Hence the account in this book relies heavily upon the written record after European contact. Thus this is basically a history of little more than the last one hundred of these fifty thousand years of human occupation.

What is clear is that prior to European conquest the region that we now call Papua New Guinea was inhabited by people who lived in small, fragmented, isolated and self-sufficient societies. It is also clear that these societies were connected by a complex web of trading relationships by which ideas and values as well as goods were exchanged across considerable distances. At the time of first European contact and in the subsequent period under review, these societies differed substantially. The most evident difference is perhaps the seven hundred languages spoken by the peoples of this region. However, they also had in common many features of social structure, a shared view of the relationship between man and the physical environment, and many other common values. The characteristics which these societies had in common enhanced the creation of the sovereign state of Papua New Guinea in 1975 and made it possible for the people of the nation to recognise and build upon their common interests in the decade after political independence.

I do not, of course, deny that there is frequently a conflict between regional and national interests but I am confident that these differences can be solved in the future as they have been in the past. Like elsewhere there are problems of violence and the difficulty of providing services such as education and health to keep pace with population growth. However, I would like to remind readers that, by world standards, Papua New Guinea is still a relatively stable, democratic, Christian, and sovereign state. There was no social group of beggars in the past, nor do Papua New Guineans starve nowadays in the rural villages or even on the urban streets. This is largely because of the continuing strength of the subsistence sector which has direct access to its customary land that provides the basis for social stability throughout the nation. I have faith and confidence that my people will continue to accept and treasure their cultural diversity, tolerate their differences and pursue their common interests to strengthen the national unity of the sovereign and independent state of Papua New Guinea in the years ahead.

John Dademo Waiko
Port Moresby
1992

Acknowledgements

This book is a by-product of the committee formed in 1984 under my chairmanship, with R. L. Namaliu, then Foreign Affairs Minister and later Prime Minister from July 1988 to July 1992, as Patron to organise the commemoration of British and German colonial settlement in 1884. I would like to thank particularly Alan Butler and Clive Moore for their substantial contributions towards the initial stages of this project.

For the sources in this account of Papua New Guinea's history I have relied heavily on the materials used in the National History course at the University of Papua New Guinea. These materials were prepared by Bill Gammage, Les Groube, Clive Moore, Wellington Opeba, Isabel Wallace, and myself.

In addition I have used material from the following: Bob Connolly and Robin Anderson, *First Contact: New Guinea's Highlanders Encounter the Outside World*; Donald Denoon, 'Changes in Rural Settlement and Marketing Co-operatives' in the *Papua New Guinea Atlas*; Ian Downs, *The Australian Trusteeship: Papua New Guinea 1945 to 1975*; Stewart Firth, *New Guinea Under Germans*; James Griffin, Hank Nelson, Stewart Firth, *Papua New Guinea: a Political History*; Ken Inglis, *The History of Melanesia*; Les Johnson, *Colonial Sunset*; David King and Stephen Ranck (eds), *Papua New Guinea Atlas: a nation in transition*; Basil Shaw, 'Yokio Shibata: a man of inspiration' and Waiko, J., 'World War II and Oral History in PNG', both in White, G. (ed.), *Remembering the Pacific War*, Occasional Paper, Center for Pacific Studies; Susan Simons and Hugh Stevenson, *Luk Luk Gen, Look Again: Contemporary Art from Papua New Guinea*; S. F. Smalley, *Contemporary Art of Papua New Guinea*; Ian Willis, *Lae: Village and City* and various contributors to the *Encyclopaedia of Papua New Guinea*. I have also used material by Donald Denoon, James Griffin, David Hegarty, Stephen Pokawin, Yaau Saffu and Ted Wolfers in the *Journal of Australian Politics and History* from 1975 to 1988.

I have used the following theses: Klaus Neumann, Not the Way It Really Was: constructing the Tolai past; Kirsty Powell,

The First Papua New Guinean Playwrights and Their Plays, MA thesis; Andrew Chalk, The King's Reward: the Australian army's execution of Papua New Guinean 'natives', 1942–1945, BA Honours thesis; Mel Togolo, Land, Mining and Redistribution: Panguna and Ok Tedi, MA thesis; Patrick Silata, Oral History and Historical Archeology of the Pacific War on the Huon Peninsula, Morobe Province, BA Honours thesis.

In addition I have relied upon personal communication from the following: Michael Hess on the labour movement; Stephen Pokawin on community government in Manus; Tony Power on the contrast between traditional land groups and the modern state; Naihuo Ahai on the social impact of the Bougainville crisis; the late Charles Valentine on social movements; Jack Golson, Wally Ambrose, Mathew Spriggs and Jo Mangi at the Australian National University for information in the field of pre-history in Papua New Guinea.

I am very grateful to all these people and while I have relied upon their specialised knowledge I accept full responsibility for any errors of fact or interpretation which might have crept into the text.

I have also much appreciated the willing and patient support of Mary Koupa, Seia Drahas, Rose Bauwai, Scholastica Mandoni and Elizabeth Morove who typed the manuscript. I also wish to thank Ann Turner without whose editorial assistance, constant support, and encouragement this book might have not been completed.

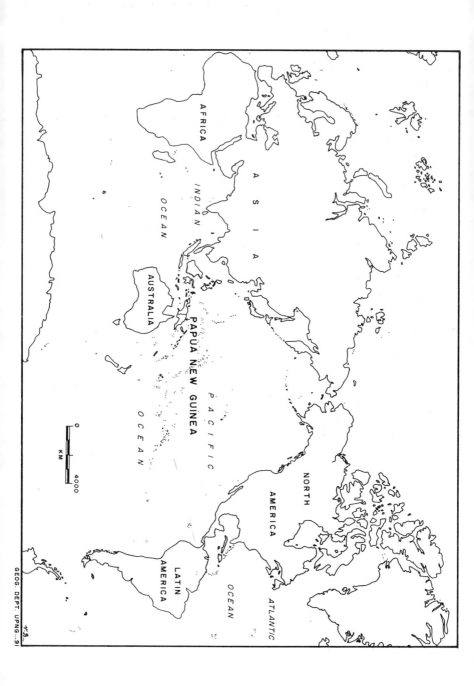

AFRICA

A S I A

INDIAN

OCEAN

AUSTRALIA

PAPUA NEW GUINEA

PACIFIC

OCEAN

NORTH

AMERICA

LATIN

AMERICA

ATLANTIC

OCEAN

0

KM

4000

1

From the Stone Age to the Steel Age

I have come from 50 000 years
So they think.
Others say I was born on 16 September, 1975.
Let my arrows fly another 50 000 years.

Kumalau Tawali, 1984.
[From a mural at the University of
Papua New Guinea]

The words of the Papua New Guinean poet Kumalau Tawali express well the feelings of many of us. Historians tell us that there is good evidence that humans have lived here for about fifty thousand years. Yet to most people, Papua New Guinea was born at independence seventeen years ago. Many of us can remember the sixteenth of September 1975, but how can we even begin to imagine a time fifty thousand years ago?

A picture of the kind of land these earliest peoples inhabited and the way in which their societies developed is gradually being pieced together by scholars from a wide range of disciplines — geology and geography, biology and botany, archeology and linguistics.

The story begins to take shape about five million years ago, that is, relatively recently in geological time, when land buckled to create the central mountain chain which forms the spine of the main island of present-day Papua New Guinea. These mountains and the mountains on a number of smaller adjacent islands were volcanic and some of these volcanoes are still active. Volcanic activity and the erosion of land caused by the high rainfall helped to form a rugged broken terrain with many pockets of rich soil in the interior of the main island. High rainfall and erosion also resulted in large rivers such as the Sepik and Fly carrying heavy loads of silt which established areas of rich soil on the coastal plains. These complex geological changes and volcanic activity have brought about rich deposits of copper, gold and oil in the main island of Papua New Guinea and a number of the smaller adjacent islands. Because of climatic and other factors, heavy vegetation and favourable conditions for agriculture occurred in many parts of the country.

The earliest evidence of human occupation in Papua New Guinea comes from the Huon Peninsula on the north coast of the main island between 40 000 and 45 000 years Before Present (BP). However, most scholars believe that it is likely that this date will be pushed back to at least 50 000 years BP very soon. Significant studies are being done in Papua New Guinea and currently-agreed dates and ideas about patterns of development are frequently overtaken by new discoveries and the introduction of new dating techniques. Current evidence of early settlement in the islands is 32 000 years BP and comes from New Ireland, and 28 000 years BP in the North Solomons. Evidence of first human settlement in the mountainous interior of the main island, the Highlands, is 30 000 years BP. However, as has been indicated, investigation is continuing in these and other areas of the country and it is generally accepted that there will be changes to these dates.

It is believed that these first settlers came from South East Asia and that they came in small numbers, involuntarily, as it is thought that their watercraft, probably solid logs and bamboo rafts, were too primitive for them to have considered a deliberate crossing.

In all areas so far investigated these earliest inhabitants were hunters, fishers, and gatherers of wild plants. It is not known which of the important food plants and animals in Papua New Guinea were available to these people, and which were later introduced from outside Melanesia. Important food plants at the time of European contact included sago palm, taro, yams,

Physical map of Papua New Guinea

GEOG. DEPT. UPNG. 91

cassava, sweet potato, breadfruit, coconuts, bananas and green leafy vegetables. Few of these were likely to have been available to the earliest inhabitants and were certainly not available in their present form. Important non-plant food at the time of European contact included marsupials such as cuscus and wallabies, reptiles like snakes and crocodiles, animals including pigs and dogs, fish, birds such as chickens, and insects. Some of these are thought to have been in the country at the time of first human settlement; others such as chickens, pigs and dogs are known to have been introduced by man.

The first evidence of gardening comes from the way in which the people established systems to manage water. In particular, it is of interest how the swamps were drained to bring water to grow crops at Kuk, near Mount Hagen in the Western Highlands about 9000 BP. If this evidence is accurate, and it is now generally accepted by most scholars, it seems likely that these highland people were amongst the first gardeners in the world.

It is not known what language or languages were spoken by the earliest inhabitants. However, at the time of European contact about 700 languages were spoken in Papua New Guinea. Linguists have divided these languages into two groups — Austronesian (AN) and Non-Austronesian (NAN). The term Non-Austronesian was given to these languages when linguists believed that they were unrelated; however, it is now believed that they probably belong to one language group which may have been spoken by the earliest settlers. There are about 200 AN languages spoken by later migrants, who arrived probably about 10 000 BP, and about 500 NAN languages spoken in Papua New Guinea. Austronesian languages are spoken in many parts of the coast of the main island, the islands in the south east, the North Solomons and the Bismarck Archipelago. Non-Austronesian languages are spoken throughout most of the main island.

The physical isolation of the many thousands of small-scale societies which our ancestors founded, and the extraordinary number of languages, made communication amongst groups difficult. However, the people managed to establish complex and substantial trade links amongst a great number of groups and over very considerable distances. Like a spider's web, the trade routes bound together the highlands with the coast, and the coast with the smaller islands. Obsidian, a glass-like volcanic rock used for tools and weapons, pottery, shells, birds of paradise feathers, stone axe blades and food were important items of trade. Some of these trading relationships, such as exchanges involving obsidian and pottery, were operating 3000 years ago over long distances both by land and sea, and there is evidence of shells reaching the highlands as long as 10 000 years ago.

Evidence also exists of trade in obsidian and pottery between the islands of present-day Papua New Guinea and places as far west as south-east Asia and as far east as New Caledonia. Trade in bronze, which was possibly exchanged for obsidian, appears to have occurred at least 4000 years ago. All these trade links and the complex exchange network systems made the present-day Papua New Guinean's ancestors some of the first traders and seafarers on earth.

The scattered small-scale societies which existed prior to Asian and European contact evolved slowly over thousands of years. Attempts to describe these societies have inevitably been distorted because our view of the past is derived only from the records to which we have access. Because the indigenous people of present-day Papua New Guinea lived in societies without writing, we are dependent for our knowledge of these societies almost entirely upon archaeological evidence, the written observations of first-contact Europeans, and the people's oral history. Like all peoples without writing, Papua New Guineans had extensive oral accounts of their past. Some of these traditions have been collected, but mostly by Europeans with limited understanding of the societies in which they were working. Readers of these records must realise that they are often flavoured by the cultural misunderstanding of the societies by Europeans, and are, of course, limited to the peoples with whom the European writers happened to come into contact. Errors have inevitably arisen when these writers have tried to generalise the social ideas relating to human origins based upon records of particular societies.

The following outline of the nature of Papua New Guinea society prior to the arrival of foreigners is restricted, except

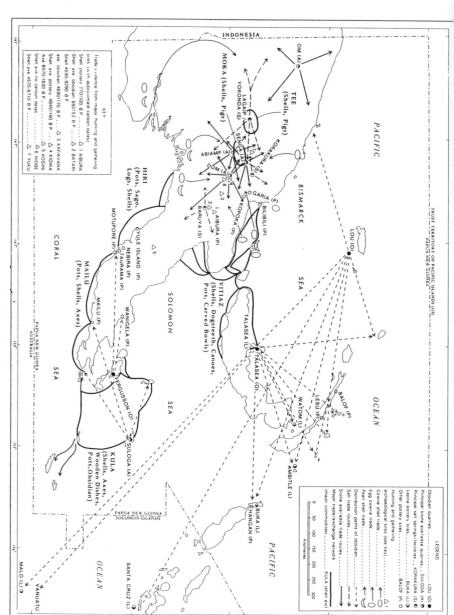

Traditional trade

where otherwise indicated, to those features which many of these societies appear to have had in common. Thus, for almost every statement made, an exception can be found in the physically and culturally fragmented pattern of societies which have joined to form our independent state of Papua New Guinea. While the past tense is used to describe these societies, many of these characteristics continue in present-day Papua New Guinea. The extent to which traditional Melanesian society has changed since the arrival of Asians and Europeans will be considered in later chapters.

Most people lived in permanent settlements that had to accommodate physical conditions which ranged from coastal plains and swamps to 4500 metres in the rugged and more densely populated mountains in the interior of the main island and a consequent wide range of climatic conditions. Styles of housing and dress, modes of transport, and tools and weapons were mainly dependent upon the local availability of materials. Complex social relationships and ceremonial practices reflected the relationship of the people to the physical environment and to the history of their societies. However, although most societies knew little of the world beyond their immediate neighbour's territory, their cultures, both material and social, were influenced by products and ideas derived from intricate trade networks which extended in some cases for many hundreds of kilometres. The differences in the physical environment in which these societies developed made it necessary to establish these trade networks in order to obtain some basic needs such as stone for tools, and food. That the people of present-day Papua New Guinea have so many characteristics in common can be partly explained by the existence of these trading networks which led to the exchange of ideas and attitudes as well as goods.

At the time of European contact, trading relationships included the exchange of cooking pots for sago between the Motu people near Port Moresby and villagers in the Gulf of Papua several hundred kilometres away; the *Kula* trade cycle amongst the islands of the south east which involved the exchange of pottery, stone and food as well as ceremonial shells; the exchange of pigs, axeheads, tree oil and salt particularly amongst highland societies and the exchange of axeheads for cowrie shells between the highlands and the coast, and fish for vegetables between coastal and inland people in many parts of the country. Most trade was conducted by barter, however shell money became important amongst the Tolai people in the Gazelle Peninsula. In some cases exchange took place immediately, but in others settlement of the debt could take many years and trade links frequently had ceremonial and social as well as economic purposes. Trading relationships had, in many cases, been gradually built up over thousands of years. Some examples include the elaborate *tee* exchange of pigs and other valuables among the present-day Engans, *moka*-making in the Wahgi Valley by the Melpa near present Mount Hagen and the *mok ink* in the Mendi region of the present Southern Highlands.

One of the basic features of the societies was that the smallest social unit was the family consisting of father, mother, and children. Each family had its extended families within a group of clans. The membership of each clan was based on kinship through blood, marriage, or adoption. Each family and relatives owned land and had direct access to hunting and fishing grounds; all natural resources were owned by the group. Apart from the trading relationships previously mentioned, each small economic unit was self-sufficient.

Early settlers cleared the bush with stone axes or adzes and prepared the ground with digging sticks. House design varied considerably depending upon materials available locally or those which could be acquired by trade. In some villages houses were arranged in rows; in others in a circle. In some regions houses included wooden beds and mat or bark cloth bed coverings. Materials and goods were transported by hand, often using poles or string bags, or by raft or canoe. In many regions baskets plaited from leaves or fibre were used for transport and storage. Dishes for food storage, preparation and serving were made from wood, bamboo or gourds. Unglazed clay pots, fired on an open fire, were used for cooking and serving food. Where pots were available food could be boiled, steamed or baked. Food was roasted on an open fire or, in some areas, baked in a sealed pit with hot stones. Bows and arrows, spears and clubs were used for warfare and hunting. The people wore little or no clothing though most societies had some form of covering for the pubic parts of adults of both sexes. Hoods of bark, bark cloth or leaves were sometimes used to provide protection against the weather. Personal ornamentation on ceremonial occasions was common to all societies. Materials used for ornamental head-dresses, armbands, legbands and necklaces included shells, feathers, fur, teeth, bones, bamboo and vegetable fibre, leaves and flowers.

In most societies among the NAN speakers, authority resided with a leader known as a 'big man' who had achieved his position through personal ability and not through inheritance. A man who rose to the position of 'big man' usually earned his status as a result of his physical strength and endurance, industriousness, organising ability, skills as an orator, and material wealth. He was a man regarded by his peers as performing most capably in social, political, economic, and ceremonial activities. A 'big man' did not exercise authority by command but by setting an example with his personal guidance and influence. His role was to initiate and facilitate activities seen to be beneficial to the group and lead members of the group to resolve issues by discussion and compromise. One way in which the 'big man' exercised influence was by periodically distributing to all members of the group food, in particular pigs, which had been produced by his wives from gardens which he had prepared. An important responsibility of a 'big man' was negotiating relationships with neighbouring groups. While in some areas the 'big man' was seen as a peacemaker between his clan and neighbouring groups, in most parts of the country warfare was common and the 'big man' was also a powerful warrior and skillful manipulator.

Exceptions to the 'big man' system occurred in relatively few societies which operated under hierarchical chieftainship systems in which the leader or chief was placed at the top of the social ladder with other chiefs of lesser status below him. This chiefly system occurred in some coastal communities amongst people who are thought to have arrived about 10 000 years ago and are often Austronesian speakers. For instance, in the Trobriand Islands the people were divided into two clans, each headed by hereditary chiefs who had inherited their titles from their fathers. In other societies such as Manus, chieftainship could be inherited only if the recipient was considered by his peers to be sufficiently worthy. Thus, some societies combined aspects of both chiefly and 'big man' authority systems.

This is a simplified version of a much more complex picture. For example, the status of women was different in the 'big man' and chiefly societies. In some societies, notably the Massims and societies in the Gazelle Peninsula, people traced their ancestors through female rather than male lines. Instead of customary rights over land being passed down from father to son as was the case in the 'big man' communities, there evolved a 'big woman' situation where women held the rights to land and these rights were transmitted from mother to daughter.

Underlying all these complexities lay the fact that social relations within the group were usually based on kinship, that is, closely related people who lived and worked together. In most societies men and women slept separately. Many villages had a men's house to which women were denied access. Women and children usually slept in separate smaller houses. Boys were normally initiated into the men's group and joined the men's house at puberty.

Disputes traditionally concerned land and women. Women captured in warfare were often forced to marry into the victor's tribe. However, women were also exchanged to cement alliances between one community and another. Payback or revenge killing for those killed in war, or thought to have been killed by enemy sorcerers, was common.

Most villages had a cleared area in which song and dance festivals usually associated with rituals, feasts, and the exchange of gifts were held. Songs and dances were handed down from one generation to the next or composed for special events such as initiations, funerals, or to prepare for war. Singing and sometimes dancing also accompanied planting of crops and building of houses. Singing, either individually or in unison, accompanied almost all activities, and men and women often sang while working. The text of some songs recorded the history of the group and provided the means by which the knowledge of the past was handed from one generation to the next. Women as well as men participated in singing and dancing at festivals, however some songs, dances, and musical instruments belonged exclusively to initiated males and were performed out of sight of women and children. Music or special sounds were often used to convey messages about special events such as deaths and feasts over long distances. The blowing of conch shells on the coast is a notable example of this. Percussion, string, and wind instruments were crafted from wood, bamboo, vegetable fibre, gourds, seeds, animal and reptile skins, bones, shells, and clay.

Religion, including magical practices, was associated with all serious events. Religious activities were interdependent with the relationship of the people with their physical environment, with people both inside and beyond the group, and with spirits and non-human forces. Spirits were frequently the recently dead and regarded as an extension of the living social structure. The help of spirits was sought in almost all important activities of the group.

Religious beliefs were an attempt to explain, and exercise control over, the physical and social environment. Papua New Guinean languages do not have words which can be equated with the European concept of religion or the European concepts of heaven and hell. There are in all languages words for particular rituals, the dead, and various forms of magic. Magic was often used in religious practices, and belief in sorcery and magic was common to all societies. Sorcerers could exercise magical powers on behalf of themselves or others often to harm enemies outside the group. Many disasters, particularly physical sickness and death, were attributed to sorcery. In societies where women exercised greater rights they often used witchcraft to manipulate and control male activities.

In some societies religion was associated with morality; however, in other societies no connection was seen between religious belief and practice and moral conduct. Religious, economic, social, and cultural activities were all interwoven, and the visual arts, singing, dancing, feasting, gift exchange, and warfare were all in some way connected with religious ritual.

Religious ritual and patterns of social relationships were supported by myths and other inherited stories. Myths concerning the creation of the universe were rare, however most societies had theories as to how people first came to inhabit particular areas. Common themes of myths and stories include the origin of staple foods (plants, animals, reptiles), land ownership, migration, warfare, and social relationships within families, amongst families in a group, and amongst groups. The correctness of these accounts was not questioned but accepted as accurate records of actual events. While each group had its own myths of origins and stories there are similarities amongst myths and stories from a number of areas. In content and in structure the myths and stories reflect both the similarities and the diversity of Papua New Guinean society.

This very brief account of Papua New Guinean society prior to Asian and European contact is restricted to noting basic characteristics which these societies held in common. It should however be recognised that each society had, in addition, many individual characteristics, and that it has not been possible in the above account to describe the extraordinary complexity of the social relationships and spiritual lives of the people of these societies.

It may, then, help the reader to give a more detailed account of the physical and social relationships in the only area in Papua New Guinea which has been studied in depth by a Melanesian scholar. In 1977 I chose to study the history of my society — the Binandere people of Oro Province. The following account of the way in which physical social and spiritual relationships are interwoven in my community is based on material collected, and exemplifies many traditional Melanesian attitudes and values. I have used the present tense in the following account because the majority of my people still view the world in this way.

The Binandere see themselves as located within a family and among a small group with whom they have built strong bonds. In turn, a Binandere views members of other societies on the basis of the kin associations and alliances that might have been fashioned between the Binandere and the other society in the past through war and trade, or today through business or politics. Much Binandere behaviour is determined by obligations and enmities within a close network of people. All are judged on how they fulfil their obligations to others. They are also very conscious of their location by place. The roots of the Binandere are anchored at the *arapa* of their hamlets, where they grew up and to which they make conscious and constant reference in later life.

The significance of the *arapa* is that this physical space binds all people who reside on it as a single entity. Its members enter into a kind of contractual obligation with one another which means that if and when one of them is affected by something, then another member is expected to act in response.

The *arapa* could be the area between the *mando*, women's house, and the *oro*, men's house, both of which face each other, or it may be just the front space of a house in a particular section of the village. The physical charter of a community contains the idea that one belongs to a fixed place or *arapa*. From there one is linked in a web of relationships that underlie rights and obligations within the confines of the *arapa*. If a person violates these rights and obligations, the rights granted to him or her by kinship will be affected.

Although the *arapa* is bare ground, usually swept by women, it is a highly respected place. This sense of honour is expressed in the killing of a pig whenever an adult falls in an *arapa* when the ground is slippery. On a rainy day, everyone grips the ground tightly with their toes to avoid falling. Even if the fall is an accident, the owners of the *arapa* make absolutely certain that relatives of the fallen do not accuse them of having set up a snare to trap intruders with evil intent who try to enter other people's *arapa*. The pig killing is a declaration that the owner is innocent and that the fall is in fact an accident.

The centre of the *arapa* in the village is marked by the fire place in front of and underneath each house. For the women, their hearth is for the fire to cook vegetables — taro, banana, potatoes, pumpkin, greens — with pieces of meat and fish in large clay pots of conical shape of various sizes.

For men, the fire place is in a hall without walls where both formal and informal meetings take place. Social interaction among male members of the nuclear family occurs here every day at early dawn and at dusk, except when it rains and the fire burns underneath the house. This is a place of informal learning as the male elders teach codes of behaviour, family history, legends, and other traditions. Almost every day this knowledge is told and repeated. By the time children reach adolescence they will have heard these various testimonies a thousand times.

The *arapa* is also a formal gathering place where men come together to discuss issues of general concern. Formal feasts and major ceremonies are conducted in this area, where the sponsors are received, entertained, and fed, and from which the distribution of pig meat and vegetables takes place. In times of disputes or conflicts, the parties stay put on their own *arapa* and speeches are delivered from them. Decisions are handed down here after the 'big men' have made their public statements. Formal negotiation about marriage and bride price also occur on the *arapa*, as well as the exchange of bride wealth. Late in the evenings, two elders might meet to discuss sorcery. Nowadays, village committees and councillors use the *arapa* to discuss community matters and business concerns.

A well-known feature of the society has to do with the manner in which discussions are conducted, decisions reached, and recommendations carried out. The *arapa* provides the forum for both private conversation and the public debate to arrive at a consensus with which the majority of people present feel comfortable. A decision reached collectively can hold together those present, at least temporarily, until the decision is implemented. If agreement can not be reached, then at least this forum contains the basis for any further debate.

Being an integral part of the *arapa* entitles household members to benefit from the fruits of one another's labour, whether in sharing garden produce, a big catch of fish, rendering services, or raising a pig for another close kin in the olden times, or even assistance to be elected to a public office nowadays. Each member is regarded as a resource person and is expected to contribute something, whether economic or emotional, towards the well-being of the *arapa* as a corporate entity.

Everyone relies upon each other as a source of material and moral support in good and bad times. As such, the household as a unit is a capital resource when any kin undergoes a lean period. Whenever an *arapa* member is in need of a valuable item such as a pig that is not easily available, then other members provide it. Simply put, every member regards the other as *ujiwo*, a capital resource, from which assistance of any kind comes forth in good and bad times through the obligation of kinship.

The underlying principle of *arapa* is goodness. Although Leo Hannett used the term 'tribe' in a loose manner, he nonetheless described this value well.

> It is manifested in that personal humane concern for others, that sense of oneness, and that feeling of brotherhood which flows in the blood of every member of the tribe. Why must such good qualities be thrown away? Isn't the world today yearning with anguish for just such qualities? I would rather be a tribalist, feeling at one with and being loved by many than be an individualist who is more likely to be shipwrecked with the inhumane disease of loneliness.[1]

In the absence of the state, the ethical system of the Binandere emphasised the importance of reciprocity among people. The cultivation of sympathy and co-operation must begin in the family, as defined by *arapa*, and then extend by degrees into the village, clan, and to the tribe. Relationships could expand from the nuclear family along definite kin lines to include the extended family bounded by the charter of the *arapa*, and through which candidates could channel their bids for election as a member of a council, a provincial, or national government. Thus, in many ways, in fact, it is possible to think of parliament as national *arapa*.

Although the above account is of one small society among many, the underlying attitudes described here are to be found in many other regions. Like the Binandere, the people of most Papua New Guinean societies had strong affinity with their land and did not separate the social from the political, or even the past from the present.

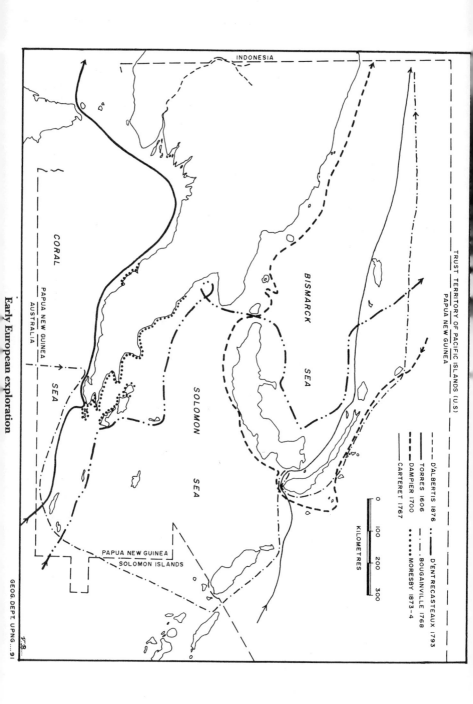

Early European exploration

INDONESIA

TRUST TERRITORY OF PACIFIC ISLANDS (U.S.)
PAPUA NEW GUINEA

BISMARCK SEA

CORAL SEA

SOLOMON SEA

PAPUA NEW GUINEA
AUSTRALIA

PAPUA NEW GUINEA
SOLOMON ISLANDS

D'ALBERTIS 1876
D'ENTRECASTEAUX 1793
TORRES 1606
BOUGAINVILLE 1768
DAMPIER 1700
MORESBY 1873-4
CARTERET 1767

0   100   200   300
KILOMETRES

GEOG. DEPT. UPNG 91

THE ARRIVAL OF THE FOREIGNERS

The Asians

Apart from the possibility of a trade in bronze and obsidian between the islands of south-east Asia and the present-day Bismarck archipelago as long ago as 3000 BP, there is little firm evidence of contact between Papua New Guinea and south-east Asia prior to the nineteenth century. However, as there appear to have been trading contacts between Indonesia and the western half of the island of New Guinea (currently known as Irian Jaya) from the thirteenth century, it is quite possible that these extended to what is now Papua New Guinea. Also, prior to the arrival of the first Europeans in the sixteenth century, Malay raiding parties captured coastal people, probably from the east as well as the west of the island, to be sold as slaves to row trading and pirate galleys. These raiding parties acquired and distributed to other parts of Asia bird of paradise feathers, turtle shell, and *bêche-de-mer* (also known as trepang or sea slug or sea-cucumber). No known settlements were established. If these contacts existed they appear to have ceased when the Europeans colonised parts of south-east Asia in the sixteenth century.

Portuguese and Spaniards

The earliest Europeans to pass by these islands were Portuguese and Spanish explorers searching for new areas for colonisation and trade, in particular spices and slaves. In 1526 Jorge de Meneses, a Portuguese, touched on the west coast of the main island and called it 'Ilhas dos Papuas', Island of the Papuans. 'Papua' came from a Malay word meaning frizzy-haired. In 1545 the Spanish explorer Inigo Oritz de Retes saw part of the north coast of the main island and called it 'Nueva Guinea' (New Guinea) because he thought it looked like Guinea in Africa. The first detailed charting of the coast appears to have come from the expedition of another Spanish explorer Luis Vaez de Torres who, in 1606, navigated the first European ship through the maze of reefs in the shallow Torres Strait which separates present-day Papua New Guinea and Australia.

Dutch, English and French

By the 1600s the sea power of the Portuguese and Spanish was challenged by that of the Dutch, English, and French. Most of the visits in the seventeenth century were from Dutch ships interested in trading for spices. At that time, the Dutch East Indies, now Indonesia, was famous for spices. Not finding any spices on these eastern islands, they soon departed.

In the eighteenth century English and French ships began to appear in northern Melanesia. In 1700 William Dampier, sent by Britain to try to chart the east coasts of Australia and New Guinea, sighted New Britain and New Ireland to the east, a number of islands to the north, and promontories of the north coast of New Guinea. Other English explorers who contributed to European knowledge of these coasts included Philip Carteret who, in 1767, explored in the east, and James Cook who sailed through Torres Strait in 1770. French explorers who were dispatched to extend their country's influence in the area included Louis de Bougainville in 1768 and Antoine d'Entrecasteaux in 1792. Many of the place names bestowed by European explorers appear on current maps of Papua New Guinea.

In spite of considerable French interest in these islands it was Britain, with its strong navy and, from 1788, its colony in New South Wales in Australia, which became the dominant European power in the area.

REACTION TO THE FOREIGNERS

Before the time of European contact no tribesman would have been admitted into the territory of another tribe unless invited for purposes of negotiation and questions of alliances; and equally no clansman would have been admitted into the territory of another clan except for similar reasons — though of course because a clan could be scattered around several villages, the clan boundaries were not as clearly demarcated as tribal boundaries. The clan or tribal boundaries were guarded against intruders. The white explorers were quite unaware of the situation and took no notice of the boundaries which the people observed themselves.

Some local people regarded the early explorers and traders in exactly the same light as they would have viewed the intruders from another tribe into their territory. These people assumed that the white men were saying that they were not going to accept the boundaries which had been accepted in the past, and therefore the Europeans were regarded as trespassers who had deliberately set out to challenge the existing boundaries. One response to this situation was to attack the intruders. Breaches of clan and tribal boundaries and the violation of hunting rights often led to bloody warfare. An example of this kind of war was the clash between the Mugula or Mailu islanders and the invading Spanish explorers in August 1606. The Mailuans were in occupation of a well-fortified place with a dangerous pass leading to the village which 'had about three hundred houses very well enclosed by planks and big canes'. The captain, Don Diego de Prado described the passway: '. . . it was about twelve feet wide, on the side, that is towards the sea, it had a great precipitous rock and on the other the high hill, also precipitous[.]^2 He led his men to within gunshot range and apparently made signs of peace but the local people defied the invaders by brandishing their spears and shields. Prado ordered his men to fire and he reported his view of the clash:

> . . . in that skirmish some fell dead, and we seized their gate and pressed on, shooting them as they fled; in order to flee more lightly they threw away their shields and lances and on reaching the village they embarked on twenty six boats flying to the great land of the Raile, and after embarking some were killed in the open sea and this caused them great fright and terror, on seeing that they killed them so far from land . . . They had withdrawn their women, and children and old men and put them on top a cliff precipitous on three sides, with only a very difficult ascent on the one at the end of the village, and on the sides it was cut off by the sea, so that for our people to get to the ascent we had to pass below this fortress. We made signs to them that they should come down and they replied with showers of stones; we passed with difficulty up to the ascent, and the chief Pilot

and a valiant Galician asked permission to go with their swords and shields up the cliff; they were allowed, and half way up there fell upon them such showers of stones that they came tumbling headlong to the bottom, without shields or hats, and came to us. The Indians raised a great shout in sign of joy but it lasted only a short time for twenty shooters and others with shields came up at once and made slaughters; the living and the wounded came down, they would be about three hundred, three parts were women and I was sorry to see so many dead children they were carrying in their arms. I selected fourteen boys and girls from six to ten years and sent them on board, the rest I let go free and they ran up a hill like goats . . . All those we carried off were baptised in Manila to the honour and glory of God. The Fathers taught them the prayers of the Pater Noster, Ave Maria, Credo and Salve Regina, and the Commandments and the articles of Catholic faith.[3]

It is evident from the remainder of the account that the Spaniards assumed that they were dealing with a morally, intellectually and technically inferior people whose only salvation lay in conversion to Christianity. Those youths that were kidnapped and taken to the Philippines certainly did not live to return to spread the gospel; they all died in Manila.

But in this instance, as in other encounters to follow, it was the superior guns that determined the issue. The Spaniards fired before they were actually attacked. No attempt was made by the Spaniards to find out why their presence was being resisted, and the slaughter continued in revenge against the resistance of the islanders long after there was any threat to the Spaniards.

For the islanders this was the first time the Mailu people had lost a large number of their warriors in one clash. The people so far had been used to battles in which there was a relatively even number of people killed on both sides. This fight was worse than anything they had experienced: it was a brutal massacre by the invading enemy, and in this fight the enemy had had no losses. Later, experiences of this kind led to the local people in other parts of the country resorting to methods of warfare such as waylaying, ambushing, and surprise attacks.

Foreign intrusion in the nineteenth century

Foreign intrusion during the nineteenth century continued as scientists and adventurers, traders and missionaries, and the German and British governments showed increasing interest in the region.

Some scientists and adventurers left their mark on New Guinea in the years preceding formal European control. The following are three notable examples. In 1871 Baron Nicolai Miklouho-Maclay, a Russian scientist, landed at Astrolabe Bay, near present-day Madang, where he lived for fifteen months, untroubled by the local people, making friends with them, and recording his observations on the language and culture of the people as well as the physical characteristics of the area. In contrast, Italian naturalist Luigi Maria D'Albertis, a collector of bird of paradise plumes and other fauna, shot his way up and down the Fly River in the present-day Western province during his various expeditions between 1875 and 1877. And Charles de Breil, Marquis de Ray, a French lord, became notorious because of his plan to establish a European colony on New Ireland in 1880. Hundreds of would-be colonists arrived from Europe but many died of fever, and the remainder gave up and shifted to Australia. The Marquis did not himself ever visit New Guinea.

Some Europeans are known to have lived for long periods on islands to the south and east of the New Guinea mainland. Some came by accident and some others by choice; an unknown number disappeared without trace, eliminated by the people they invaded. In September 1858, the ship *St Paul*, carrying 327 Chinese migrants from Hong Kong bound for Sydney, was wrecked on Rossel Island at the eastern end of the Louisiade Archipelago. When the wreck was eventually seen by a passing steam ship in January 1859, only one of the passengers was left alive, the rest having been massacred and eaten. However a stranded Englishman, Thomas Manners, who spent ten years on New Ireland from 1825 to 1835, was more fortunate and lived to tell the tale.

The most influential contact in the early nineteenth century was that of the traders. Passing ships traded with the coastal villagers for food, wood and water. Following the founding of the British settlement in New South Wales in 1788 shipping routes from Australia to Bengal in India, Batavia in the Dutch East Indies and Canton in China passed through Melanesian waters. The most easterly route to Canton went around the Solomon Islands and ran parallel to the east coast of New Ireland. The inner route which passed through the Bougain-ville Strait west of the Solomon Islands and St George's Channel between New Ireland and New Britain, was recom-mended to ships requiring food, fuel, and fresh water en route to Bengal. Ships using the Queensland coastal route, inside the Great Barrier Reef, either attempted the hazardous Torres Strait or passed through the Barrier Reef. Certainly the coastal villagers over several centuries must have seen a wondrous array of ships and crews pass by. Some coastal people even travelled on the ships. Before 1847 men from Woodlark Island had travelled to Sydney as ships' crew. The use of Pidgin English as the common language for communication probably began slowly between 1790 and 1850, intensifying in the second half of the nineteenth century as trade increased.

Increasingly, itinerant traders came for sandalwood, cedar, and copra, to catch and smoke *bêche-de-mer* or to dive for pearls and pearl shells. During the nineteenth century, north Melanesia was a whaling ground, hunted in by British and American ships. Local people were employed by the traders as crew on ships, as interpreters, carriers, and labourers, usually only for short periods of one or two months. Some traders employed local agents to supervise the smoking of *bêche-de-mer* which they had left to cure in sheds along hundreds of kilometres of coastline and returned to collect every few months. Many of the individual or small company traders were based in Cooktown or on Thursday Island in Australia's north Queensland. Ah Gim, from China, worked out of Cooktown in the 1890s collecting *bêche-de-mer* along the coast from Torres Strait to the Louisiade Archipelago. His ships were equipped with bamboo shields three metres across for the crew to hide behind when attacked by local people. However, not all village people were prepared to defend their territory, and generally the traders were accepted.

Towards the end of the century companies based in Australia, Britain, France, and Germany were formed to exploit our resources. The German company J. C. Godeffroy and Sons, which had been trading in South America since the 1830s, established a base on Matupit Island near Rabaul in 1871 and in the Gazelle Peninsula in New Britain in 1875. Both bases were closed when company representatives were finally driven out. They had more success establishing a base in the Duke of York Islands in 1875. In 1879 this was transferred to the Deutsche Handels-und Plantagen-Gesellschaft, also known as the 'Long Handle Company', and in 1884 incorporated into the Neuguinea-Kompagnie, a consortium organised by Adolph von Hausemann, a leading German banker.

Another important German-based company was established by Thomas Farrell and his part-Samoan de facto wife Emma Coe Forsayth who had arrived to manage the Godeffroy's Duke of York trading station in 1878 and established their own company in 1880. The Farrells realised that trading stations buying copra from villagers would be replaced by copra plantations, so, at the cost of the local people, they invested in land on which plantations could be established.

Another German trader in New Britain was Eduard Hernsheim who set up a company working out of Hong Kong in 1872. This increased German presence increasingly involved the coastal people. Hansemann's New Guinea Company controlled trade on the northeast coast, while the Farrell and the Hernsheim companies controlled trade in the Bismarck Archipelago. It was these areas which became the focus of European settlement in northern New Guinea.

European and Asian commercial activity in the south of the islands prior to formal British annexation was limited to individual traders and collectors of *bêche-de-mer*, and occasional labour recruiters and gold prospectors.

The labour trade

During the nineteenth century many of the local people were

recruited to work on plantations within New Guinea or in Queensland, Australia. Some accepted recruitment; others were taken by force. Kidnapping Pacific Islanders and forcibly transporting them to the Queensland plantations was called 'blackbirding'. The practice of blackbirding was outlawed in 1884, however this did not stop blackbirding, and not all those who had been taken by force were repatriated. Recruitment of labour on one island for service on another island was also widely practised and here too the local people were sometimes forced into employment.

All recruits faced problems adapting culturally and physically to work on the plantations. One by-product of the labour trade was the introduction of European technology into traditional society. In particular, iron and steel products came into everyday use and filtered into the elaborate, extensive exchange networks. Another important by-product of the labour trade was the further development of Pidgin English as a common language of communication amongst Melanesians and between Melanesians and foreigners.

The missions

The first mission stations were established by French Marist Catholics on Woodlark Island in 1847 and Rooke Island in 1848. The French Catholics were replaced by Italians but neither group made any progress and when the missions closed in 1855 the Catholics had made no converts. Following several other unsuccessful attempts the Mission of the Sacred Heart finally established Catholic communities in New Britain in 1882 and on Yule Island in 1885. The first permanent Protestant mission was established by the London Missionary Society (LMS) in Port Moresby in 1874 and this was shortly followed by the founding of a Methodist mission in the Duke of York Islands in 1875. The denomination which made greatest initial progress was the London Missionary Society. By 1884 there were 140 students at the Port Moresby mission and 1000 students at the twenty mission stations which had been established along the coast and in adjacent islands.

However, although the Christian missions were to have a significant influence on the lives and culture of many of the people, they were unable to consolidate their position until after formal colonisation by the British and the Germans in 1884. The first German Lutheran mission, at Finschhafen on the north coast, was not established until 1886. In spite of the expanding influence of the Christian missions, for many people belief in the Christian religion coexisted with traditional beliefs in the spirit world and the power of magic and sorcery.

Formal takeover by European powers

The Australian colony of Queensland had long been interested in the southern coast of the island of New Guinea, and in 1864 had established a base at Somerset on Cape York to monitor its interests. In 1872 Britain authorised Queensland to extend its northern border ninety-six kilometres north of Cape York, only thirty-two kilometres south of the mainland island coast, and including most of the Torres Strait islands. In 1877 the Somerset base was moved to Thursday Island in Torres Strait and in 1878 the border was extended yet again — this time almost to the mainland coastline. Queensland's interest, and that of the other Australian colonies, was mainly strategic, though Queensland was also interested in securing Melanesian labour for its sugar plantations. In 1883 Queensland boldly sent an official to Port Moresby to annex the southern half of the island on behalf of Britain. Britain refused to accept Queensland's action and would not consider adding the territory to its empire unless the Australian colonies agreed to pay the costs of administration. Australia accepted this provision in 1884 and Britain agreed to formal annexation. As elsewhere in the British empire the local people were not consulted and, by most European officials, not even considered. However as the vast majority of the people (even those who had some contact with Europeans) did not know their land was being formally annexed, the question of formal opposition did not arise.

The German government was interested, for strategic and economic reasons, in the north-eastern section of the island where German traders were already well established. With the establishment of the German-based New Guinea Company which would, in effect, pay for the administration of the territory, the German government was willing to add the north-east of the island to its colonial empire.

On 3 November 1884 the north-east section of the island of New Guinea was declared a German protectorate and on 6 November the south-east section of the island was declared a British protectorate. The western half of the island remained in the hands of the Dutch. Thus, the fact that the people of the present-day nation of Papua New Guinea became part of the British and German colonial empires, and not the Dutch, was an accident of European history over which they had no control.

Thus, by 1884 only some mainland coastal and island people had experienced foreign intruders. The Asians and Europeans who had come to New Guinea not only had no contact with the vast majority of the population, those who lived in the highlands of the mainland, but were completely unaware of their existence. The mistaken belief that the population would become sparser in the interior was to continue until well into the twentieth century.

What, then, was the effect of the Asians and Europeans on those limited number of island and coastal people with whom they had made contact? The overriding features as far as the villagers were concerned were their initial curiosity in regard to the strange pale foreigners, the introduction of iron and steel and other products of European technology, and violence. Violence came from Melanesians protecting themselves and reacting against the intruding foreigners; violence also came from Europeans protecting themselves from attack. Before European colonial governments were established, and usually for a long time afterwards, coastal and island people came into contact with a variety of Europeans who were beyond the control of their own governments. The foreigners dealt with situations as they thought best. When in situations where their main objective was to stay alive, often by using their superior technology, they gave little thought to the lives and rights of the people they encountered. Europeans viewed resistance by villagers as unprovoked attacks by savage people. But the reactions of villagers defending their homes and families were rational and correct within the rules of their societies. Try as they might, they had no chance against the new arrivals.

Eighteen eighty-four marked the end of several hundred years of informal contact between the independent small-scale societies of northern Melanesia, and Europeans, Malays, and other Asians. In the century since the formal declaration of British and German power in northern Melanesia, enormous changes have taken place, the most important being the declaration of the independent state of Papua New Guinea in 1975.

2

British and German colonial powers

Pokupoku was the noise in the distance
That chilled the marrow of my bones
There appeared a white skinned spirit
Who took my name
I wondered why he left in a hurry
I feared he may return.

[Anon].

BRITISH NEW GUINEA 1884–1906

Commodore Erskine of the British Navy declared south-eastern New Guinea a British protectorate on 6 November 1884 and established headquarters in Port Moresby. This declaration gave notice to other European powers to keep out, and gave the British a limited degree of control and a greater ability to protect its Australian colonies. Although Britain promised the people that she would protect their lives, land, and other properties, the legal limitations of the Protectorate did not allow Britain to interfere in domestic matters such as local forms of government, law, and religion.

The people charged with administering the Protectorate were called Special Commissioners. The first, Sir Peter Scratchley, took up office in December 1884. Scratchley, a retired British Army General, was considered to be an ideal person to send to a British Protectorate where the main concern was the security and defence of Australia — the most important British colony in the region. Scratchley had a budget of only 15 000 pounds sterling a year and very limited legal powers. He died of malaria after only three months in office, however, he travelled as far as was possible in this short time in an effort to extend British control. On his death, the Protectorate was temporarily under the control of Hugh Hastings Romilly, then Deputy High Commissioner for the British in the Western Pacific. In 1886 the British appointed John Douglas, formerly a premier of Queensland, as administrator. Douglas advised the annexation of the territory and in 1888 the British government formally annexed the Protectorate and appointed Sir William MacGregor as first administrator of the new colony.

MacGregor, a medical doctor by training who had risen from a working-class background, was an extremely capable man. He is best known for the way he established an administrative system which linked Port Moresby with the rest of the colony. This system remained the basis of administration until the 1950s. MacGregor divided the colony into four divisions with a resident magistrate in each. The Western division was based at Daru; Central was based at Port Moresby with administration agents at Rigo and Mekeo; Eastern was based at Samarai, with an assistant resident magistrate at Tamata on the Mamba River near the border with German territory; and the south-eastern division, controlling the islands, had a resident magistrate first at Sudest, then at Misima, and later at Nivani in the Louisiade Archipelago.

Under the control of the resident magistrates, the main force of the colonial administration was the police, called the Armed Native Constabulary. From a small beginning in 1890, with Fijian instructors and Solomon Island constables, the force grew steadily until by 1898 there were 100 constables. The armed constabulary did a great deal of the basic patrol work in the colony, and very often it was the police who decided what happened at first contact between the villagers and the administration.

MacGregor explored nearly all the navigable rivers in Papua, crossed the island, and climbed the highest mountain, Mount Victoria. Physically strong, he was driven by the desire to make

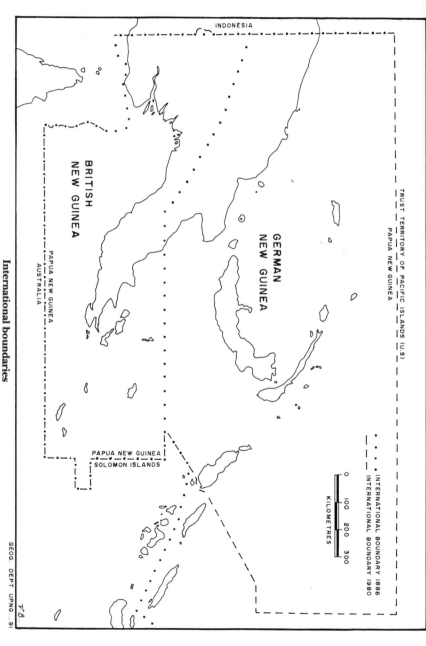

International boundaries

INDONESIA

TRUST TERRITORY OF PACIFIC ISLANDS (U.S)
PAPUA NEW GUINEA

BRITISH
NEW GUINEA

GERMAN
NEW GUINEA

PAPUA NEW GUINEA
AUSTRALIA

PAPUA NEW GUINEA
SOLOMON ISLANDS

• • • • INTERNATIONAL BOUNDARY 1886
—·—·— INTERNATIONAL BOUNDARY 1980

0   100   200   300
KILOMETRES

GEOG. DEPT UPNG....91

the administration known to the local people and by his ambition to be the first European to penetrate the interior of the island. He and his constables were the first foreigners to meet many of the people in our small societies, and met with the same type of reception as earlier foreigners had met on the coast — sometimes hostile, sometimes friendly.

The first official contact was usually with an administration patrol led by European patrol officers and including native police, interpreters and carriers. The police frequently went ahead of the patrol officers and the behaviour of the police often influenced the way in which the patrol was received. For example, if the police stole food or molested women, the local people might either hide from the patrol or attack it. When patrols came to villages they had to rely upon the villagers for food, however the residents often fled as the party came to the villages. When the officers could not buy food because there was no-one with whom they could negotiate, they took it. But the people understandably regarded this as ruthless raiding and looting, and the white officer and his party were regarded as members of a thievish mob. For example, C. A. W. Monckton carried out a punitive patrol inland from Wanigela, Northern District, in 1903, and captured a warrior whose wife summed up the activities of the colonial party: 'You are a set of murdering thieves, I have not killed the Maisina [from the coastal group] but you have looted my house.'[1] Contacts were complicated by the fact that villagers who had joined the police force sometimes used the patrols to attack their traditional enemies.

In potentially hostile situations, the bushcraft and experience of indigenous police sergeants often saved the white patrol officers from making mistakes which might have led to an attack. Generally, the skill and courage of the bush policemen did much to bring together the local people and the foreign colonial administration.

The main aim of the Special Commissioners before MacGregor's arrival was to impose peace, and their immediate task was to stop violence between villagers and foreigners. MacGregor took the process one step further. He set up a government, and (as already mentioned) established an administrative system which linked Port Moresby with many other parts of the colony. In villages where colonial power was introduced, MacGregor appointed village constables. This was a separate body from the armed constabulary. The village constables had no special training; they were clan leaders who had assisted colonial officers, or men who had acquired some knowledge of the outside world by serving as policemen, labourers, or prisoners. Such men were given a cap, a uniform, and one pound sterling a year to act as administration representatives. They met officials on patrol, reported disputes, sickness, and other problems. The officers expected the village constables to encourage their people to keep the villages clean, maintain the rest houses, supply information, help officials on patrols, and surrender suspected criminals and deserters from labour contracts. The village constables had no power from the central authority to settle disputes or impose penalties, but like members of the police, strong men added to their power by using their position as informants to administration officers.

During the initial contact period all the European officers who reached the villages to establish political relations with the people were men. However, in two exceptional circumstances in Papua, females were given the status of village constable. One was in the Gulf division and the other in the Northern division. When the Binandere people in the Northern division joined the police, they were able to use the social network well. Bakeke, for example, accompanied a European official to a village in the Aega territory where all the residents ran away except Uripa, a woman of powerful personality. She was related to Bakeke, so he told the officer to recognise her as the village constable of the area. This was done and she carried out her duties as well as her male counterparts. Oral tradition has it that Uripa's powerful role in a male-dominated society did not affect her husband.

The main problem for MacGregor was that the administration and the people had opposing attitudes towards law and order. MacGregor insisted that his law be obeyed, even where the villagers were used to different customary laws. For example, the administration wanted to end warfare and killing, but these things were customary for many of the people. It seemed unfair of the administration to punish people who were only doing what was their custom. But on the other hand, if the administration accepted those customs, it would never be able to end war and killing. MacGregor was willing to use force and always tried to make the power of his administration obvious to his officers and the people. As MacGregor put it:

> I look on it as my first duty to impress on the natives that white men are not to be robbed and murdered and I was determined to teach them by an awful lesson that killing is murder and the punishment for it death.[2]

MacGregor was

> . . . determined to make an example of the perpetrators if possible, acting in the belief that severity would under the circumstances be mercy.[3]

However, it was hardly surprising that this use of force seemed only to produce more violence.

To promote peaceful behaviour and to spread European values, MacGregor made use of the various Christian missions. To avoid conflict between different missions, he called a conference in Port Moresby in 1890 between representatives of the London Missionary Society, the Methodists, and the Anglicans. Probably under MacGregor's influence the Europeans agreed on 'spheres of influence', and decided not to compete in the same areas. Like the four divisions of his administrative system, the missions were to establish their spiritual influence in the following manner: the southern coast 'belonged' to the London Missionary Society; the Methodists restricted themselves to the islands of the east; and the Anglicans were given the north coast. This left the Roman Catholics, who did not take part in the 1890 conference, the limited area of Yule Island and the adjacent mainland. This was a clear example of how the administration imposed its power and beliefs on the local people. It is quite clear from the records that there was no indigenous representation in the conference, and that the people had not been consulted.

The colonial administration had meagre material and human resources at its disposal. This is why both the administration and church authorities shared a common interest in being two edges of the same sword: carriers of Western 'civilisation' and the word of God. MacGregor discouraged sectarian rivalry and was on cordial terms with the London Missionary Society, the Anglicans, the Methodists, and the Catholics. He encouraged the missions to help the administrative officers to make friendly contacts with the people. In particular he supported the work being done to teach the English language and give instruction in hygiene, and by those missionaries engaged in writing down the local languages.

Before MacGregor's arrival the only industry which had taken the white man away from the coast was gold mining. During his ten year administration gold was still the most important export, and the reason why most Europeans came to the colony. At first, the miners worked gold fields at Sudest and Misima islands which reached their peak in 1889–90 when about 400 Europeans and 1200 Papuan labourers were working there. As activity on these islands decreased Woodlark Island became a more important centre. At the end of MacGregor's period the miners were moving into the northern fields, first to McLaughlands Creek on the middle Mamba, then on to the Gira River and later to the Yodda Valley at the source of the Mamba River.

Trade in pearl, pearl shell, copra, *bêche-de-mer*, and sandalwood continued. However, there were virtually no plantations by 1898. MacGregor and others believed that colonies should pay for themselves and not rely on the colonial power to provide a grant or a subsidy to the colony. He needed economic development by planters so that eventually he could tax them and so obtain revenue for the administration. In the end he felt that large plantation companies were the best means to develop the colony, and though he also supported the idea of the people as small cash-crop farmers, little came of this.

MacGregor supported very strongly the policy that the people must not sell their land to Europeans. He established a land ordinance under which land sales were to be made only through the administration, although he did relax the land laws a little to attract Europeans. MacGregor had a good understanding of the local system of land ownership and made a strong attempt to protect the people's rights. However, the local landowners were protected as much by a lack of demand from European investors as they were by MacGregor's legislation.

Labour was another area where MacGregor showed his concern. He would not allow labourers to be employed outside their own district, which was defined as being ten kilometres from home. This concern appears to have stemmed from the fact that MacGregor intended to protect the source of labour supply. He knew that the village people needed a workforce to establish coconut plantations near their villages in order to obtain cash to pay the administration's head tax; and the colonial authority required cheap local labour for the purposes of exploration, mining, and work on plantations. Eventually the colonial authority aimed to establish a system of exploitative social relations, and the labour policy was tailored towards achieving this goal[4,5]. In 1891 legislation was passed to order the men of each village under administration control to plant a given number of coconut palms each and to tend them properly[6]. In 1892 MacGregor passed a labour ordinance in which he sought to safeguard labourers from the exploitation they had faced in the earlier labour trade where people had been taken to work on sugar plantations in Australia. Taking men to Australia undermined the all-important subsistence economy; the 1892 ordinance reversed this trend because it was essential to maintain a supply of cheap labour for exploitation within the colony. The colonial practice of recording births and deaths, as well as the collection of data on adult males and females in the villages during the 1890s, also indicates that the administration wanted to protect and maintain the source of labour supply.

Health and education services received little attention. Although MacGregor had both the desire and the training to improve health in the colony, he had neither the staff nor the money to do more than suggest simple rules for village hygiene. No schools were established by MacGregor's administration; he relied on missions to provide what little education there was.

Reaction of the people

There is not enough evidence available for us to accurately tell how our people responded to colonial policies. As has been indicated earlier, there is little written evidence, and it usually describes the European reaction to us and not our reaction to the European. Where Europeans have tried to interpret the reaction of our people they have frequently been mistaken. In some areas the situation was not as simple as 'villagers versus Europeans'. In certain regions, where the villagers realised they could not defeat the Europeans, they used alliances with the Europeans to pursue local grievances against rival clans. The following example again comes from the Binandere people in the Northern division — one of the few peoples who have been the subject of a systematic study which takes into account both written and oral accounts of contact events.

Contacts between the Binandere and the administration began in March 1894 when MacGregor travelled up the Mamba River for forty kilometres. Europeans might see first contact in terms of it being 'friendly' or 'hostile', but the Binandere view of the situation was in terms of 'ally' and 'enemy'. Each clan had its own enemies and allies, and everyone was concerned with killing or wounding a member of the enemy to avenge previous deaths or wounds. During initial contact Europeans sometimes reported that they had entered into 'friendly' relations with a number of clans. But to the Binandere, friendship with one clan meant enmity with traditional foes of that clan. The Binandere fitted the white men into their networks of alliances and their own accounting of the balance of the dead.

A good example to illustrate the point is the Pure clan, which was hostile to clans upstream of the Mamba River that had combined to kill Pure clansmen. At the time of contact the Pure allied with the whites to avenge previous killings. The response of the upper clans was to combine to resist what they saw as the Pure's first subtle move in the building of an alliance. Seen from the Binandere vantage point, MacGregor's writings reveal misunderstandings which occurred. During his first trip MacGregor had done several things that determined subsequent relations. The lower villages imposed taboos to prevent him from landing, but he had ignored them, mistaking them for a 'welcome'.

Official contact was not the only contact between Europeans and local people. Following reports of the presence of gold, a prospecting party led by George Clark, an experienced north Queensland prospector, arrived in Binandere territory in June 1895. Once the party entered the territory of the upper clans, stones were thrown at them, a warning that the whites should not go any further. The miners ignored the warning, which was taken as a gesture of defiance. The upper clans could have had no idea of the real reason why miners and their convoy of canoes were coming. The only logical conclusion for them was that the Pure had a very strong and powerful ally. It was also the conclusion shared by the Pure, who came in force in the accompanying canoes.

The plot of the Pure clan was for one group to attack the enemy at Dabo, about 50 kilometres from the mouth of Mamba River. The rest of the warriors were given the task of appearing to help the foreigners by pulling the boats up the rapids with ropes, while unknown to the miners, a man cut the rope of one of the boats. George Clark was in the boat holding the steering oars. The warrior cut the rope and the strong current of the river at the rapids pulled the miner's boat down towards the warrior Jiregari. When he saw Clark on the boat, Jiregari, holding the pole with his left hand, threw a spear with his right hand, hitting Clark. Tamanabae thrust most spears into the body. He picked the fatally wounded Clark up and threw him overboard. After Clark was killed, the other miners gathered together and drifted downstream on their boat until they met another party coming up the river. They combined forces and returned to the scene. They not only plundered the villages of those involved in the killing of Clark but also the village of their Pure ally. In their ignorance the miners did not discriminate between their allies and enemies. This vengeance, at least temporarily, united all clans on the Mamba River.

The news of Clark's death reached MacGregor, who came

with a punitive expedition. But when MacGregor arrived with his half dozen police he was faced by a united opposition, so that he did not dare to arrest any of the killers. He did not act until reinforcements of twenty more police arrived. MacGregor's force arrested six warriors and killed a further half dozen men. This meant that the network of clans with a grievance against the Europeans was extending. MacGregor had made a mistake, and his staff were to pay dearly for it. On 14 January 1897, the warriors attacked and killed John Green, the first colonial officer in Binandere territory, who had previously shot two local men. The killing of Green and all of his party was by far the greatest defeat imposed on any administration party in Papua. The news of the vengeance killings reached MacGregor, who again led a punitive expedition to Binandere territory.

Thus, between 1894 and the end of 1905, the Binandere were unaware that the Europeans were not mainly interested in trying to stop the Binandere from killing one another. In fact the Europeans were undermining the warrior tradition which would otherwise be used against themselves. Although pacification stopped fighting and killing in open warfare, its real effect was to prevent the people from continuing payback and using the techniques of traditional warfare to attack the new regime.

This was also achieved by imposing an alternative system of law and order. The Europeans had double standards. On the one hand they said that the payback must stop, but on the other hand they carried out punitive expeditions which were exactly the same as traditional revenge parties to avenge the deaths of whites or their policemen. This was just like the Binandere indulging in vengeance.

When Anglican missionaries arrived in November 1899, the church's teaching increased the divisions in the Binandere by separating the Christians from the heathens. The church further prevented the Binandere from seeing the new regime as the enemy because it offered justification for collaborating with the whites. Payback as an index of political power was changing among the Binandere. Although the payback system continued, the methods shifted from open warfare to using sorcery and the penal law, the courts, and the local prison administered from Ioma.

In 1904, buildings at Ioma consisted of a residence for the officer-in-charge, barracks for single policemen, quarters for married police and non-commissioned officers, and a gaol. Some land was cleared to grow vegetables, mainly sweet potatoes, to feed the people on the station. With its buildings and personnel, Ioma was a physical presence; it was the post from which the colonial administration agents would come in force to punish offenders. The penal station was a miniature version of the headquarters in Port Moresby. The resident magistrate, who exercised considerable power, represented the higher colonial authority. His immediate subordinates, the assistant resident magistrate and the patrol officer, were invariably white. Below them were the black policemen, carefully ranked with the sergeant at the top, then the corporal, the lance-corporal, and the private constables at the bottom. The police were required to arrest people, accompany officers on patrols, carry mail, supervise prisoners while gardening, and do construction work.

The agents for the administration of law and order in the villages were the constables who took the colonial shirt, the black uniform, given to leading men. It would not have surprised the village constables to learn that their utility was defined by the white administration almost exclusively in terms of the services they could perform for the new regime.

Dumai, a Binandere, was among the first men arrested and taken to Port Moresby in 1896. On his return he advised his people that there were not many white men there, and he provoked the people to kill the whites as they came to Binandere country. Dumai underestimated the effectiveness of the enemy's weapons. Though few, the Europeans continued to arrive, and consolidated their colonial rule.

Dumai died and his relatives created a series of vivid and characteristic images of the man who defied the white officials. The chanter spoke of *gugumi*, the carpenter bees, which bore holes through which the whites came. *Orowa*, a variety of a stinging bee, and *dubemi*, a poisonous wasp, are also mentioned to evoke the angry reaction of Dumai.

Stinging and stinging,
Like the wasp,
He made a mark.
Drilling and drilling,
Like the carpenter bee,
He bored a hole.

For the Binandere the wasp is a metaphor: it bores, penetrates with its head, and stings with its tail. The Binandere see the foreigners as entering and damaging their society, while they themselves respond by penetrating the whites through the police, and stinging by directing the whites against their old enemies. They had used the deception of the wasp with its unexpected tactics of attacking with its tail.

Not all communities had such complex and violent relationships with the European intruders as the Binandere. For many communities the experience was less traumatic. When Captain John Moresby surveyed the south coast and parts of the northeast coast he encountered mostly friendly people. In 1875 representatives of the London Missionary Society received a boisterous welcome from the Mekeo people on Yule Island. Ten years later the Yule Island people were prepared to welcome the Catholic missionaries.

The reaction of the people was often dependent upon their experience in the first few years of contact. For some people, such as the Binandere, European contact created a violent and confused situation which significantly disrupted their relationships with neighbouring groups. For others, such as the Mekeo, the desire to have access to the white man's goods overcame their distrust of the intruders' motives. However, it is important to remember the limit of European control in the period. The majority of societies in the British Protectorate were beyond effective administrative control, and were not significantly affected by the European settlement.

GERMAN NEW GUINEA 1884-1914

The function of the German Protectorate established by the German government in north-east New Guinea in 1884 was to protect the interests of Germans seeking to exploit the land

and local labour. German exploration and exploitation of the coastal areas was severely hampered by lack of natural harbours and the many flood plains and malaria swamps common to the area. It was hard to explore inland areas because the country was so mountainous. So the Germans, who initially gave administrative authority to the privately-owned New Guinea Company, kept their activities almost entirely to the coastal area, made little attempt to explore the mountainous inland, and made no systematic contact with the people in the highlands.

The New Guinea Company control 1885–1899

For almost half of the thirty-year German occupation of north-east New Guinea, the territory was administered through the New Guinea Company, which hoped to make its profits from using local labour to work on copra, cocoa, and tobacco plantations. The German government delegated to the New Guinea Company the authority to buy or take the land from the local people for this purpose. Company policy was designed by businessmen based in Berlin. In fact the company director, a powerful and wealthy banker, Adolf Von Hausemann, never visited this outpost of his commercial empire, and day-to-day administration of the Protectorate was in the hands of company employees, not German government officials.

In June 1885 the first company expedition set out from Berlin for the territory to prepare the way for German settlers. When they reached Finschhafen in November 1885 they were welcomed by village people as relatives who had come back from the dead and it was reported that one old man threw his arms around Captain Dallmann of the company. Prior to the arrival of the New Guinea Company, villagers' contact with Europeans had been confined to occasional visits from missionaries and explorers. On the mainland coast the company men were among the first Europeans ever seen by villagers, and traditional village life had hardly been touched by foreign influences. The people used stone axes, wore bark clothing, and had travelled no further in their trading canoes than the near neighbouring islands.

Company activities on the mainland

Initially the company was regarded by the people in the area as a novelty and its activities were welcomed. Whole families and clan groups came to the company settlement offering to work clearing bush and carrying rocks. In return they earned hoop-iron, axes, beads, and mirrors. The Germans believed that the people valued the company presence and were confident that they would become willing labourers.

However, the Germans were soon shown to be mistaken. The company expected labourers to work all the time but the village people would only work when they wanted to. After they had replaced stone with steel axes and obtained cloth and beads for decoration, they lost interest in working. The company's labour problems were compounded by the fact that they had failed to attract German settlers and thus had no source of European labour. In consequence, they were forced to recruit labour from the nearby islands. Even Indonesians and Malaysians were imported to work on the large cacao (cocoa) and tobacco plantations which were established on the mainland coast. However, thousands of these imported labourers died of malaria, dysentery, and influenza, and between 1891 and 1896 the company lost three-quarters of its total workforce.

As conditions on the plantations worsened the people of the smaller islands became increasingly resistant to the foreign presence. Eventually the islands' labourers refused to go to the place of *'no kai kai, no Sunday, plenti pait, plenti die'* (no food, no holidays, violence and death). Thus, the company activities on the mainland were a disaster for all concerned. The local people lost land, many labourers lost their lives, and the German investors lost their money.

Company activities in the Gazelle Peninsula and the islands

Even under these circumstances, the New Guinea Company received some return from its investments in the Gazelle Peninsula and the islands although they had lost money on their investment on the mainland. This region had been settled by missionaries and had had European trading contacts since the 1870s. There were villagers who had worked as labourers in Queensland, Fiji, and Samoa and who could speak Pidgin. They wore *lap-laps* (loincloths) and leather belts and had long since adopted steel in place of stone for implements and weapons. Villagers who had benefited from these contacts were initially happy to work on the German plantations.

Relationships between the local people and the company benefited from the fact that the foreigners employed by the company included British, Scandinavian, and mixed-race Samoan settlers who had a better appreciation of the local culture and recognised that the local people could exercise real power. They knew that if they offended islanders by breaking taboos, shooting pigs, taking village women or by not bringing back labour recruits, they could expect to be killed by villagers or have their houses burnt down. These early foreign settlers came for a variety of reasons: some to trade with Tolais for coconuts and pearl shell, others to grow copra, others to convert heathens to Christ; but, unlike the company men on the mainland, most of them believed that local people deserved respect, for the power of their spears, if for nothing else. However, the company soon encountered difficulties in recruiting labour to develop plantations in these areas also. The Tolai people of the Gazelle Peninsula resented the loss of their land to the planters and the interference with their sacred places. The resentment sometimes erupted into violent conflicts.

Tolai uprisings 1890–1893

A major confrontation took place in 1890 when a Filipino overseer was killed near Kokopo. In retaliation the expatriate community organised a punitive expedition. For several days there was war on the Gazelle Peninsula. Europeans with guns, a few trusted local labourers with guns, and the many island labourers with axes, spears, bows and arrows attacked the Tolai. Two hundred Tolai houses were destroyed, but within a few days a return party of several hundred Tolai warriors attacked one of the plantations. Peace was negotiated in 1890, and, although the Tolai had to pay compensation in *tambu* shell money, they had substantially improved their position. The Germans realised that they faced a united enemy who outnumbered them, and that the settlers could only proceed by negotiation. They had to learn to take notice of the Tolai point of view and to discuss compensation for land taken.

The conflict flared up again in 1893 as the plantations extended further into Tolai land. The arrival of a German warship made little difference to the Tolai. The ship shelled their villages, and troops were used against the Tolai, but without much success. As will be seen, the relationship between the Tolai people and the administration improved with the arrival of Governor Albert Hahl. Although Hahl believed in asserting the authority of the white man, he also recognised that the local people had rights. Hahl respected the right of the Tolai to their land; he received a measure of co-operation, and introduced a limited system of village-level government. Eventually the Tolai made peace, but remained undefeated. These early uprisings established the Tolai reputation as proud warriors who could not be ignored by colonial governments.

Imperial German government control 1899–1914

In the second half of the thirty-year period of German colonisation the New Guinea Company administration was replaced by direct German government control. The German government appointed as Governor Albert Hahl, an experienced colonial administrator with instructions to extend German influence in the region and encourage the development of the plantations.

The Imperial administration had ten times as much money to spend as had been available to New Guinea Company administrators. This enabled Hahl to build colonial district offices, extend the road network, establish police posts, and expand the police force. Hahl soon recognised that difficulty in recruiting labour was hindering the progress of the colony. When he visited Lihir Island in 1900 the people told him that they had plenty of food at home, so why should they go to the plantations? In 1901 very few people in the Madang region were willing to sign on as labourers, although some said that they would spend a month in Kokopo in the Gazelle Peninsula in order to see the place. The people in the Huon Gulf refused German money and demanded to be paid in pigs' teeth. Initially Hahl tried to improve recruitment by introducing more liberal labour policies. However, the German planters were desperate for labour and convinced Hahl to impose his control on the villages as fast as possible in an attempt to secure a more stable labour supply.

In 1899 the Germans had only two colonial stations, one at Madang to cover the mainland and one at Kokopo to cover the Gazelle Peninsula and the islands. New stations were rapidly established. Kavieng in New Ireland was the first to be established because the area was thought to be a rich source of plantation labourers. By 1905 three more stations had been established in the islands — at Namatanai, Kieta and Rabaul. Between 1906 and 1914 stations were established at Aitape, Morobe, Angoram and Lae on the mainland and at Manus in the Admiralty Islands.

In order to exercise more direct control over the villages the Germans appointed local headmen, known as *luluais,* to act on their behalf. Supposedly as an inducement, *luluais* were each given a portrait of the most powerful *luluai* of all — Kaiser Wilhelm II.

Each district was controlled by an officer who had to make his district safe and profitable for Europeans. He had to protect European lives, extend colonial law through *luluais,* build roads, make sure that labour recruiters were getting all the villagers they wanted, and return escaped labourers to their masters. He commanded a force of up to eighty armed local police. If hostile locals were too much for police, a German warship came to aid with off-shore firepower detachments of German troops. From 1911 district officers had the assistance of the mobile expeditionary troops based in Rabaul, a force of 100 to 125 locals available for service anywhere in the colony. By these means the Germans succeeded in gaining control of much of the mainland coast, although most of the inland region remained untouched.

The results of German control

Imperial German government control was good for the exploitation of the local resources by European planters. In this period successful plantations were established along much of the mainland coast, the Gazelle Peninsula, and many of the adjacent islands, and the number of men signing on as contract labourers increased from 1000 in 1899 to almost 11 000 in 1913.

Some locals liked the new jobs brought by the white man, and made careers away from home as policemen, personal servants, boats' crew, and mission catechists, but men who did not like the new jobs also had to work for the white man. The *luluai* who wanted to keep his job made sure that the young men of the village volunteered as labourers and carriers. Under the forced labour regulation of 1903, native people were required to work up to four weeks a year for the administration, usually on building roads. From 1907 villagers were allowed to pay a head-tax instead of working. To earn this money they had the choice of selling copra or vegetables, or working for cash on a plantation. The Tolai people, who lived near the big plantations in the Gazelle Peninsula, had no trouble paying the head-tax from money they made at the markets, but in other areas, many people were forced to work for the Germans in order to pay the tax.

Villagers on the advancing frontier of German control experienced similar German tactics. An officer with thirty or forty armed police would arrive, persuade one man to accompany them to a European town to learn Pidgin, or if there were Pidgin speakers already, appoint a *luluai* and a couple of *tultuls* or interpreters. The cap and stick would be presented as badges of office for the *luluai*. The *luluai* would be told that he was to help the labour recruiters and that the government wanted every unmarried man to work at least one contract of three years. All the young men might be conscripted to build roads, and orders would be given that twenty new coconut palms had to be planted for every able-bodied man in the village.

Opposition and retaliation

Some people asked why they should lose men who were needed to fight in local wars? Others wanted to fight the Germans. ToVagira of Tomanairik village in the inland Gazelle Peninsula was said to have killed a man for doing roadwork for the whites. A southern New Ireland man, Geges, threatened in 1906 to kill two *luluais*, eat them, and feed pigs out of their *luluai* caps. Some Bougainvillians were prevented by villagers from doing forced labour for the Germans south of Kieta in the same year. Two villages near Hatzfeldthafen on the coast west of Madang sent a message to the district officer in 1910 saying that they would kill him if he came with his police. People near Aitape killed a policeman in 1913 as he tried to catch escaped labourers. The Germans did not tolerate disobedience. They punished the local people with surprise dawn raids, naval bombardments, or the landing of German marines to march through the villages.

The arrival of missionaries was also resisted in some areas. Talili, a Tolai leader from inland of Kabakada at the neck of the Gazelle Peninsula, declared war on the Wesleyan Methodist mission in the late 1870s because mission activities were interfering with trade networks which he dominated. The mission considered him responsible for the deaths of four Fijian teachers from the mission in April 1878. Reverend George Brown reacted by arming Europeans and declaring war on Talili and his people. In 1879 Talili was alleged to have burnt down the local mission house, threatened the Fijian missionaries, and made himself ready for protracted warfare. The British-based Wesleyan mission reported the incidents to Captain Richards of the British naval ship HMS *Renard*. A patrol from the ship went ashore at Kabakada, destroyed houses and banana gardens, and shot a rocket inland, hopefully in the direction of Talili's village. He was later caught and deported to the mainland by the German administration.

The Germans used more force than the British or Australians in Papua, and they killed more people. The Mussau Islanders who killed a party of explorers in 1901 lost ninety-three dead in battles with a German punitive expedition. The German force lost no-one. The people of Paparatava in the Gazelle Peninsula and their allies who killed a planter's wife and child in 1902 mourned eighty to ninety dead kinsmen after the event. About forty mountain warriors died in a single battle against the Germans and their Buan allies on 1 February 1911. A German expedition into the mountains of southern New Ireland in December 1913 consisted of five Europeans, ninety-two police, and fifty-one carriers. The fully-equipped native 'police-soldier', as the Germans called him, with his M88 rifle and bayonet, was a more powerful enemy than the villager had ever known, especially when he was joined by German troops with machine guns.

The following story provides an example of the German policy that allowed extensive alienation of indigenous land which, in turn, aroused intense hostility from the people.

Killing of a planter's wife

Klaus Neumann[7] has written an account of a Tolai incident in which he allowed the indigenous view to emerge more clearly than the view of colonisers. The killing of a planter's wife in April 1903 led to an uprising in which many people were killed. A dispute arose between a German planter, Rudolf Wolff, and a local landowner, ToKilang, concerning Wolff taking over ToKilang's land. The dispute escalated and ToKilang gathered local villagers, including a local leader ToVagira, to kill Wolff's wife and regain the land by force.

The group approached Mrs Wolff after her husband had left the house and offered to sell her a pig, copra, and eggs. While negotiations on the price were continuing one attacker moved behind her and hit her with an axe on the back of the head. That was the sign for the others to thrust their spears into her body. In an ensuing fight between some of Wolff's men and the attackers, one man from Paparatava was killed and five of Wolff's labourers seriously wounded. ToKikile killed the baby, and Turpele killed the black maid Sophie.

Wolff, hearing screams, rode back to his house. One of his labourers, Sotelle from Buka, rushed to meet him. The planter saw many Tolai men, some aiming guns at him, running around in excitement. Later Wolff claimed to have been shot at and to have fallen from his horse three times. Presuming that his wife and child were dead he shouted to the labourer Toraki to get help from the mission station at Takabur and he himself rode to Giregire Plantation owned by Emma Kolbe and sent a labourer to Kokopo to alert the police.

The attackers looted and ransacked the premises and took at least eleven guns and ammunition with them. They retreated towards Paparatava and Tomanairik. People from Malakuna appeared and continued the looting until the first Europeans arrived.

The reprisal

Some hours later, about eighty native policemen, led by Assessor Wolff and accompanied by Rudolf Wolf and some other whites, arrived in Tabaule. They went to Paparatava where they burnt all the houses. On the next day the administration put Assunto Costantini, a former Catholic missionary, in charge of the operations. He was later credited with their success. Over the next few days the police tried in vain to get hold of the Paparatava people who were held responsible for the murder. A price was put on ToKilang's and ToVagira's heads. On 6 and 7 April about 2000 labourers supplied by Emma Kolbe and the New Guinea Company destroyed the gardens in and around Paparatava. On 11 April the police, apparently again supported by plantation labourers, occupied Tamanairik and killed eight men. But ToKilang, ToVagira and their men had fled. On 24 April 1902 ToKilang was shot by a police patrol after his hide-out had been betrayed. Some time between 19 May and 5 August 1902, ToVagira, tracked down by people from Paparatava, was also killed by the police. According to figures supplied by members of the police force, between eighty and ninety 'enemies' had been killed.

Apart from the guns taken from Wolff's house, the police captured forty-five firearms, nearly all of them usable. The Tolai had adapted Wolff's ammunition for their own weapons, either by making bullets from shot gun pellets removed from their cartridges, of which they had captured about 600, or by swathing Mauser cartridges so that they could be fired from Snider rifles. The colonial troops had no casualties from bullets. In his report Assessor Wolff noted that the Tolai did not use a deadly weapon applied in earlier confrontations, the sling stone. To sling the stone the warriors had to operate in the open. Wolff believed that they were afraid to do so because of the sophisticated firearms used by the police and their allies.

The details supplied in reports written before the end of the hostilities suggest that the police could rely on a network of informers among the Tolai. Wolff reported that from the very beginning Costantini 'was in close touch with the natives, was well informed about their plans and managed to approach the peaceful elements at the right moment'.[8]

From the beginning, the avengers of Mrs Wolff took the offensive. The colonial troops declared an operational zone between Tabaule and Mount Vunakokor, the north-western boundary of which was to be held as a defence line. People living inside this zone were shot dead, fled to villages outside the zone or to mission stations, or were brought to Kokopo, where women and children from Paparatava seem to have been kept in a camp. Gardens within the zone were destroyed.

'This seems to be an irregular and unrestrained Grenskrieg which is conducted without mercy by both sides', commented the *Socialist Vorwarts* on 30 May 1902, relying in its assessment on information provided by Father Eberlein and published in the Catholic German press.

A later Tolai attempt to reclaim the alienated land

When the Australians took control of the German Territory in 1918 they, in turn, confiscated what they mistakenly believed to be German-owned land. Early in the 1950s a descendant of ToKilang called ToVetenge attempted to reclaim the land on behalf of his people. His claim was based on an oral history version of the 1902 incident. The following is part of ToVetenge's account of his attempt to regain possession of the land.

> My name is Josep ToVetenge. I will tell you about this court case we had. I have forgotten which year it was. It was about the piece of land which is called Tokota. We began it like this: we knew that [the Germans] had confiscated this particular piece of land without paying for it. So we asked: 'What does the law say about this? They seized our land, and they killed women and they killed children and they killed

men and they burnt down houses and they killed pigs and
chickens — and all that as a payback for one woman, for
one white woman?' That's what we asked the court. We went
to court, the first time in Rabaul. Mr Kampari [name is spelt
phonetically] was the judge . . . Mr Kruksen [name is spelt
phonetically] was our lawyer . . . We argued that according
to our knowledge of the law, if one person was killed by two
people, those two would be killed in return. The ones who
had killed will be killed, and that's it. And in this case, many
men were killed, and houses were burnt, some women were
killed and some children and so forth. We asked the Government and we asked the court: 'How come there was only
one woman, just one white woman, but they have retaliated
many times?' The court replied that in those days people
were not enlightened. 'It was probably done in order to
prevent them from taking up arms again.' We said: 'If they
had killed only [the leaders], there would have been no
more hostilities.' That's what we told the court. We asked:
'Which law applies here? We, too, know that when one
person is murdered, they kill the one who has killed. If there
were two of them, they would kill the two. If there had been
three who killed, those three would be killed in return. If
there had been four or more who killed, all of them would
be killed.' That's how we presented our case. The court
heard our argument and put them into the right words.
They ruled that this particular piece of land, Tokota, be
returned to us, because it had been seized illegally as just
another compensation for Mrs Wolff. The people rejoiced
because we had got back the land . . . So far, so good. The
masta, Tom Garrett, heard the verdict and appealed in
Australia to the High Court. We collected one hundred
pounds to support me, or rather, to assist the Government
which paid for my air fare, so that I could attend the court
case at the High Court in Australia.

I arrived in Australia at night time. They put me up in a
hotel. I slept. In the morning, a white man by the name of
Mr Brown met me at the hotel and accompanied me to the
court. I arrived at the court. The court proceedings began.
I sat there, I did not say anything. My lawyer did the talking.

I did not say anything. The court was adjourned. We rose, we knocked off. On the next day we went to the court again. Only the lawyer spoke, I just sat there like an idiot. Nobody interpreted for me, so that I would know what was going on and could say something. Nothing. I just sat there. I simply sat there. On the third day, a Friday, we went again to the court. I sat there again and did not speak. I just sat there. Nobody interpreted for me or asked me to speak. No, I just sat there until they wound up the court proceedings. And they told us to get ready to return to Rabaul. We rose. Mr Brown, the white man who was taking care of me, told me that I would return to Rabaul. I arrived back in Rabaul and then went to my village, to Tagitagi No. 1. The people asked me: 'So what? Did we win?' 'Oh, I was like a statue, I did not say anything. I just sat there with my eyes wide open. Like a piece of wood I sat there. Just like a statue. I did not speak.' The people were furious. The Australian won the appeal and the Tolai lost the case[9].

As has been seen, the reaction of local people to the arrival of Europeans was mainly hostile. Many local people such as the Tolai resented the alienation of their land and hated the Germans. However, others, such as the people of the Huon Gulf area whose contact was mainly with missionaries, had a more favourable impression of the European invasion of their territory. It is important to remember, however, that even under the considerable extension of German control in the period from 1899 to 1914 there were still many people in the inland areas who did not know that the Germans were supposed to be in charge.

The missions

In those areas in which the first significant European contact was with missionaries, the people often accepted the European presence more favourably. The administration encouraged the establishment and expansion of German-based missions of various denominations as a way of spreading German language and culture amongst the people.

Along the coast of the mainland, mission stations

representing Lutheran sects or Catholic societies concentrated their activities at Aitape, Astrolabe Bay and the Huon Gulf. Catholic societies were also active in the islands. The earliest of the mainland missions were established in the 1880s and by 1914 there were missions in most areas with which the administration had made contact, and in some areas over which the administration did not have great control. All these missions were financed and predominantly staffed by churches in Germany. A missionary society in the area without a German base was the Methodist Missionary Society of Australasia, which had begun work in the Duke of York Islands as early as 1875 and extended into other island areas. The Methodist Missionary Society sought to overcome this disadvantage through the use of some missionaries who had been ordained in the Methodist Episcopal Church of Germany.

Apart from religious instruction, the missions usually conducted a school which offered basic number and German language skills. Most missionaries learnt local languages, taught in the language of the people, and recruited indigenous people as teachers. Some missions also tried to provide basic health services, although in most cases their own European staff were severely affected by common local diseases.

The missions were most readily accepted by the people when their activities were thought to be of some benefit to the community. In many areas they were allowed by the people, who did not at that stage realise that their land was being alienated, to set up mission stations peacefully. The pioneer Lutheran missionary, Johannes Flierl, for instance, established a mission at Simbang, near Finschhafen in 1886 without serious incident.

SUMMARY

The British interest in the south of the island was mainly strategic; they saw little economic advantage to be gained from their colonial possession. In consequence they alienated very little land and did little to encourage settlers. The administration was very poorly funded and could not afford to establish a marked physical presence except in Port Moresby. The main Christian denominations operated missions in areas agreed upon between themselves and the administration and provided what few health and education services that were offered to the people.

The Germans, on the other hand, saw the colony of New Guinea as a economic venture and hoped to establish profitable trading companies and produce cash crops through the exploitation of a cheap supply of local labour. The missions were seen as channels for the introduction of German culture as well as Christianity. The Germans hoped to see the colony become a substantial economic asset and they established a durable physical presence on the lowlands. The villagers were mainly unco-operative and serious clashes in which the Germans were invariably the victors occurred.

Although the motives for the establishment of the colonies were different — mainly strategic on the part of the British and chiefly economic on the part of the Germans — neither colonial power consulted the people when making decisions which affected their land and their lives.

3

Papua 1905–1940

Across the raging waves
Beyond the blue waters
They saw the scattered islands
Clad in colourful horizons
Blown by the cool breezes
Great masses of unknown land
Exploration, exploitation,
Determination were their common aim
Winning and glorification their common faith.

Adapted from Arthur Javodimbari, *Return to my Land*, **Papuan Pocket Poets Series, Port Moresby, 1974.**

By 1905 most Papuan societies were very much as they had been in pre-colonial times. Less than one hundred Europeans were based in Port Moresby and Samarai while even fewer were scattered in isolated stations such as Daru in the Western division, and Ioma in the North-eastern division. With their warrior traditions the Goaribari had killed James Chalmers of the London Missionary Society in 1901, and the killers were either in prison in Port Moresby or still at large; the Binandere had fought the colonial administration and the miners with more open violence than other Papuan communities, though they made peace with the Australian colonial officers and the Anglican missionaries by 1900. Both the Kiwai and the Binandere men turned their warrior spirit in a different direction to serve in the police. Itinerant gold prospecting parties reached a few places in the Papuan interior such as YoddaValley, but most of the local communities

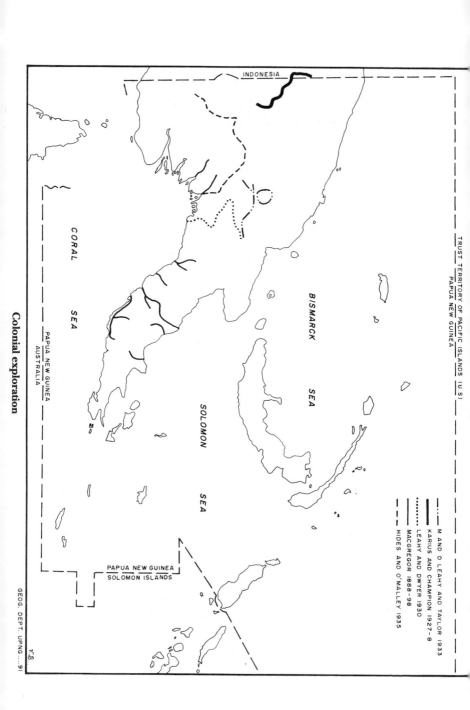

Colonial exploration

TRUST TERRITORY OF PACIFIC ISLANDS (U S)
PAPUA NEW GUINEA

INDONESIA

BISMARCK

SEA

CORAL

SEA

SOLOMON

SEA

PAPUA NEW GUINEA
AUSTRALIA

PAPUA NEW GUINEA
SOLOMON ISLANDS

.... M AND D LEAHY AND TAYLOR 1933
━━━━ KARIUS AND CHAMPION 1927-8
•••••••• LEAHY AND DWYER 1930
———— MACGREGOR 1888-98
– – – – HIDES AND O'MALLEY 1935

GEOG. DEPT. UPNG.....91

remained unaffected by miners, missionaries or administration patrols.

It was the spread of the steel axes, knives, fish hooks, nails, and other trade items ahead of the white men who brought them that began to bring about change in some communities on the coast and a few inland. The introduced steel technology made the local people aware of their less-efficient wooden tools and weapons. In the next two decades this technological change was to make more impact in the villages than the administration's attempt to impose colonial law and order.

Under the Papua Act, adopted by the Commonwealth of Australia in 1905 and brought into effect in 1906, Australia formally accepted responsibility for the British Protectorate and renamed the territory Papua. Australia took responsibility for the British colony reluctantly. It appears that the young nation was too concerned with its own internal issues to pay serious attention to the outpost of the British empire immediately to its north.

The period between the departure of Sir William MacGregor in 1898 and the appointment of Hubert Murray as Australian administrator in 1907 was one of marking time. Although gold prospectors, and hence the government, went into some parts of the country previously unknown to them, the three British administrators G. le Hunte (1898–1903), C. Robinson (1903–04) and F. R. Barton (1904–07) who succeeded MacGregor were mainly concerned to protect the policies laid down under the previous administrations.

It was evident from the outset that there was a basic division of opinion in Australia as to whether to adopt a policy of protection of the rights of the Papuans, in particular their land and labour rights, or to encourage economic development by Europeans. Advocates of each of these policies inevitably clashed, because economic development by Europeans required the use of Papuan land and Papuan labour and, of course, their use would interfere with Papuan rights.

The Royal Commission of 1906

In 1906 a Royal Commission was appointed to enquire into the efficiency of the administration of the then-administrator

Captain Barton, and the suitability of the territory for European economic development. Land and labour policies were of course basic questions addressed by the commission, as economic development could not go ahead without taking more Papuan land and Papuan labour. The commission was in favour of rapid development of large areas of land to grow tropical crops such as copra, rubber, hemp and tobacco. However, the commission also recommended that the land should be leased by Europeans, not taken by force, and the people should not be sold guns or alcoholic liquor.

The assumption of the commissioners was that the Papuans would work on the European plantations and for European prospectors on the gold fields for very low wages. The administration justified this exploitation of Papuan labour on the grounds that this work would be socially and morally good for the people. In presenting the Report of the Royal Commission on Papua to the Australian Parliament the commissioners asked the colonial administration to intervene in the recruitment of labourers. The commissioners believed that:

> Government officers would more readily obtain recruits. The native would place greater reliance, and we think rightly so, upon receiving fair treatment from their employers if the Government were the go between. The Government, by monopolising the right to recruit and desiring to make no profit thereby, could afford to do so at least cost to the employers, who would consequently be benefited[1].

As Michael Hess has pointed out, the detailed regulation was seen by the colonisers at the time 'as an evil necessity created by the Papuans' "level of advancement" '[2]. One official wrote

> the Administration looks forward to the time when the Papuan native will be so far advanced in education, civilisation and the spirit of self-reliance as to no longer need the protection of a Contract of Service and Native Labour Ordinance, with all the present restrictions and safe-guards[3].

While the Commission took evidence from Europeans in many parts of the country, the most important evidence came from Hubert Murray, who came to dominate the colony over the next three decades. Born in New South Wales, Australia, in 1861, Murray was the son of a landowner and politician. A lawyer, trained at Oxford University, he arrived in Papua as Chief Judicial Officer in 1904. To the Commissioners, Murray criticised both the efficiency of Barton's administration and his implementation of MacGregor's policy of protecting Papuan rights to their land and their labour on the grounds that this policy discouraged the development of the colony by Europeans. Many people thought Murray's attack on Barton was unfair, but the Commission accepted his evidence. Barton resigned, and in 1907 Murray became acting administrator, and in 1908 lieutenant-governor and administrator of Papua.

However, as will be shown, in practice Murray continued to implement the basic policies established by MacGregor of giving some protection to the people at the expense of short-term economic development. Murray and a few far-sighted foreign investors recognised that it was in the long-term interests of Europeans not to implement policies which could result in wiping out the labour force. This was partly on humanitarian grounds, but mainly because local labour was necessary for the foreigners to exploit the natural resources in the colony. As Michael Hess has said, the real effect of the labour regulation was that 'it served to protect the pre-colonial society while labour was extracted from it' and some areas were 'to be closed altogether to indenture where officials felt [indenture] was endangering subsistence production[4].' Thus, the protectionist policy towards the people stemmed from both humanitarian and materialist motives.

The Land Ordinances of 1906

The Land Ordinances of 1906 gave effect to some of the major recommendations of the Royal Commission. Under the Papua Act land could not be bought, but it could be leased for ninety-nine years. However, under the Land Ordinance of 1906 no rent at all had to be paid for the first ten years of a lease, no survey fees had to be paid, and by simply paying a nominal deposit a settler could obtain a lease of up to 1000 acres of land suitable for a plantation. If the land was for raising cattle he could acquire a much larger area for the same amount.

The settler was required to work the land. One-fifth had to he planted within five years; two-fifths in ten years; and up to three-quarters eventually had to be kept cultivated. If a settler did not cultivate the land he lost the lease. The interests of the people were protected to the extent that they could not sell or lease land to settlers. All land had to be purchased by the government, which had a duty to make sure that the owners were willing to sell and were unlikely to need the land in the future.

These seemed attractive conditions for Europeans wanting to settle in the Australian territory. The administration did much to encourage settlers, describing in advertisements how suitable the land and climate would be for tropical agriculture. Some Europeans responded to the new laws and the official publicity and came to the colony to establish plantations. In 1906 there were 550 Europeans in the colony; in 1907, 690; in 1909, 720; in 1911, 1032; and in 1913, 1219. But then there was a slight decline, and it was not until 1924 that the 1913 figure was again reached. Overall the European population had not increased as quickly as the administration had hoped.

There is no direct evidence to suggest that Papuans expressed opinions in the Royal Commission to give away permanently or to lease for ninety-nine years large areas of their customary land to Europeans. No Papuan could even understand the concept or the implication of the term 'lease'. Some officials declared extensive areas as 'vacant land', and steel axes, knives, as well as other trade goods were used to pay for the land. It is obvious that the Papuans did not know what they were doing with their land.

The same pattern of an early period of growth, followed by a levelling off, can be seen in the figures for land that was leased. In 1906 just over 22 000 acres were under lease. By 1910 this had shot up to 363 425 acres. However, many of these leases lapsed as investors were unable to comply with the ordinance requiring leased land to be used for agricultural purposes. By 1914 only 220 000 acres were under lease and this figure was not exceeded until 1940. The area actually planted was much less: 10 000 acres in 1910, 43 000 acres in 1914, and not much more in 1940.

Up to 1914 most of the planting, about 67 per cent, had been of coconuts, 15 per cent had been of rubber, and 7 per cent of sisal hemp, which was used for rope and twine making. This spike-leafed plant grew well in the dry Motu-Koita area, and the British New Guinea Company had large plantations of it at Bomana. Tramways were put down to carry the leaf. The industry declined during World War I, revived briefly in the middle of 1920s, and then disappeared altogether.

But in 1914 gold, not crops, was still by far the most important export from Papua. The most valuable field was Woodlark Island, which had been worked since the 1890s. Other important fields were at Misima in the Trobriands and Yodda and Gira in the Northern district. The Lakekamu River, in the Gulf district, was the only important gold field started during this period. It had a rich but brief life between 1910 and 1912. The gold fields also provided opportunities for local communities which supplied miners' labourers to earn cash to pay for trade goods.

After 1910 copper was also exported through Port Moresby from the Sapphire Creek field in the Astrolabe Range. By 1914 there were plans to build a railway line from the copper mines to Port Moresby to carry the copper ore. Casuarina trees which are still along Ela Beach in Port Moresby marked the route that was planned for the railway, but the war came and the plans were abandoned. When the copper industry was revived in the 1920s, a railway was built, but the route was down to Bootless Bay, east of Port Moresby.

Why did Papua not develop rapidly as an exporter of plantation crops? Europeans who were the ones to gain from the exploitation of cash crops blamed the administration, but it was not really the fault of the governing authority. There were more basic factors. All the crops that the territory could produce could be grown in other countries which had a climate and soils at least as good as the colony's and which were closer to markets. Those who predicted riches for the territory overestimated the resources of Papua and the demand of world markets.

Many European settlers did not recognise this and believed that a colonial administration of their own countrymen was abandoning them. Many planters believed that they had to work hard with little help, and resented Murray's attitude towards them. Most did not recognise that Papuan labour was being exploited to work the plantations; they believed that Murray was favouring the plantation workers at the expense of the planters.

Exploration of the interior

By about 1920 the administration had made contact only with the people of the coast and those island and inland areas where profits could be made from gold: that is, in the Northern district and around the Lakekamu River in the Gulf district. Murray was anxious to explore the mountainous interior and in the 1920s and 1930s mounted a number of well-organised expeditions. By 1939 Murray was fairly confident that the whole of Papua had been explored by Europeans.

In the initial stages most Papuans who had met with representatives of the colonial administration had done so through foot patrols of one white officer and six to ten police, and carriers. Murray knew that it was a risk to send small parties into new areas, but he said that, even if he had the funds to pay for large expeditions, he preferred small parties. A small party was easier to control, it was easier to see that carriers and police did not interfere with local people, and he wanted his officers to establish colonial control with as little disturbance as possible. They were not to subjugate the people; they were to associate with them, he said. In 1932 he wrote:

> In practice the natives always have the first shot, for a government party does not open fire until it is attacked, and not always then. Even if the spears are poised and bows are bent there is still a chance of preserving the peace and making friends[5].

If a patrol fired shots, Murray demanded sufficient information to satisfy himself that the patrol had no alternative. If a patrol took food from a garden or possessions from a village, Murray wanted to know what payment had been made. Of course sometimes patrols in Papua shot people. But Murray was demanding this standard at a time when the Germans and, after 1918, the Australian administration in the Mandated Territory of New Guinea carried out punitive raids. Murray accepted that using small foot patrols was a slow method of extending colonial influence. He liked the description used by a French administrator, 'the policy of the oil stain'. Murray wanted his administrative stations to act like a drop of oil, spilt on water, which would gradually spread outwards.

Murray read carefully the reports of his 'outside men', his field officers. He gave his officers little praise to their faces but he praised them to others. He was also proud of the Royal Papuan Constabulary, 'Judge Murray's police', as they were called. His pride in his field officers and the police was probably justified. Their co-operation was essential to the process of extending European control in the colony.

By 1940 at least a quarter of the people of Papua still did not recognise the authority of Murray's administration. These were mostly the people of the southern highlands. In 1937 a base had been established at Lake Kutubu, which was supplied by flying boat from the Kerema station. But Kutubu was a fair way from the main centres of population in the southern highlands, so that the populated areas around Ialibu, Mendi, Tari and Koroba knew little of the invading foreigners, and neither did the less-populated areas to the west.

In one of these early patrols an incident occurred which has become a part of the folk history of initial meetings between the invaders and the local people. This particular event happened at Kero village in Ialibu probably in the late 1930s or early 1940s. Kelly Keleli of Mokai clan, Kogibungi village, and Thomas Lapi, both of Ialibu, have interviewed some of the people who were involved in the incident, and in 1985 translated the material for the Social History course at the University of Papua New Guinea.

At Kero, it was the second or third time that a group of policemen had led a patrol officer and came to the village. The residents took to the bush for fear of being shot, as had happened on the first contact occasion. The official party apparently offered trade goods and invited the people to come out of the bush to receive steel axes, knives, lap-laps, salt, and other things. Kombea, a 'big man' and renowned warrior, was chosen to destroy the weapons of the intruders. Whilst other villagers were diverting the attention of the European officer and the policemen with the presentation of the gifts, Kombea moved swiftly but stealthily to the spot where a gun was lying near a tree. Grabbing the gun he chopped it with his heavy stone axe and broke the weapon. Everyone, including Kombea, ran for their lives into the nearby forest.

The policemen and their officer pursued the people and arrested many of the villagers, but the culprit was still at large. The prisoners were put 'in a huge hole', probably a cave, near Kero. Apparently the policemen built a hut at the mouth and posted a guard who sometimes entered the dungeon and raped women prisoners.

Kombea was still at large, but Kakaye, another 'big man' of the Akai clan, joined the prison voluntarily because he had been responsible for organising the attack. Kakaye noticed a digging stick in the hands of Kaite, a female prisoner, and he realised that a tunnel could be dug from the cave to the nearest valley. Kakaye organised some men and women to sing songs and play near the mouth of the cave so that the police guard would not suspect what was going on inside. Kakaye, who was alive in 1987, told Thomas Lapi in his language:

> I took this digging stick and started to dig a tunnel towards the direction which I thought would be easy to escape. It took me some weeks before the tunnel was completed. All the prisoners crawled through it like a herd of pigs and escaped to their homes. We spread the horrible way in which we were treated in the prison. The next morning word was spread around the nearby villages to make a revenge attack on the whiteman and his party. We invaded the outpost but the whiteman shot Ekai Kerandi with his gun from the distance and this manner of quick death frightened us. We called off the attack and the white man left Kero with his party. This is how we reacted when the second white man arrived in our village[6].

The people of the coast, its hinterland, the islands, and the lowlands gold areas were most affected by the European presence. For these people the administration meant an uncertain peace, some European goods, and the occasional visit of a resident magistrate who forced them to line up. Sometimes he asked them their names and then wrote something in a mysterious book. At other times he told them how good the colonial authority was but the people feared the resident magistrate because they were uncertain what he wanted, and they were relieved when he moved on to the next village. By 1940 many more people had learnt about the colonial administration, but they usually looked on patrols as something that appeared rarely, and for whom something of a show had to be put on. During the times of initial contact some people believed that the members of the patrol, whether white or brown, were the kin returning from the dead, and for this reason those patrols were welcomed.

Those Papuans who were under the control of the central authority were given virtually no chance to play a part in the government that the administration was trying to establish in their communities. Some continued to be appointed village constables and to join the armed constabulary, and in these areas their duties had changed little from the time of MacGregor. The only institution that Murray added to the administration system was that of village council.

The first village councils were established in the 1920s. The Port Moresby Council, established in 1927, had twelve members and was more active than most. In 1933 it talked about problems associated with gardening, putting in a water supply, buying a truck, banking, and the education of girls. However, the Port Moresby Council was exceptional, in that it had some money to spend. Most of the councils had no money and no power. At best they just talked and perhaps handed on requests to the village constable or directly to the resident magistrate. But to make requests or to supply information is not to govern. The main effect of the establishment of village councils was to help the administration to strengthen control over local communities. Murray expected little from the councils and again he expected change to be slow. 'It may be desirable', he wrote in 1935, 'to arrange for the amalgamation of different councils into one large conference on matters of common importance'[7]. But he warned that this change should not happen too quickly and he made no plans for a meeting of representatives of councils in his time.

Murray also gave Papuans a slight involvement in the colonial courts by appointing what he called assessors. These were village leaders; often they were also councillors, and they sat alongside the resident magistrate when he heard a court case. They might give the resident magistrate advice about local customs and about the severity of the sentence that should be imposed, but they had no power of their own and could only talk to the resident magistrate, who might accept or reject the advice of the assessor. Murray was in no hurry to give responsibility to Papuans.

Education

In 1921–22 only seventy Papuans passed standard 2, then the highest standard that was examined by an official inspector. In 1938 seventy-seven Papuans were given certificates for having passed the highest standard, that is standard 5; in 1939 fifty passed; in 1940, ninety-one. The schools which taught them were all mission schools which Murray subsidised with money collected from Papuans under the Native Taxes Ordinance. Murray spent approximately one-third of the revenue collected from Papuans on education. Some money was given on the basis of how many students passed at various levels. For each student passing standard 1, the mission received five shillings, and ten shillings for a student passing standard 5. But most money was in the form of grants covering the cost of salaries, buildings, equipment, and so on. Murray particularly wanted to promote technical and agricultural education and he was ready to give a thousand pounds per year to missions prepared to provide technical education.

Several of the missions expanded their technical courses as a result, and by 1940 a number of Papuans had acquired skills, mostly in carpentry, at Salamo on Fergusson Island where they were taught by the Methodists, at Kwato near Samarai where they were taught by Papua Ekalesia, at Bogani, Dogura, and Abadi where the Anglicans had mission stations, at Port Moresby, at Aird Hill near Kikori where the LMS gave some technical education and practical training, and at Yule Island where the

Catholic Mission had a small technical school. The Department of Works employed some Papuans as apprentices. In spite of Murray's hopes that an agricultural school might be established, only one was started — by the Methodists in the Trobriands. Its aim was to teach the Papuans to be better traditional farmers, but it had little success.

Both Murray and the missions have been criticised for providing little education for the people. The reasons were economic, social, and ideological. Murray had little money. The headtax on Papuans did not provide adequate funds, and little money was available from outside sources. In addition, there were few opportunities for employment for educated Papuans; many came to town with their certificates safely stored in a bamboo tube to find there were no jobs available. It should also be recognised that the type and length of education given to Papuans was related to Murray's beliefs concerning their preferred future. Murray wanted the Papuans to be first — better gardeners, second — good craftsmen, and only third to be given a good basic education.

However, although the education given to Papuans was very limited, those who received it, by their learning and by their ability to communicate with Europeans, greatly changed traditional patterns of village authority. Educated mission workers, in particular, gained much status, and the mission pastor and teacher became new figures of authority in the village.

Village plantations

Murray hoped the Papuans would become more than employed labourers for Europeans by working their own plantations on their own land. To some extent this happened later. People on the coast grew more copra than they had done before, and the Mekeo attempted to grow rice, and for a while they were successful. In 1940 the people in the Northern district received over 2000 pounds sterling for the coffee they produced. But generally village plantations were not much of a success. They were often kept going by resident magistrates gaoling people who did not work on them; in effect this was forced labour. The profits had to be divided among so many people that usually a man only received a few shillings for his

share of a year's work. He could have made more as an indentured labourer, and most Papuans who found a way into the
cash economy did so as indentured labourers.

Labourers

Indentured labourers were men who signed an indenture,
which was a contract to work for cash and trade goods away
from their villages. Most indentured labourers worked either
for planters or for miners, and their conditions were set down
in the Native Labour Ordinance of 1907. Each recruit signed
on before a resident magistrate or some other official who was
supposed to ensure that the recruit understood and accepted
his indenture. He then recorded the recruit's name, home
village, and details of employment on the indenture, and tried
to make sure that the indenture was fair. Although these
legalities were not always observed, and some men were forcibly recruited, generally these rules meant that Papuan workers
were, better off than workers under the German and the subsequent Australian administration in New Guinea.

In Papua, there were usually enough men wanting to work
on plantations, mainly because they wanted trade goods such
as steel axes, salt, tobacco, and beads. Some also went away to
escape traditional obligations like paying bride price, or even
to avoid conflicts within their families. In 1906 there may have
been 1500 to 2000 plantation labourers; by 1914 about 7000;
by 1940 about 10 000. Between 1906 and 1940 there was very
little change in plantation labourers' conditions.

Plantation labourers could work for a maximum of three
years, though in the early days most signed on for only eighteen
months. The pay was ten shillings a month, and health and
housing standards on the plantations were laid down by
ordinance.

When the labourers arrived at the plantation, they were assigned to a gang, told to work hard, and given the rest of the
day off.

Often the labourers came from different areas. Sometimes
this was a deliberate policy of the plantation manager. He
thought the labourers would be easier to control if he had
them from different areas.

On arrival the recruit was issued with a blanket and two *ramis*, also known as loincloths or *lap-laps*. Six months later he would get another two *ramis*, a mosquito net, a dish, and a spoon. He wore nothing on the top half of his body. In the morning he was fed and then had to line up. Those the manager thought were ill were called out, and the rest went to their jobs. By 7 o'clock the men were at work. Under the labour regulations a man had to work no more than fifty hours in the week, and he was to have Sunday off. Interestingly enough, these were shorter hours than Australian farm labourers worked at that time. In fact, labourers were sometimes 'punished' by being made to work on Sundays, especially where there was no mission nearby. Perhaps the labourers might stay in the labour gang clearing scrub for new plantings, cutting grass, or making copra. Or perhaps someone might become a driver, or operate a machine making rubber, or work in and about the house.

Whatever his position, he was unlikely to be spoken to by a white man other than as a servant, and if he was slow to act he was likely to get a bang on the ear. That was illegal, but even Murray admitted that it did happen. If he did not work hard enough, or ran away, he was fined or gaoled. His sleeping quarters had to be kept clean and dry. Sometimes they were inspected by administration officers, and if they were not in good condition the plantation manager could be fined. Rations were adequate, not appetising. The labourer had to get at least one and a half pounds of rice a day, and one pound of meat or fish a week. On Saturdays, after cleaning up the quarters, he might be issued with a little extra black twist tobacco and perhaps something else, such as fish, which his boss thought might make him more contented. When the labourer's contract expired, he had to be paid 18 pounds sterling before a magistrate for the three years work, and no deductions could be made. If he died on the job, compensation and his pay had to be paid to his relatives.

The work was hard, the diet uninteresting, and there was little justice. But there is much evidence that labourers went back to their villages much bigger and physically healthier than when they left. They brought back with them knives, axes, tin dishes, tin whistles, pieces of cloth, kerosene lamps, and many other things which had a significant effect on the lives of the villagers.

The labourer distributed these goods among his clan, among this friends, to pay debts and bride prices, and in order to create debt among others which would be returned in the future. Of course, what actually happened on the plantations varied from manager to manager despite the rules — although by the 1920s Europeans were being prosecuted fairly often for breaking labour regulations.

Miners' labourers could be engaged for eighteen months, but most signed on for only a year. In 1914 there were about 1000 miners' labourers, and their numbers still fluctuated at around 1000 in 1940. Many were carriers, supplying miners who worked in the interior. The maximum load for a carrier was fifty pounds, or thirty pounds if he was being asked to walk more than twelve miles a day. In addition, the carrier had to carry his own blanket and food. If he was carrying from Buna to Yodda near Kokoda in the Northern District, a journey of approximately fifty kilometres, he had to have thirty-six hours rest before returning to Buna.

As these regulations might suggest, life was tougher for miners' labourers than for plantation labourers. Work was hard, and conditions were severe. Often the miners' labourers worked in cold rivers shovelling gravel onto the banks or into the sluice boxes which washed out the gold. Usually they were coastal people unaccustomed to the cool wet interior. Often it was difficult for the miner to get the supplies to feed them adequately, so hunger and sickness were common, and the medical facilities were completely inadequate. On the Lakekamu field dysentery broke out and 255 Papuans died in five months in 1910, out of a total of about 600 labourers on the field at the time. While conditions for the miners' labourers were generally tough, it is clear that the Papuans went knowingly and freely to work for the miners. By 1914 some men from villages on Milne Bay and Goodenough Island had been working for miners for twenty years. Where men from the villages signed on, they certainly knew what to expect, and given the choice of staying home, or risking the hardships of the goldfields for six to twelve pounds sterling for a year's work, they chose to work.

Some labourers were forced to work as carriers for the colonial administration[8]. If a man refused to carry goods for the administration he could be sent to prison for two weeks[9]. Moreover, an ordinance of 1897 made it possible to punish a man who failed to fulfil his agreement with the administration. He could also be forced to resume his service after spending time in prison. It was also expected that carriers who returned to the villages after they had carried supplies for the colonial administration would also carry back some ideas of the white man's law to the villages.

A distinction should be drawn between the carrier or labourer of the colonial administration and the carrier or labourer of the miners. The miners' labourers were recruited only from 'declared labour districts' or areas that were brought under control. Labourers entered into agreements with the miners to work for a term of contract. Carriers for the administration, however, were recruited from their villages whenever they were needed, to carry the rations for the policemen and the colonial officers engaged in the punitive or exploratory patrols within each division.

As has been seen, the desire for European goods attracted some young men away from their villages, while others were more interested in the adventure. Indeed, there was a certain status associated with ex-labourers once they returned to their villages. Although working on the plantations meant that they had missed the usual manner in which men climbed the social ladder to achieve the status of 'big men', the men who returned had with them the new trade goods and the steel tools which they used or exchanged in the society, and this undermined the status of the established 'big men'. For example, some ex-labourers were able to marry more than one wife because they were able to pay the bride price with the white man's goods instead of the customary wealth such as feathers and dogs' teeth.

Boatmen and police

Perhaps the two groups of Papuans with the positions of

greatest responsibility were boat crews, including some men who captained small launches, and the police. Small boats belonged both to the government and to the traders, and operated all along the Papuan coast. The seamen were comparatively well paid and were probably the most-travelled Papuans in the colony.

In 1914 there were 287 native men in the police force, many of them recruits. The police wore a black *rami* and jumper and carried their heavy Martini-Enfield rifles and cartridge belts with pride. They were much photographed, and numerous visitors commented on their appearance. A newly recruited policeman came to Port Moresby for six months' basic training. He may not have been able to read or write or speak English. He commenced his training day with drill at 6.30 each morning and finished with another drill session at 4 o'clock. In between the periods of drill he learnt to use his rifle and other practical skills such as setting up camp, rowing a boat, and carpentry. Once he had completed his basic training he was posted to a station. In 1914 there were twenty policemen at Daru, eighteen at Kerema, and sixteen at Nepa on the Lakekamu.

The police had numerous duties. They went on patrols and they carried the mail on foot for long distances. At many stations the police were also builders, and built many of the earliest buildings on colonial stations. For the first year of employment the recruit received ten shillings per month, the same basic wage as was paid to a labourer. In his second year he received fifteen shillings, and in the third, one pound. One man, Simoi, from Katatai village just off Daru, who once saved Murray's life, and reached the rank of sergeant-major, was paid five pounds per month in 1914. By 1914 other Papuans had reached the rank of sergeant. Many of the police were Kiwais from the Western district or Orokaivans from the Northern district.

A resident magistrate relied on the policemen to enforce law and order. A policeman could be called upon to go on sentry duty whilst he was on the station. He supervised the prisoners and the labourers in planting the gardens and building roads. He could be sent to arrest killers or to escort carriers along the tracks. He went with his white officers in exploratory and punitive expeditions. Early recruits to the police force often had motives other than just acting as mercenaries for the Europeans in establishing and consolidating colonial law and order. The Kiwais of the Western division and the Binandere of the Northern division, for instance, were more interested in traditional payback killings of their enemies than advancing the frontier of the European presence. The Binandere clashed with the white men but they realised that sustained conflict would not bring about anything to their advantage. Therefore, the Binandere tried to resolve the situation by joining the police force, and using their position inside the force to manipulate the police force in order to enable them to take punitive action against the neighbouring local people who were the Binandere's traditional enemies.

Government officials, tradesmen, and clerks

There were men at the other end of the employment scale who were not indentured labourers. A handful of Papuans, educated at the administration-subsidised mission schools, were employed as officials, craftsmen, and clerks. These were the only Papuan men allowed to wear clothes over the upper half of the body. In the 1920s the police in towns would literally tear the shirt off a Papuan found wearing one illegally.

Lack of training meant that, until the 1920s, there were very few Papuan officials, tradesmen, and clerks. By 1940 there were still only sixty local tradesmen in the Department of Public Works. They repaired boats and buildings and did painting and plumbing. They ran the telephone exchange and installed telephones. They looked after the engine that produced electric power in Port Moresby, and they did electrical wiring. They set the type for the *Papuan Courier* and at the Government Printing Office. They serviced the siren that signalled the 9 p.m. curfew in Port Moresby.

A few Papuans became clerks. In 1929 Murray reported that Nansen Kaisa had been made a collector of taxes. It was, he said, the first time a Papuan was given responsibility for money, so we can assume that most Papuans who became clerks were assigned only minor tasks. Many of the graduates of mission schools went back to the missions as pastors and teachers, and a few went into private enterprise as drivers, tradesmen, or shop assistants.

All Papuan workers were severely discriminated against. They were not allowed on European premises from dusk to dawn. Between 9 p.m. and 6 a.m. all Papuans were forbidden to enter the perimeters of Port Moresby or Samarai. Papuans were, in this period, denied access to their own land. There was segregation of toilets, public transport, especially buses, and residential housing in Port Moresby. Segregated public transport was formally abolished in the 1950s whereas the urban housing restriction withered as Papua New Guinea approached self-government in the early 1970s.

Prisoners

Another group of Papuans who made close contact with Europeans were those who went to gaol. The prisoners were either Papuans captured during the initial conflicts with administration patrols, or Papuans who breached colonial laws and regulations. They were arrested by uniformed policemen, often on the recommendation of the village constables who were appointed by the administration, and taken away from the villages to serve gaol sentences ranging from a few weeks for minor offences such as failing to keep clear the tracks between villages, to several years for murder. Over 500 Papuans, for example, were in gaol at Koki Point near Hanuabada in 1913–14. Prisoners worked harder, at duties such as quarrying, than indentured labourers. They rose at 5.30 and were not back in the gaol until 5 o'clock at night. Much of the public works such as road building, reclaiming land, and painting public buildings in Port Moresby and Samarai was done by prisoners. They were often seen working about the town during the day wearing a *rami* decorated with broad vertical arrows.

Confinement in prison was a new experience for the people. In one way, this experience was like the customary practice in some societies whereby a captive might be taken from the enemy. However, in the latter case, he would be taken to the village to be killed and perhaps eaten. Hence, at the initial stages of contact, a captured man might have feared that the white man and his police would kill him. But later he would learn that he would be allowed to return to his village.

A prisoner served out his sentence under close guard by the police. By day he would work hard in the garden, on the road, or cut materials for a house in the bush. The pattern of life in the prison was different from the pattern of living in the village. All the men who were sentenced to gaol had been used to working very hard all their lives in the village. However, when they were in gaol they were forced to work at a pace imposed upon them by the prison authorities. A new pattern of life was forced upon the prisoner. He worked for a specified length of time determined by someone else, and he ate and slept at a time determined by someone else. The daily routine in gaol was a totally new experience for the prisoners. The life determined by bells or tin whistles was distinct from the social pattern of behaviour in the villages where they worked, ate, and went to sleep almost at will.

One of the worst experiences was the lack of food that led to a loss of weight. This changed the appearance of prisoners so that some looked like different people when they had completed their sentences. They also suffered greatly from loneliness, and longed to return to the warmth of their loved ones. One impact of being in gaol was the disruption it caused to social relationships in the villages. Payments of debts were often deferred, and traditional feasts to honour the dead could not be held. However, as has been noted earlier, once the prison system was well established, some men used the gaol to escape from their villages after they had committed serious offences such as adultery, for which they would be more severely punished under traditional law.

There were at least two purposes for gaoling the men. One was to deter the men from committing crimes again and to make them cautious about doing anything that might offend the colonial administration. Secondly, it was considered that the gaoling of convicts would make the people in the village realise that the law and order of the white men had to be obeyed or they would be punished.

Being in gaol was in some ways like going away to school. Many prisoners were sent to remote areas. On their return to their villages they were the ones who knew most about the colonial officials and the outside world. Often they became men of influence in their villages, working for the Europeans as policemen or village constables. As the governing authority extended its influence, the prisoners who had served their sentence became agents of contact between Europeans and Papuans.

Health

By 1908 little had been done for the health of Papuans, but gradually Murray increased the money spent on health services. Most, but not all, of this came from Papuan taxes. By 1940 there were four hospitals. These were located in Port Moresby and Samarai, where patients were treated by trained doctors at Misima where they were cared for by a European medical assistant, and at Gemo Island in Fairfax Harbour where tuberculosis and leprosy patients were treated. Apart from hospital treatment, there were a few European and Papuan medical assistants who went on regular patrols.

In the mid 1930s, three groups totaling thirty-eight Papuan students did a six months medical course at the University of Sydney. A professor there thought their ability equal to that of Australian students, but Murray doubted this. On the other hand, Murray disagreed with the majority of foreign residents, who did not think Papuans should be sent south for education at all, and who were scandalised by reports of Papuans embracing white women and children in farewell before they left Sydney for home. This European opposition was partly responsible for the decision to stop training Papuan medical assistants in Sydney.

From 1927 some Papuan medical assistants went on patrol alone and gave injections for yaws, treated wounds and common sickness, and kept records. By 1940 there were about sixty Papuan medical assistants, but government health services remained slight. Papuans still suffered from old diseases such as yaws, eye and skin diseases, and malaria; and from new diseases which had come in from overseas through colonial contact like dysentery, pneumonia, and tuberculosis. The colonial administration did, however, operate a relatively effective quarantine system which protected the people from some of the diseases such as measles and smallpox which had decimated native populations in many other South Pacific islands.

Race relations

E. P. Wolfers has discussed in detail the Native Regulations and Ordinances, including the Native Labour Ordinances by which the colonial administration controlled the local people and maintained a strict system of racial discrimination. In Papua, curfew laws were strictly policed, and from 1920 Papuan men were forbidden to wear clothing on the upper parts of their bodies. Only members of special categories like the police, mission teachers, and administration workers were exempted. David Marsh, a former district commissioner, rationalised this piece of discrimination on health grounds:

> A native wasn't allowed to wear clothing on the upper part of his body. This [regulation] was brought in because they tended to leave their clothes on and get wet and catch pneumonia or skin diseases.

In addition:

> A native wasn't allowed to drink. He couldn't go into a picture show with Europeans. When walking along the footpath the native was expected to move aside. We had the White Women's Protection Ordinance which more or less said that if you smiled at a white woman it was rape . . . They also had a Native Women's Protection Ordinance which seemed to say something quite different, and didn't mean much anyway[10].

Europeans were concerned that their women should be 'protected' and preserved for their own kind. They regarded Papuans as an inferior race which did not have the capacity for normal sexual relationships, and believed that the men possessed abnormally large sexual organs. Their fear was based on European prejudice that persisted until the 1960s when human desire from both races began to break down these attitudes.

Death of Sir Hubert Murray

When Sir Hubert Murray died in February 1940 at the age of seventy-eight during a tour of eastern Papua, he had been governor for thirty-three years and had been responsible for one colonial territory longer than anyone else in the British empire.

Murray was regarded by many Europeans as one of the most advanced colonial administrators of his time. While Murray believed Papuans to be inferior to Europeans, passed discriminatory legislation, and provided only limited educational opportunities, he thought more highly of Papuans and credited them with more ability than did most other Australians at that time. Our judgement of his attitudes and policies depends upon whether we compare them with the attitudes and policies of other Europeans of the time, or what, in hindsight, we believe he should have done. Murray believed it important to progress slowly. If Murray had been told in 1920 that he was changing the ways of Papuans very slowly, he would have been pleased, for he believed that his most important task was to ensure that the Papuan people survived, and that they were most likely to survive if they and their societies were disturbed as little as possible.

Examined more closely, however, Murray simply consolidated the colonial legacy established by MacGregor that the local labour supply had to be protected and maintained in order to provide a healthy workforce for continuous European exploitation. For instance there were the underlying exploitative motives inherent in Murray's labour policies. As Michael Hess has pointed out,

> . . . early Australian colonial labour policy demonstrated a capacity for a long range view in which overall goals of creating the social relations needed for colonial exploitation were primary. Considerations of immediate profit as expressed by individual entrepreneurs, such as the private recruiters and plantation owners, were overturned by administration policies where they were seen to threaten long term development of exploitative social relations. The fact that the latter were typically expressed in terms of the

'advancement of natives' and that the colonial exploitation
. . . was limited by lack of capital have led to the perception
that Australian colonialism was characteristically paternalistic and weak ... Certainly the rhetoric of colonial
administration was consistently paternalistic and the
policies were limited by weak investment and inadequate
funding. Within such limits, however, colonial officials
strove to create a willing labour force capable of partnering
foreign capital. When criticised for the protective nature of
their labour regulations, they consistently pointed to the
long term utility of their policies . . .[11].

Many Papuans respected Murray and appreciated what he had
achieved. Ahuia Ova, one of the few English-speaking Papuans
in 1904, and an old man when Murray died in 1940, spoke
movingly at the memorial service held at Tanobada after the
traditional forty days of mourning.

> Governor Murray is dead. He worked until he died. He was
> governor for more than thirty years. During all that time,
> we saw his work and his laws and we have seen his good
> deeds also. When our people were in trouble they went
> to him and he did not turn them away. In our trouble he
> gave us help and made us happy again. There was no man
> like him in this way. Wherever he went in Papua he spoke
> friendly words. He was never harsh towards men, women or
> children . . . He was the best of men; our children and their
> children will talk of him. He promised us all 'I will not leave
> you. I will die in Papua'. His words were the words of a true
> man, for his body lies in our ground[12].

Ova was, however, more generous in his attitude to Murray
than many fellow Papuans who had less sympathy with
Murray's motives, resented his patronising attitude and saw
him as the architect of European intrusion into their villages.
Some of the older people who cherished traditional ways
recognised that their societies were being disrupted by
European intrusion. Amongst those who accepted the
Europeans and had successfully completed primary schooling,
and in a few cases acquired a few years of post-primary

education, there were those who resented not being given an opportunity to further their education.

In the southern highlands there was, as elsewhere, a mixed reaction to the penetration of Europeans. While Murray initiated exploratory expeditions, they did not make contact with highlands people until the late 1930s when Hides reached Kikori through the Samberigi Valley and Claude Champion's party walked into the Tari and Wage valleys. Thus, the first European penetration from the Papuan side was with explorers, whereas contact with the central highlands through routes from the north had been almost simultaneously with prospectors, administrators, and missionaries. Hides' expedition led to a number of violent clashes in which Hides shot at least thirty-two highlanders believing, rightly or wrongly, that he was attacked. By contrast, the expeditions led by Champion were mostly peaceful, and good relationships were established with the people whom they encountered.

SUMMARY

In 1906, when Australia formally took responsibility for the British Protectorate and renamed the territory Papua, it appointed a Royal Commission to advise on the suitability of the region for European economic development. In the course of this inquiry the advocates of rapid economic development clashed with those who believed the interests of the indigenous people should be paramount. The commission adopted a compromise position and appointed as administrator, Hubert Murray, who could, they believed, implement a compromise policy. In practice, Murray's paternalistic policies on land and labour proved to be only slightly modified versions of MacGregor's policies of the Protectorate period.

Under Murray's administration gold and copper production grew, and transport, communication and health services and the commercial sector were expanded. However, the agriculture sector languished and little attention was paid to the education of the people. Murray mounted a number of successful exploratory expeditions for the Europeans; substantially extended European influence through patrols; and established village councils which allowed the local people a very limited degree of participation in governance. Murray encouraged the missions, to whom he entrusted with the responsibility for what little schooling there was for the people.

Murray's administration met with a mixed reception from the people. On the whole his paternalistic policies were tolerated and in some areas well accepted. However, as has been seen, Europeans sometimes met with a hostile reception, especially in the early years of colonial encounter.

While Murray believed in disturbing the indigenous people as little as possible, European contact inevitably disrupted traditional societies and by 1940 Papuans in those areas under the colonial administration's control were being inexorably led into the Western world.

4

Australian military occupation and the Mandated Territory of New Guinea 1914–1942

The Germans came and exploited us.
The Australians drove out the Germans.
I have seen them both in my time.
Germans or Australians, their presence
    persisted.
Change of masters with the same magic
    command.
No change for me in store.

[Anon].

Australian military occupation 1914–21

In 1914 the direction of the history of Papua New Guinea was once more determined by events thousands of kilometres away in Europe. The dominant European industrial powers, Germany and Britain, clashed over the expansion of their colonial empires through which they acquired the raw materials which supported their factories. When this happened, their Pacific colonies, including Australian-held Papua and German-held New Guinea, were inevitably affected. When the conflict erupted into a major European war, which came to be known as the First World War, one British tactic was to get Australia, no longer a British colony but a staunch ally of Britain, to despatch 2000 troops to take over German New Guinea.

The Australian force which arrived on 11 September 1914 met little resistance. They occupied Rabaul, captured the radio station, and within twenty-four hours proclaimed Australian military rule. The only serious losses were suffered by the native constabulary, some of whom fought bravely for the Germans although they did not understand the cause for which they were fighting. From Rabaul the Australians moved rapidly to occupy the entire German colony.

The change of masters, from the Germans to the Australians, probably did not matter much to the local population as they were all white-skinned people after all. If there were any reactions at all they must have been based on how well or badly the Germans or the Australians treated the people. In places where the Germans were kind to individual communities the people may have resented the Australian takeover. In regions where the Germans had grabbed extensive tracts of land, such as around Madang and the Gazelle Peninsula, the people most likely welcomed the Australians, at least during the early stages before they realised that the Australians had no intention of returning the land which the Germans had taken.

The Australian military administrators, Colonel W. Holmes, Commander S. A. Pethebridge, Colonel S. S. MacKenzie, Acting Brigadier G. J. Johnston and Brigadier R. Griffiths, were confronted by problems new to Australian colonial administrators. As well as controlling the resident German population, the administrators were expected to take responsibility for local people over whom the Germans had established only partial control. One major concern was the attempt to reconcile Australian military law with established German law. German businesses and plantations were left intact. Un-co-operative Germans were deported to prison camps in Australia, and those who undertook not to help Germany, mostly officials and a few planters and missionaries, were allowed to stay. Profits from German enterprises could not be sent back to Germany, and some Germans invested in local

Australian-controlled enterprises such as Burns Philp and W. R. Carpenter.

While the German administration had acted as a restraining influence on the planters, the planters managed to convince the Australian administrators that they should enforce harsher labour laws. Hence, the people suffered more under this military administration than they had under the Germans. It is not too much to say that whatever attempts Albert Hahl, the last German administrator, had made towards promoting the welfare and progress of the people of New Guinea disappeared under the Australians. The German official stations near Lae and Angoram were closed, patrolling was reduced, projects to develop local educational and medical facilities were shelved, roads, jetties, and buildings fell into disuse, and qualifications earned in German times were often ignored. The head tax continued to be collected, but whereas the Germans had at least argued that the head tax was a means of encouraging local participation in the cash economy, to the Australians it was often simply a means of raising revenue. At the same time ordinances which favoured plantation interests made villagers' participation in the cash economy more difficult. The most thriving local industry, copra, suffered especially from this practice.

Overall Australian policy, as much from ignorance of administration as intent, further reduced the limited chances for economic and political advancement of the people of the former German colony. For instance the Australian military administrators did not understand the *luluai* system, introduced by the Germans to help extend the administrator's influence, and allowed it to collapse.

The Australian mandate 1921–1942

After the 1914–18 war, the League of Nations gave Australia a mandate, or permission, to govern the former German colony, and from 1921 to 1942 the area was known as the Mandated Territory of New Guinea.

Under Australian policy, established following another Royal Commission in 1919, it was decided, against the wishes of administrator Murray in Papua, that the two territorics,

Papua and New Guinea, would continue to be administered separately. One of the effects of this decision was that in Papua, under Murray's administration, native rights such as land and labour were to some extent protected at the expense of European economic development, while in the Mandated Territory the administrators encouraged economic development in the interests of the Europeans at the expense of the rights of the local people.

Policies in the Mandated Territory

The authority of the three Australian generals who administered the Mandated Territory from 1921 to 1942, E. A. Wisdom, J. Griffiths, and W. R. McNicoll, was restricted by the operation of the Expropriation Board. This three-man committee was established in 1920 to supervise the transfer of property that Germans had developed when they had taken over the land and people in the area. Instead of deciding to return the property to its rightful owners, the committee gradually assumed control of almost all economic activity in the Mandated Territory, including matters which were, in theory, the responsibility of the administrators.

A partial explanation of this extension of the Expropriation Board's influence lies in the position of W. H. Lucas, chairman of the Expropriation Board, who was also the president of Burns Philp, the largest single commercial enterprise in Papua or in New Guinea. In addition, Lucas was the technical advisor to the Australian government on all matters relating to the Mandated Territory, and had direct links with the Australian prime minister of the day.

Some historians believe that the board was even more important than the administrator. Certainly its functions, which extended to influencing policies about land, labour, finance, and immigration, were considered the most important business of the governing authority. In addition the Board aided the administration policy of extending European influence further into the interior.

The Board reversed the policy of the previous military occupation towards the Germans. Instead of looking into the legality of the ownership of the property and transferring some of it to the local people, the Board took over all property previously held by Germans. Deported Germans were allowed to leave with only fifty pounds sterling in cash, their clothing, and a few belongings. In theory, the deportees were to be compensated for their properties after they had returned to Germany. However, by the time the money was paid to them it was practically worthless, because the value of German money declined rapidly after the war. Thus, the Australians did not take advantage of the opportunity to return alienated land back to the rightful owners.

The Board then listed former German properties, and sold them by auction to British and Australian buyers. Australians who had fought in the war were given preference and financial assistance by the Board, and many of them bought former German properties. Until 1926 the Board usually sold properties outright to buyers, but after that date it gave long-term leases instead. Most of the property was plantation land. Local landowners who felt that their land had been unfairly taken from them by the Germans could lodge objections with the Board before a property was sold, but in fact very few did so, probably because they did not know how to lodge objections. Thus most land went to British and Australian buyers. Within a few years, however, many of these found themselves in difficulty. They had borrowed money to buy their properties, and low copra prices and high freight and interest costs soon forced them into debt. Many borrowed from the large companies to pay off their debts. When they could not repay these loans, their plantations were taken over by companies such as Burns Philp and W. R. Carpenter. The villagers were equally disadvantaged by large and small plantation owners alike.

Economic change

Most of the local population continued to live in the subsistence economy although some communities were now affected by the cash economy. A group of Chinese was doing very well as retailers and wholesalers, and the Chinese commercial interests increased rapidly. By 1912 there were about 200 Chinese businesses; two years later only 186 out of 1377 Chinese in German New Guinea were described as labourers, while the rest were businessmen. Ah Tam in Rabaul, for instance, was reported to own 'trade stores, shipyards, a hotel, several plantations, a brothel, an opium house and a gambling den'[1].

The area under copra continued to expand during the 1920s and 1930s. By 1924 over 95 per cent of the Mandated Territory's exports were copra, and in 1937, the most profitable year, 1 231 90 pounds sterling worth of copra was exported. However, attempts by the Department of Agriculture to increase copra production on plantations owned by the people had limited success and only a very small proportion of exported copra came from those plantations. There were other crops grown by Europeans: cocoa, rubber, and coffee, and oil palm and tea were grown on an experimental basis. Of these, cocoa was most important, although by 1939 less than a fifth of the total exported was produced by native growers.

By 1933 the Mandated Territory's most valuable export was gold, which rapidly came to dominate the cash economy. Australian prospectors had been getting worthwhile gold yields from the German colony even before 1914, particularly from the Waria River. After the war, prospectors travelled from the Waria over to the Bulolo River on the edge of the eastern highlands and in 1922 found gold. In January 1926 a rich strike was made at Eddie Creek near Wau. Thousands of prospectors flocked to the area. Although payable gold was also found in the Sepik area, Wau–Bulolo remained the most productive area and attracted the operations of large mining companies such as the Bulolo Gold Mining and Dredging Company and the New Guinea Gold Company.

Gold exports softened the effects of the 1929 worldwide economic depression on the cash economy. The gold companies were wealthy enough to experiment with air freight, which was still a new concept in the mid 1920s. They designed the huge dredges which can still be seen at Bulolo and built them so they could be flown in piece by piece. Each dredge weighed about one and a half tonnes, and required over 3000 plane flights before it was fully assembled. Yet by 1939 eight dredges were at work in the Bulolo area and much other equipment had been flown in besides. From the late 1920s and for most of the 1930s the Salamaua–Bulolo air freight route was the busiest in the world.

When gold replaced copra as the Mandated Territory's most important export, there was a shift in European activity from the copra-producing islands and coastal areas to the gold-producing centres on the mainland. The administration recognised this change of emphasis when it moved the capital of the Territory from Rabaul to Lae in 1937. This move also encouraged Europeans to push deeper inland, and in the 1930s they had established contact with villages in the eastern highlands. Another effect of these economic changes was greater contact between Europeans and the local people employed on the goldfields and plantations, and an increase in the revenue available to the administration to extend administrative services, and its influence on the people. However, changes in the cash economy did not make much difference to the lives of most of the people who continued to live a subsistence life.

European contact with the Central Highlands

The first Europeans to reach the central highlands were miners and administration officials who came from the north-east coast through the Markham and Ramu valleys into the Wahgi Valley. In 1933 gold prospectors Mick and Dan Leahy and patrol officer Jim Taylor organised both air and ground expeditions in the Wahgi Valley. The expeditionary parties were astonished by the rich and populous territory that they had entered, and the highland people were astonished to see them — particularly those who arrived by air.

Towards the end of 1933 a Catholic missionary, Father Schaefer, led by a local 'big man' Kavagl, reached the Waghi where they were shortly joined by Father Ross who had been given instructions to establish a station between Bundi and Mount Hagen. The Catholic missionaries were very soon followed by the Lutherans, Reverends Bergmann and Foege, who flew into the area and in the middle of the following year established a station at Kundiawa.

Thus, within twelve months the Europeans had established

a significant economic, administrative, and mission presence in the highlands which had been beyond European contact for so many years. As has been noted, the extremely rugged country and the belief that the interior of the island was unpopulated or only sparsely populated and of no economic value had acted as disincentives to exploration. However, by the 1930s aircraft could survey the interior, greatly reducing the problem of the difficult nature of the terrain. The discovery of gold and people who were potential coverts to Christianity led to very rapid penetration of the region by Europeans.

The speed with which contact was made with many peoples of the highlands is in sharp contrast with the slow progress made by Europeans in the coastal and island regions. The rapidity of the establishment of the European presence in the highlands significantly effected economic and social changes in these areas. The results of these contacts on the people were dramatic. By 1938, for example, the Melpa society was already caught up in a new kind of economic exchange with a growing number of Europeans at Mount Hagen where about 700 white foreigners required a daily supply of food and workers from the local community. Miners and missionaries alike found that Australian money was worthless and they turned to the local currency, the pearl shells, to buy food and labour. Even when the administration officials paid the local people in cash for the work done, the labourers demanded *kina* shells. According to Bob Connolly and Robin Anderson, Mogei Yaga, a Hagen man, refused to be paid in cash:

> We said no. We don't want that (cash). Just gives us more shells. They told us they were giving us something of value and we should take it. And we said, 'What we do with it? Thread it and wear it? What use is it to us? All we want is shells, nothing else!'[2]

There was no doubt that the demand for shells far exceeded the supply. According to Ian Hughes, Europeans airlifted virtually millions of pearl and other shells of value from the coast and Torres Strait Islands:

> A chartered DC3 aircraft brought supplies from Thursday

Island, 1000 lb. load fetching ten times the price in Mt. Hagen[3].

One of the effects of this trade was that some people became rich too quickly. As the pioneer Catholic missionary, Father Ross observed:

> Thousands of these shells were passed around the area in ten years of white occupation. The result was that the native of the Hagen area became the millionaire. He could go out to the fringe of the area and buy wives with the shell he was gradually hoarding. Where a chief would formerly be a great men with three wives, now he could buy eight or ten. Young men who formerly had no standing could now raise their status by working for the white man, receiving payment in shells[4].

The sudden influx of Europeans with precious shells reduced the value of this local shell money and undermined the local exchange economy. The exchange relations of the 'big men', whose prestige and power had until that time dominated the Melpa society, were severely curtailed within a decade of European invasion of the central highlands of Papua New Guinea. By 1948 Dan Leahy had built the first trade store in Mount Hagen to sell Western goods to the local people. These goods were flown by air from Lae on the coast, as there was no road between the highlands and the coast.

Land policies

The Australians initially followed the policy of land acquisition laid down by the German administration and it was not until the Land Ordinance of 1922 that the Mandate administration established its own land acquisition policy. Under the ordinance, only the administration could buy land from indigenes. It had first to confirm who the land owners were and ensure they were willing to sell. Even if they were willing, further checks were required to ensure the people were not likely to need the land for a further fifty years. A district officer on the spot had to sign a certificate confirming this agreement before a land purchase could be made. In practice these conditions were often ignored and land was taken even when the district officer had advised against it. When European development was planned, land could be obtained for the project.

Europeans bought relatively little land during the Mandate period. Most land settled by Europeans had been alienated during the German period or immediately after the First World War. By 1914, 702 000 hectares of land had been taken away. By 1939, towards the end of the Mandate period, the total had increased to 894 000 hectares. However this total does not include large areas of land taken by Europeans under mining leases in the Wau–Bulolo area.

Although the Mandate took relatively little land, most acquisitions were of good agricultural land. Whereas less than two per cent of the total land of New Guinea had been taken by Europeans by 1942, this represented perhaps a quarter of the good agricultural land. On the Gazelle Peninsula, New Ireland, Manus, and the Madang Coast, the people had lost large areas of their most useful land.

The administration failed to resolve dissatisfactions which had begun under the Germans and which were to erupt into a whole series of land claims in the late 1960s and the 1970s. This does not mean that the people in 1914 or in 1940 accepted land losses. After all, Europeans had taken the land because they were stronger, and superior strength was a traditional method of land acquisition.

Labour policies

Although the Mandate transferred relatively little land, that acquired in German times was already more than the available labour force in New Guinea could work. There were simply not enough local labourers to plant all the land taken by Europeans. During the Mandate period, as in German times, there were never enough people who were prepared to work for Europeans. Employers were therefore constantly demanding that the administration be more active in labour recruiting, or more tolerant to private labour recruiters. Labour was essential to rapid economic development, so demands by European and Asian employers put considerable pressure on the governing authority. There were many abuses of the labour regulations which the administration failed to prevent. There were many occasions when the law was not respected by labour recruiters on the plantations and on the goldfields, and conditions were much tougher for workers in New Guinea than for workers in Papua. At the same time the administration gradually brought a little more humanity into regulations governing labour conditions, and at least it did what Hahl, under the German administration, had tried and failed to do: it created conditions which attracted a greater number of labourers onto the plantations.

Employment figures show that a great many men were in European or Asian employment. In 1921–22 there were almost 27 000 indentured labourers in the Mandate. By 1929 the number had risen to about 30 000, and by 1939 to about 40 000, although the figures fluctuated slightly in the intervening years. There were also about 2400 non-indentured, casual, or temporary labourers employed by 1939. The 1939 statistics, for example, show that about a third of all men who had been counted or estimated by census were labourers in the cash economy. However, it must be remembered that many parts of the Mandated Territory were still beyond European influence and thus had no involvement with the cash economy.

It would be difficult to estimate the total impact of the labour recruitment, particularly recruitment of men from one district to work in another. For instance, one effect of recruiting indentured labourers from the highlands to work on the plantations on the lowlands was that they were exposed to malarial attacks because these labourers had not developed a natural immunity to malaria.

Miners' labourers

In the 1920s many local people worked as miners' labourers or as carriers whose role in carrying supplies up from the coast was an essential one. In the 1930s the development of air freight and of large gold mining companies changed the pattern. By 1939 there were about 13 000 indentured labourers on the goldfields, mostly employed by large companies in the Bulolo area. Many came from the Sepik, and around Bulolo now there are communities of Sepiks which began before the 1939–46 war.

In the early years, the late 1920s, life was pretty tough for miners' labourers and carriers. There was some legal protection. Their contracts were limited to a minimum of two years, a minimum wage of ten shillings was set, there were load limits for carriers, minimum clothing and food rations were laid down, and after 1931, hours of work were limited to eight hours a day, six days a week. However living conditions were poor. Often they went short of food because supplies could not always be brought from the coast, and some died of pneumonia and dysentery. They also suffered greatly from being so far from their homes and families.

Plantation labourers

Legal conditions for plantation workers were not as liberal as for men on the goldfields. This was because plantation conditions were not as difficult for coastal people as in the cold mountains of Wau–Bulolo. The usual contract period was three years, though, after leave, men could sign a further contract. Officially plantation men worked ten hours a day, six days a week. They had one and a half hours off in the middle of the day and usually Sunday was free. Later the working week was reduced to fifty-five hours. Each labourer was to be issued with one blanket a year, a loincloth each month, and at the beginning of the contract period a bowl, a spoon, a mug, and a box with a lock on it. Minimum scales of rations were laid down and after 1927 these ration scales were quite detailed. In fact they were too detailed for most employers, so by and large they seem to have been ignored, and the old standbys of rice and tinned meat issued instead.

All in all, life was hard for plantation workers also. Although the hours were similar to those being worked by rural labourers in Australia, they were longer than most villagers were used to, and the food was often strange and unpalatable. Wages were low, although even the little a man did get, in money and goods, made him appear comparatively wealthy when he returned home to his village.

Both the mining labour and plantation labour schemes were

subsidised by the work of the women back in the villages. Traditionally, men had responsibility for clearing the land for gardens, building houses and fences, hunting forest animals and crocodiles, and fishing. When the men worked away from home, women were forced to undertake much of this work, particularly the clearing of land for gardens and maintenance of the houses, in addition to their traditional responsibilities of supplying the day-to-day needs of the family through gardening, tending pigs, and foraging in the bush for berries and insects, or on the seashore for shellfish. Women also suffered from the disruption of traditional life caused by the absence of their men. In addition there is evidence that some women were seriously disadvantaged when men took the opportunity of paid employment away from home to escape family responsibilities. These disadvantages were partly compensated for by the Western goods, such as metal cooking pots, brought back by the men and used by the women to lighten their work load.

Other workers

Some workers lived under better conditions and were paid much more than the average plantation or miners' labourer. As in Papua, the best paid were boat captains and police. The most senior of these were paid about five pounds a month, and they held positions of some authority and responsibility. Those employed in the towns were better off. They worked closer to Europeans, which could be stressful, but there were more fringe benefits like food, housing, and entertainment. There were better opportunities for higher wages because more skilled jobs were available. However, most town workers were indentured labourers, paid a fixed and usually low wage. They knew it was low, because men in town were able to compare their poverty with European wealth more easily than could those men on plantations.

By today's standards local workers during the Mandate, even the better-paid workers, were not well off. Today's standards, however, are not relevant to the period before the war, although a comparison with pre-war Papua certainly is. Europeans in the Mandate justified their policies by saying that they were necessary if there was to be rapid economic development, and that economic development benefited everyone, including the people of the New Guinea region. Did the local people think this? Did they believe they were well treated? We do not know what most of the people thought about the treatment they received. However, we do know that the only people who gained from this kind of development were the foreigners. Jim Leahy, for instance, admitted frankly why he had come to Papua New Guinea:

> I didn't like the climate, I didn't like climbing mountains, and I wasn't particularly mad about the people. I went there not for the natives' benefit but purely for my own. I was a colonialist from way back, and I didn't mind being one, either. I couldn't see anything wrong with it; it was the way things were in those days . . .[5].

Race relations

As elsewhere, the white men established, protected, and maintained a dominant political and economic position by claiming to be a superior race who regarded New Guineans as inferior to them. Because there were so few Europeans, most felt very insecure and saw the local people as a potential threat, either real or imagined, and they were in constant fear of local uprisings against them. Under such circumstances Europeans believed that they had to have a common approach in their relations with the local population in order to maintain white power and prestige. Economic factors as well as insecurity were behind the master–servant relationship. The white men believed that 'the natives' needed to be 'kept in their place', in an inferior position, in order to exploit their labour more effectively. In addition many Europeans were obsessed with the idea that all black men wished to rape white women, and they used this mistaken belief to support racially discriminatory legislation.

Race relations took a different form in some parts of the highlands. Michael Leahy, a practising Catholic, was persuaded by his human urge to cast aside his Christian ideals as he could not resist the physical attraction of the highland women. After less than two years in the highlands without access to his kind of the opposite sex he made the following entry in his diary on 1 November 1934:

> I am afraid this walking about among these kanakas especially their good looking womenfolk, has not been conductive [sic] to the persistent observances of my early religious training. And if I was to be bumped off suddenly, I would certainly become a permanent resident of Old Nick's Domain . . . When I left Queensland for New Guinea I was full of high ideals and religious fervour. But a few years among the natives, with no chance of ever being able to make a home of one's own, where a person could settle down with a member of the opposite sex and justify his existence by perpetuating the race, very soon woke up to the futility of trying to suppress one's urges to copulate, and the longer one looked at the black, brown and coppery coloured girls, with essentially feminine mannerisms, the prettier and more seductive they become. And I still think I done the best I could under the circumstances, and I am sure the Good Lord, who instilled the sexual urge in all of us, perhaps in some stronger than in others, will not be too hard on the poor sinner who has fallen by the wayside with one of these seductive damsels of this hinterland country.

His brother, Dan Leahy, rationalised his affairs with the local women as follows:

> The women would come to Kuta bringing food, and they'd get paid the same as anyone else. And when they found that we wouldn't rush out and grab them, or wheel them off somewhere, that we treated them quite normally, the women got very friendly. The fathers or brothers – they sort of tee it up with the women before they came along. And they'd, say, 'Well my sister wants to come'. And as long as she was quite willing and everything. I mean sex was a normal thing. There would be something wrong with you if you didn't want sex. That's the way they look at it[6].

Europeans who had lived in the territories for a long time gave explicit instructions to new arrivals on how they should behave and what they should expect from New Guineans. In 1939, for instance, the *Rabaul Times* said:

> Imagine the young men (or women) arriving for the first time in this territory without any previous experiences of the tropics or advice having been supplied as to the general deportment expected from a member of a superior race residing in a native country . . . [T]he new arrival has no knowledge of restricted hours for house servants and that the boy whom he finds has become his personal servant must be supplied with a signed permit to be out after 9 p.m. and is violating a regulation if he makes unseemly noises after that hour. Neither is he aware that betel chewing in and around the house is positively *tambu* among self-respecting servants, and is only done by 'hard heads' to try out the Master or Mistress, even as the same boy will answer with a cigarette in his mouth and test out his new employer, with a dozen forms of studied disrespect and insolence, and getting away with it[;] repeat such actions with a frequency that eventually becomes a habit, with a result that his employer is powerless to instill any degree of discipline . . . How few Europeans exact the respect which is due to them from the native? Smoking while being addressed, sitting down when spoken to, the absence of 'Sir' etc. What is the use of the few exacting respect if the majority do not? The average native is particularly amenable to discipline, but needs to be told by authority the extent of his limitations, what he may or may not do[7].

Often the white planters and other commercial traders were hostile towards the various missions because they felt that the missionaries were undermining white prestige by educating the local people and attempting to 'civilise' them. Stephen Reed observed:

> Working intimately with natives, missionaries cannot and do not observe all strict canons of white prestige, the code of caste. This alone sets them apart from the rest of the Europeans. More important, however, is the fact that the missions interfere in European exploitative undertakings

and even in some cases, actively compete in the European economy of the Territory[8].

In towns Europeans lived in close-knit communities set apart from the local population. When gold was found at Eddie Creek above Wau in 1926 an airstrip was built at Lae to cater for the growing gold industry in the hinterland. Within a decade Lae was a bustling centre of the aviation industry. In 1935, *Pacific Island Monthly* reported:

> Lae is now a township ranking high in the Mandated Territory of New Guinea. It is a centre of great activity . . . and one of the biggest (if not the biggest) aircraft centres in the southern hemisphere. The European population is around the hundred mark and increasing with each steamer. Accommodation is being taxed; so much so that a new hotel has been commenced and is expected to be completed in a month or two.[9]

According to Ian Willis the social grouping of the white residents in Lae consisted of the staff of Guinea Airways and the Bulolo Gold dredging company, then the managers of Burns Philp and Vacuum Oil, and the assistant district officer, and below them the mechanics, clerks and storemen. The pilots were in the top group. Most whites of whatever social standing were racist towards Papuans and New Guineans, from whom they were completely socially separated.

By 1942, when the Japanese destroyed the town, there were 120 European residents, about sixty Chinese just as racist as whites but not in such positions of power, and probably several hundred New Guinean labourers, who were socially distinct from the local villagers as well as from Europeans and Chinese. Willis described the social pecking order in this manner:

> Away from work there was little contact, formal or informal, between the three communities, European, Chinese and New Guinean, and each group kept to itself. The society of the town was stratified into a strict caste system with the Europeans occupying the upper level, the New Guineans the lower, and the Chinese an uncertain position between them. The main contact between the groups was on the job,

where the class structure was implicit and was rigidly maintained. Any dealings between the races proceeded on assumptions of white superiority[10].

Accordingly the social life of the whites revolved around the newly built Hotel Cecil and a few sports clubs, which New Guineans were strictly forbidden to enter. However, the seemingly invincible 'white prestige' was challenged, if not dented, during the Rabaul strike of 1929.

The Rabaul strike of 1929

A group of New Guinean workers went on strike for more pay in 1929. This was the first significant action by workers in showing their discontent over conditions of employment. An account of this strike tells us much about European attitudes as well as prevailing employment conditions and workers' discontent.

Bill Gammage[11] has thoroughly studied the leaders of the strike and their fate at the hands of the Australian administration between December 1928 and January 1929. The leader was Sumsuma of the Boang clan of Sasa village, about fifty kilometres from Namatanai in New Ireland District. While Sumsuma had little education, he was regarded by his employer as 'a most extraordinary and outstanding native' who, when he was in his twenties, became a captain of the motor schooner *Edith.* Sumsuma was paid five pounds sterling per month and, with bonuses, sometimes received twelve pounds sterling per month, at a time when his contemporaries were receiving only five or six shillings per month. Sumsuma's hope was that he would secure such wage rates for all local workers. Also closely involved in the strike was Bohun from Buka in the Bougainville District who was a cargo master of the ship *Ralum*, which belonged to the Melanesian Company. Both men felt that those workers who received only twenty-one or thirty-one shillings a month should ask for an increase in wages.

They were supported by other seamen and, having agreed to take action, they approached the most senior local men of the police force. These sergeant-majors were N'Dramei of

Manus Island and Kateo of Wewak. There was a slight disagreement between the two men as to whether the proposed strike was proper, but Sergeant N'Dramei insisted: 'Those who are women can stay! Those who are men, follow me!'[12] It was resolved that the core of the police NCOs should go on strike. The strike leaders then proceeded secretly to enlist the support of the sympathetic workers. The leaders' tactic was to use the mission stations as bases from which to negotiate an increase in pay to £12 a month for all workers. The strikers chose the Methodist and Catholic missions at Malaguna and Ropolo along Kokopo road because they imagined the missionaries might be more sympathetic to their cause.

The plan was to strike on the night of New Year's Day 1929 but this was postponed to 2 January. As Bill Gammage has pointed out:

> The choice was perfect for on that night at least half the senior Administration officers were in Australia, many of the *mastas* left in Rabaul were either contending with or intensifying the effects of the season's festivities, and the night was dark and stormy, and not such as men liked to be about in.[13]

The strike was carried out with speed and skill, and caught the administration officials and planters by surprise. The Rev. J. H. Margetts of the Methodist mission alerted the acting police inspector W. B. Ball by 7 a.m. the following morning:

> All over town *mastas* had woken to find their shaving water cold, their breakfasts not cooked, their servants missing. Angrily they rang the police station to see whether their boys had been arrested, or shouted to their neighbours to find out what was bloody going on. 'My coon's not here', called one, 'and the damned stove's not even lit'. 'Me too', replied his neighbour, 'my boy is gone.' I'll teach the young bugger when he comes back'. But soon annoyed exclamations about unreliable natives gave way to a realization of what really had happened: overnight almost the entire work force of Rabaul had vanished![14]

And a white woman resident echoed:

Upon arising, I called for my washboy to get my bath. No response from the slave, so I called for the Mary . . . She got my bath . . . [and] off I went to the office, and not a sign of a boy on the way there. Reached the office and heard all about it then. During the night practically every native had departed out of the town . . . whilst we slept so peacefully, only a mile away there were thousands of blacks just needing the slightest thing to make them finish us properly. Of course . . . being comparatively a mere handful of people, it wouldn't take much to wipe us out . . . the trouble is . . . generally thought to be due to a certain mission[ary] . . . who has told the boys they should get more money . . . also . . . the Government . . . [is] disgustingly lenient with the natives, and if one dares to strike a native, no matter how insolent he may be, one gets fined for it . . . Why, the only thing a native understands is a beating. Anyhow . . . we are too small a community of whites to let the blacks get the upper hand[15].

A commission of inquiry was set up to determine the cause of the strike. It concluded the disturbance was related to 'the talk of the foreign coloured sailors; Sumsuma; Sergeant–Major Rami (N'Dramei); and that there were no other or no more complex causes'[16].

Most *mastas* were not prepared to forgive and forget. They were determined to teach the natives a lesson, they believed that civilization had been challenged, they suspected a traitor, probably a missionary, among them, they asserted that the strike proved the Administration's laziness and inefficiency. So they made almost hysterical demands: that the strike leaders be hung or shot and the remainder be sent to prison or to work on the goldfields or in the Madang swamps where they might die, that the missionaries be deported, that police and senior Administration officials be dismissed, that a battle ship be sent to protect the town, that the police barracks and all boy houses be shifted outside town limits, that flogging be legally reintroduced, and that the curfew and the penal and disciplinary laws dealing with natives be made as tough as they were in German times[17].

All of the ringleaders were tried in a court of white men's law and most of them were convicted, expelled from Rabaul, and dispersed to serve their sentence away from their home areas. As Bill Gammage has aptly concluded:

> The law men had searched their books to find such penalties. The Police Force Ordinance then in force allowed neither for the charge nor the penalties actually used against the strike leaders, and the police NCOs must have been dismissed from the force on a charge not known, then arraigned as labourers before the court. But the Native Labour Ordinance under which the leaders were reportedly tried also allowed neither for the charge nor the sentence imposed upon them, and they were sentenced under the Queensland Criminal Code of 1899, adopted in New Guinea [in] 1921, a section of which laid down a penalty of up to three years imprisonment for any conspiracy to commit an offence in Queensland. Even the Citizens' Association might have admitted that the Administration tried hard to punish the strike leaders severely[18].

The penalty ranged from six months to three years gaol. Most of the leaders completed their sentences and returned to their own villages. Sumsuma concentrated his effort on encouraging his people to plant coconuts and make copra — an activity which formed a co-operative movement. He was arrested on an allegation of organising a 'cargo cult' but released. During the Second World War his own men elected Sumsuma as 'king' and upon the Australians' return, he was gaoled for a year for allegedly again trying to form a cargo cult. In 1953 he established a Copra Marketing Society which bought a trading schooner — a dream fulfilled.

Sumsuma did not receive recognition in his lifetime, and on his death in 1965 was simply buried under a plain concrete slab. However, as Bill Gammage has correctly suggested, an appropriate epitaph could be:

> While the Sumsuma led strike failed to achieve the aim of better wages for local workers, he and N'Dramei had, by uniting people from different tribes in opposition to

colonial power, planted a seed of nationalism amongst the people throughout the country[19].

The Rabaul strike of 1929 was, however, a unique event. No other strikes occurred in either the Mandated Territory or in Papua until well after the Second World War. While many workers were undoubtedly unhappy about their conditions of employment, the most usual reaction to exploitation was to do the job badly, or desert the job altogether and return to the village.

For those people who were not coerced into employment, such as those in the highlands who were first contacted in the 1930s, the European presence was often welcomed. It was welcomed by those who thought, as some people on the coast had thought, that the white men were spirits returning from the dead. White men such as the Leahy brothers were also welcomed in the highlands when they brought much-prized traditional items of trade such as cowrie shells, as well as modern, useful goods such as axes and knives.

Education

Educational opportunities for the people were very limited under the Mandate administration. In 1922 an Education Ordinance empowered the administrator to set up schools funded from a Native Education Trust Fund financed by a special education tax levied upon certain categories of the people. In the early 1920s ambitious plans were made for the establishment of a primary education system, however, the enthusiasm generated by the 1922 Education Ordinance was not sustained and by 1942 primary schools had been established only at Malaguna Nodup, Tavui, and Pila Pila, all near Rabaul, and Kavieng in New Ireland and in Chimbu in the highlands. These schools were attended mainly by boys because neither the administration nor the villagers thought it important to educate girls in even basic literacy and numeracy.

The curriculum was modelled on the early years of Australian primary schools, with an emphasis on English language literacy and numeracy. Those who successfully completed primary schooling were employed in clerical positions or became trainee teachers. A technical school established in Rabaul taught basic trade skills and its graduates also entered the paid work force.

Administration attempts to involve the missions in providing general education were unsuccessful. The missions were unwilling to accept subsidies for this extension of their activities partly because they lacked sufficiently literate staff. The missions saw their role as being the providers of basic learning in the local languages to allow pupils to read Bible stories and hymns. In most missions further education was given only to those boys whom it was hoped would become mission teachers.

However, the various missions took advantage of the literacy programme because it hastened the spread of the Word of God. For example, the Catholic schools in the Bougainville District benefited from such a scheme. Hugh Laracy pointed out that:

> By 1920 the desire for literacy had become an important factor in the spread of Christianity. The ability to read and write, particularly in English, seemed to be the crucial difference between Melanesian and European, the key to the latter's astounding prosperity and a means of dealing with him on his own terms[20].

However, in spite of the lack of interest shown by the administration in the education of the people, the average annual per capita expenditure on education in the Mandated Territory was considerably higher than that provided by the Murray administration in Papua in the same period.

Health

During most of this period the limited funds available for medical services tended to be allocated to centres of European settlement. In 1921 the administration established a Department of Public Health under a Director of Public Health staffed by six medical officers. In addition there were approximately twenty medical assistants, all European, mainly based in Rabaul. The number of medical personnel doubled during the period of the Mandate but they did not include any local people and were still mainly concentrated in Rabaul and Lae. The lack of general basic education meant that there were very few local people who were qualified to enter the skilled workforce and thus few available for para-medical training. Some medical work and hygiene instruction was carried out by the missions, and towards the end of the period several European doctors were established in private practice. When the Wau–Bulolo gold rush began, the administration recognised that it would have to take steps to combat the inevitable outbreak of disease, particularly dysentery, which had accompanied gold rushes in other areas. Medical officers were sent to the gold fields but could do little to solve the problem.

Apart from dysentary, the most common complaints were tuberculosis, respiratory infections, venereal diseases, tropical ulcers, and malnutrition which was caused by the dependence of many labourers, particularly in the plantations, on a diet largely of polished rice from which vitamins and minerals had been removed. The administration seemed to be aware of the importance of preventative medicine, but it had neither the staff nor the funds to implement preventative medical policies.

As in Papua, the sick in the villages were still treated mainly by women, or by recognised male healers, with traditional medicines. However the local women were powerless to deal with the diseases introduced by Europeans and spread into the villages by labourers returning from the plantations and the mines.

Reaction of the people

It is even more difficult to generalise about the reaction of the people to the Mandated Territory administration between 1914 and 1942 than for other regions and other periods. This is partly because the administration covered people in the coastal and island regions who had been in contact with Europeans for perhaps two generations, and people in the highlands who saw a white man for the first time in the late 1930s. However, in other areas the people's reaction was mixed, and although exploitation was greater in New Guinea than in Papua, opposition to the exploitation was, with the notable exception of the Rabaul strike of 1929, scattered, sporadic, and largely ineffective.

SUMMARY

Australia took over the German colony in 1914 at the beginning of the First World War and established a military administration which was replaced in 1921 by a League of Nations Mandate administration which lasted until 1942.

Under the military administration, the previous German attempts to build up the economy were abandoned and harsher labour laws introduced. In the Mandate period, administration was officially the responsibility of appointed administrators — however, in practice, power lay with an Expropriation Board which sold plantations established under the German administration to British and Australian capitalists.

Until the 1930s the main export was copra, followed by cocoa, rubber and coffee grown mainly in foreign owned plantations. In the 1930s, following important finds in the Wau–Bulolo area, gold supplanted copra and the administrative headquarters was moved from the copra-based town of Rabaul to Lae, which was better placed geographically to take advantage of the economic activity generated by the gold discoveries and the penetration of the highlands.

A major problem for the administration continued to be recruitment of labour for the plantations and the mines, and in an effort to increase the labour supply some protective legislation was introduced which provided for minimum wages and conditions of employment. While the provisions of this legislation were frequently ignored, improved conditions did attract a greater number of labourers into the work force, particularly after the opening of the highlands. When able-bodied men were recruited to work away from home, the women in the villages were disadvantaged by having to undertake a number of tasks that were normally the men's responsibility.

Western medical and educational services were inadequate or non-existent and the people depended almost entirely upon traditional medicines and the nursing care provided by village women.

The small white population took very strong measures to ensure that they maintained their position of economic, political and social supremacy and, on the assumption that the New

Guineans were an inferior race, introduced and policed a wide range of racially discriminatory legislation.

When the Australians were driven out of the Territory by the Japanese in 1942 they left a colony in which foreign settlers and gold companies had, on the whole, prospered, and a native population much further integrated into the cash economy and European culture than had been the case in 1921.

5

The Pacific war
and wind of change
1939–1960

War has come
The young men are leaving
To defend alien land
The foreigners will be saved
What has called
The young men away
To become enemy victim?
The conquerors will be happy
The mother is deserted
Lonely without her son
A barren beggar.

[Gavide][1]

Papua and New Guinea in the Pacific war 1939–1946

As has been seen in chapter 4, Germany had been driven out
of New Guinea in 1914 by troops sent by Australia who was
supporting Britain in a war against Germany. Though defeated
and humiliated in 1918, the German nation recovered and
during the 1930s became a strong and aggressive power, which,
supported by Italy, invaded a number of neighbouring
European states. In an attempt to stop German expansion,
Britain, supported by France and the former British colonics
of Australia, Canada, South Africa, and New Zealand, declared

war on Germany in 1939. In 1941 Japan entered the war in support of Germany and Italy and bombed Pearl Harbour, in the United States Hawaiian island of Oahu, and the British colony of Malaya. Japan's complex motives included a desire to continue her conquest of east Asian countries, which had begun with the invasion of China in 1933. Japan also planned to invade islands in the south-west Pacific, including Australia and New Zealand. In response to the bombing of Pearl Harbour the United States entered the war and despatched troops to both Europe and the Pacific.

Despite Australia's involvement in the war in Europe and the determined southward expansion of the Japanese at the beginning of 1942, Papua New Guinea remained a quiet colonial backwater. Europeans continued to live in Port Moresby, Rabaul, and on their plantations as if nothing was happening in the outside world. Most of the local people would not have been aware of the great war raging to their north. Slight fortifications and preparations for war had been made in the south, but the League of Nations' Mandate forbade the construction of fortifications in New Guinea. On 4 January 1942, the situation changed abruptly when the Japanese bombed Rabaul in East New Britain. This was the first attack ever made on Australian-held territory, but for the people of Papua New Guinea it heralded yet another invasion by a foreign power. (Henceforth the term Papua New Guinea will be used because from 1942 Australia regarded Papua and New Guinea as a single administrative unit.) From 1942 to 1945 Papua New Guinea became a battlefield over which a million Americans, 300 000 Japanese and nearly 500 000 Australians fought. At the time this was almost one foreigner for every member of the indigenous population.

On 23 January 1942 a Japanese sea-borne force captured Rabaul after a brief battle; on 3 February Japanese planes bombed Port Moresby; and on 19 February Darwin, on the northern coast of Australia, was bombed. But the Japanese had no plans for invading Australia. Indeed they had advanced with a speed which surprised even themselves. After they occupied Lae and Salamaua on 8 March 1942, only three months after they entered the war, they paused to consider

their next objective. It was to be Port Moresby. The problem
was how to take it. The Japanese had few maps and little information about the country, and already the length of their
supply lines was causing them concern. Yet they had to maintain the forward momentum of their advance, to prevent their
opponents from regrouping to mount a counter-offensive.
After a month's hesitation, they decided to attack Port Moresby
by sea, around the coast of eastern Milne Bay District, and
from Tulagi Island, near Guadalcanal, in the Solomon Islands.
In 1942 Arthur Duna of Northern District graphically gave his
eye-witness account of the Japanese invasion of Buna:

> As if you had a dreamlike spirit chasing you and you want
> to run; [but] you cannot run and the spirit catches you. It
> was just like that. There was a great panic. That afternoon
> you have run away from where you were at the time of Japan
> landing. There was not time to go to your village to gather
> your family or collect your valuable belongings. Wife ran
> naked without her husband and children. Husband ran
> naked without wife and children. A child ran without his
> parents and even if he was with his small ones, he deserted
> them. All ran in different directions into the bush. All ran
> like rats and bandicoots in the *kunai* grass. The night fell
> and each individual slept either in the grass or under trees.
> The soil was your bed and the rotten logs your pillow. You
> go to sleep wherever you happened to run into. The noise
> of the guns died down in the night[2].

The people involved in the fighting

There were four main groups involved in the fighting: the
Japanese, the Australians, the Americans, and the people of
Papua New Guinea.

Although their supply lines were over-extended, the
Japanese were determined and maintained their resistance to
the last. Even when they were desperately short of food and
supplies and had sustained very heavy casualties and were completely cut off, they clung to their positions. With a conviction
that Europeans regarded as fanatical, they refused to surrender. Although exact figures are not obtainable, we know

that almost 200 000 Japanese died in Papua New Guinea alone and very few were captured.

The Australian infantry was undoubtedly better fed than their enemy. However, in most encounters the Japanese had the advantage of greater numbers. Despite this, in victory or defeat the Australians developed a skill and an aggression in jungle fighting which few except the local soldiers were able to equal. It was the Australians who fought in the most decisive battles of the campaign. Australians were also involved in the campaign as coast watchers, or as members of the Australian New Guinea Administrative Unit (ANGAU), though ANGAU was intended mainly to continue the civil administration of those areas not occupied by the Japanese.

The Americans were allies of the Australians. The experience of contact with American troops had a deep effect on the people. Some remarkable changes were seen. A seemingly endless stream of goods arrived from the United States, and the people saw a large number of black men serving in the American Army — black men who apparently had all the privileges, cargo, and wealth of white men. The Americans brought war supplies to Finschhafen, Saidor, Manus, Bougainville, and Port Moresby in such huge quantities that both locals and Australians were amazed. Perhaps neither group has yet recovered from that experience.

Those most affected by the war were the people of Papua New Guinea. The war was not their war, though it was fought on their soil, but nonetheless many fought bravely. Some fought for the Japanese, others for the Americans and Australians (the Allies). As soldiers, they endured hardship and showed skill in jungle fighting; as carriers, stretcher-bearers and labourers, whether as volunteers or as conscripts, they were obliged to suffer disease, hunger, and exhausting conditions for causes which usually had little meaning or attraction for them. Many died, particularly under the Japanese, who were themselves short of supplies. Many on both sides ran away; many struggled gallantly on. The Australians, particularly on the Kokoda Trail, depended completely on them, and this brought Australians and native people into a new relationship.

Physical and psychological effects of the war

An obvious effect of the war was the great damage done in areas where the fighting had been heaviest, in the Northern, Morobe, Madang, Sepik, Milne Bay and Bougainville districts where practically everything Europeans had built before the war was destroyed. Almost all the solid buildings and government and mission stations were destroyed, and valuable government and mission records dealing with the period prior to 1942 were lost.

Much of the people's property was also destroyed. Villages were burnt and the people evacuated. Gardens were pillaged and left to the jungle, and possessions were destroyed, some never to be replaced. Along the Madang coast, Allied bombing destroyed the great sea-going canoes of the Bilbil people, and during the war the old people with the skills to build them died, so that after the war the destroyed canoes could not be replaced. Allied bombing, ground fighting, the Japanese search for food and, to a lesser extent, looting by both Allied and Japanese soldiers caused most of this destruction.

As well as this outright destruction, people suffered from the recruitment of their young men to work for the Japanese or the Allies. As a result, gardens and village work were neglected. In some areas Papua New Guineans were shot by the Japanese or the Allies for disobedience, and towards the end of the war starving Japanese soldiers sometimes shot villagers and enemy prisoners for food.

After the war the Australian government paid the people money as compensation for damage and loss of property, whether the damage had been caused by Australians, Americans, Japanese, or by the local people themselves. The confusion of the period inevitably meant that these payments did not always seem fair. Some people were paid compensation for property they never lost, while others are still trying to claim compensation for war damage.

In general, the war was most difficult for the people in areas where there was fighting, or labour recruiting. Many died and many old ways were unsettled. It produced a mood for change so that in the post-war period the people were looking for new ways of life and were ready to listen to new ideas.

Different areas of Papua New Guinea experienced physical effects of various sorts. All the invading armies, and particularly the Americans, undertook large-scale construction works which dramatically changed a countryside which had altered little in thousands of years. For example, one million Americans passed through Manus, and in 1945 there were more houses and more jeeps on Manus than there are people now! At Oro Bay, in the Northern District, a town was built in a few months to house 250 000 people (about double the present size of the capital city). The town had seven hospitals, more than nine hotels, and two wharves each over a mile long. Nearby, at Popondetta, there were twenty-three aerodromes. Airstrips and hundreds of houses were built in such places as Konedobu, the Trobriand Islands, Woodlark Island, Cape Gloucester, Torokina, and Wewak. The scale of building amazed both locals and Australians.

Wartime labourers

The experience in which most people were involved during the war was the same experience which many had shared before 1942: working as labourers. Not much has been written about what it was like working for the Japanese, though quite a lot of people had that experience. We know more about the people who worked for the Australians and the Americans. Men were recruited for both these armies, and supervised by ANGAU, troops, and the police. In May 1942 ANGAU issued an order that not more than 25 per cent of the adult male population of a village could be recruited as labourers, carriers, policemen, and soldiers, and that labourers and carriers were to be employed in their home districts. However these regulations were frequently ignored.

While there is no doubt that the people suffered death and destruction from bombing and shelling from the Allied and the Japanese forces alike, the heaviest burden for the village people was the provision of labour service towards the war effort. The exact figure of the total labour strength between

1942 and 1945 is difficult to obtain. However, Peter Ryan provides the following figures which show that labour service increased dramatically as Papua New Guinea became increasingly important theatres of war:

> On 31 October 1942, total labour strength was 7,914. By the end of the year it had doubled to 16,050 and three months later, it had risen to 18,446. In September 1943 it was 30,000 and by July of the following year it had jumped another 30% to a total of 40,000 under contract of service[3].

These figures do not include many people who served short terms near their homes. However, the point is that during the war many well-populated districts were held by Japanese, so that less than half the population of the controlled areas were required to supply the entire levy. According to Peter Ryan's calculation:

> Recruitment in some villages was 100% of fit male adults . . . I myself knew villages where, in 1944, recruitment exceeded 100%, since partly unfit men were impressed for lighter duties. The villages suffered severely, without men to clear gardens, hunt, maintain houses and canoes etc. Diet was deficient, disease mounted, the women were strained from overwork, there was in some places near starvation and very high infant mortality, there was all the grief of separation and bereavement and that frightening apathy and loss of will to live noted by many observers[4].

In 1943 Peter Ryan, walking up the Lakekamu River in the Papuan Gulf, crossed the Bulldog Track to Wau within seven days. In the Morobe district he observed the carriers' conditions:

> The carriers each had a load of about 50 lbs. Their daily ration was one meal of boiled rice, which they cooked for themselves each night. They had each a packet of army biscuits in the mornings, usually eaten on the march, and they set out from Bulldog with a small tin of meat a piece which they ate the first day, so as not to have to carry it. Apart from his loincloth . . . each carrier had one 'trade' blanket. I have

slept in 'trade' blankets often enough to know what they are worth in a cold place[5].

The ration was inadequate for the kind of service required by the war effort. Peter Ryan continues:

> Simple scientific measurement shows that this ration lacks protein, fats and vitamins, and even for ordinary work could be deficient in crude calories. For arduous labour in cold mountains it was quite inadequate. Sickness rates sometimes rose higher than 25%, 14% was accepted as reasonable. Beri-beri, New Guinea mouth and tropical ulcer — all diet deficiency signs — were common[6].

The toll was heavy and there was great suffering and considerable loss.

Arthur Duna was at the Buna government station when a Japanese plane bombed it and he describes how he and a relative escaped from the station:

> As the plane came very low it started to fire its machine gun and went ta-ta-ta-ta-ta-ta-ta, like coconuts falling from the trees, and everything was totally smashed. Wilfred and I were near a house with an iron roof and we felt that the machine gun was going to destroy the roof of the house and bring the house down to the ground, so Wilfred and I hid under some planks of timber that were laid on top of one another nearby. We were hiding there when the plane came and fired its guns and then passed by. Then it returned and fired at the station again. I came out from the planks first and pulled at Wilfred's legs saying, look if we stay here the bombs will come and kill us all, so let's run away. So I pulled him out and we ran to the sea. Wilfred and I left all our loin cloths and our waist bands, arm bands, everything, under the planks — we just ran naked into the sea and dived under the water. All other parts of our bodies were under the water with mouths shut though the noses were above water to breathe and eyes to watch the planes were in the air. It was like lying in a grave except we still breathed. Each time the plane came over we dived under the water, and each time it went away we

came out of the sea and ran along the beach, just ran and ran and ran[7].

Arthur Duna was subsequently captured by the Japanese, escaped and was recruited by the American forces to work as a labourer.

Another villager, Raphael Oembari of Buna has described assisting George Washington, a wounded American soldier whom he helped to a nearby camp where a doctor treated him.

> After the bridge crossing he asked for water and I fetched some for him. He had hardly finished drinking it when a Japanese bren-gun burst out like thunder at us, and we dived under the kunai grass — George on one side and I on the other side of the track. I crawled up first and picked him up slowly. We were walking again when he said, "I am hungry!" I gave him one hard biscuit. But he said, "break it in half and let us share it". So I broke it and gave him one half and I ate the other half. After sharing the biscuit, he began to limp instead of walking: the pain was too much and he was dizzy. I embraced the man and tried to carry him but he was too heavy, so I half carried him to the Siremi Camp[8].

As indicated earlier, an order had been issued which allowed for the recruitment of only one quarter of the total adult male population as labourers, carriers, policemen, and soldiers. In order to appreciate the overall problem of recruitment, it is worth examining in detail a small Binandere community. A population of about 2538 adults and children occupied twenty-one villages on the lower reaches of the Mamba, Gira and Eia rivers. The total adult male population was 354 of whom twenty-one or six per cent were recruited as soldiers in the Papuan Infantry Battalion (PIB), thirty-five men or ten per cent joined the Royal Papuan Constabulary as policemen, and 110 or 31 per cent of the able-bodied men were recruited as general labourers and carriers. This meant that 188 males or 53 per cent of the male population were too old or too young to render any services towards the war effort, or be of any use to the women in the villages.

Stephen Reed noted the sexual frustration of women as a

result of the long absence of their men from Angoram in the East Sepik.

> Deprived of their lawful sex-partners, the women indulged in random love-affairs with men who remained in the village. An extreme type of maladjustment came to my attention on the Lower Sepik River. A group of women of a village from which almost three-fourths of the able-bodied men had been recruited appeared before the Assistant District Officer at Angoram to 'make court'. They accused the *tultul* [or the government agent] in the village of neglecting his duties by refusing to have intercourse with them. They argued that since the Government had sanctioned the recruitment of their men, it was up to the village official appointed by the Government to keep them sexually satisfied. The *tultul*, speaking on his own behalf, wailed that he had done his best, but that he had reached his limit. 'Mi lez long pushpush', he cried, 'baimbai sikin bilong mi i lus finis' [sic]. 'I am exhausted of sexual intercourse. Soon I will become a physical wreck (as a result of too much orgasm)'[9].

Work as soldiers

As the war progressed, police and other local people were taken into the Australian army and trained as special fighting units: first the Papuan Infantry Battalion, and the two New Guinea Infantry Battalions, which were later all joined together as the Pacific Islands Regiment. Because of their knowledge of the environment, their experience and their skills, these small units achieved much and produced some distinguished war heroes. Simogun Pita, Somu Sigob, Katue and William Metpit, and Yauwiga are some of the most famous. Some Australian soldiers had respect and affection for the local people with whom they worked and fought, and treated them as equals. Others accepted what had been the prevailing view of the pre-war colonists that the local people were inferior and should be segregated from Europeans. An anthropologist reported a not-unusual incident which occurred at Madang immediately after the war:

> Two tanks were installed near the wharf for drinking, both

full of the same chlorinated water but labelled respectively 'European personnel' and 'Native only'. As I passed one morning I heard an ANGAU officer in charge of the natives roundly abusing a private who had gone to the wrong tap. 'Have you no pride of race?' he asked. 'Don't you realise that this water is for coons?'[10]

The Australian soldier may have been an innocent person who probably did not think of the people as 'coons'. In spite of official segregation there was often a very close bond between the soldiers of different races. Don Barnett reports a toothless Australian being fed by a Melanesian driver when huge floods chased the soldiers up in the trees:

> After an uncomfortable and wet night there was a little cheer in the morning when a small wild pig was captured. Miraculously a fire was made and soon the tempting smell of cooking pork was causing mouths to water. Watering freely was the mouth of Lt. Harry Read who was also bemoaning the loss in the flurry of the previous day of his denture. Pig cooked, Read's batman Pte Lalun produced a tasty meal assuring Read the pork was tender enough to eat without teeth. It was. 'How was it done?' queried Read. 'Simple', said Lalun, 'I chewed it first!'[11]

Japhet Jigede, who rose to the rank of sergeant-major, believes that the war ended because Pacific islanders used their age-old customary magical power, and not because of the dropping of the hydrogen bomb on Hiroshima in August 1945. Jigede believes that it was the use of the ashes resulting from the burning of a piece of bark of a tree, a leaf of a plant, a piece of animal, and a portion of his father's hair, that saved the men under his command. He describes the process and the effective use of the magical power:

> I told all the members of the PIB under my control to sit around the fire that I made to burn these things. They had to be there when the power in these things evaporated into smoke so that they could inhale it. After the things were burnt to ashes, I filled their tins with the ashes. I ordered each soldier to come, one by one, and pick a tin of ashes

and my instructions followed: This [war] is not ours, but we have entered into it, and you may die at any moment. This stuff is your protection, derived from our deep-rooted customs established by our ancestors who used it against their enemies[12].

The Australian New Guinea Administrative Unit (ANGAU)

After the Japanese captured Rabaul the Australians used colonial administrative officers and planters to establish military units to administer those parts of Papua New Guinea not occupied by the Japanese. In April 1942 these units were combined to form the Australian New Guinea Administrative Unit (ANGAU) which operated until the establishment of a Provisional Administration in October 1945. ANGAU's main functions were to provide all requirements for fighting and to maintain law and order. The main divisions of ANGAU were the Field Services Division, the Native Labour Section, and the Production Control Board. Through these divisions Papua New Guineans were recruited into war service as carriers, stretcher-bearers, road workers, air field construction workers, and plantation labourers.

The most common experiences for those recruited by ANGAU were in the Kokoda campaign in 1942 and on the Eloa Trail (Bulldog Track) campaign which followed the tributary and moved from Lakekamu to Wau to Bulolo and Salamaua, as the Australian army pushed the Japanese back from Kokoda during 1944.

The villagers

Many of the people in remote places such as Telefomin and much of the Western and Southern Highlands had little or no contact with the war. However for others the war was very real. Many villagers experienced the terror of the might of the warplanes, battleships, mortar, and machine gun fire; they watched as their homes and gardens were destroyed; they were conscripted by both sides; and sometimes they felt like refugees in their own land. The war was not of the villagers' making and was beyond their understanding.

During the Second World War many mothers expressed their heartache when husbands or sons were recruited to be labourers, soldiers, and policemen. For instance, Gavide, a woman of the Binandere clan from Kotaure village on the Gira River, wept when her son was taken away as evident from the chant at the beginning of this chapter.

Wartime attitude towards the Europeans

The war affected the people's attitudes towards Europeans, although it is sometimes difficult to say exactly how. The people had seen Europeans retreating in defeat from the Japanese, but they had also seen them returning in victory and driving out the Japanese. Therefore, the picture remained of Europeans being very powerful, but the possibility that they might not stay forever was raised in the minds of some people. After the war Europeans seemed less superior and less all-knowing than before.

Some people also saw new Europeans. These were Australian and American soldiers, most of whom were far more ready to treat them as equals than the pre-war Europeans. They saw carriers, police, and Pacific Infantry Battalion men helping the Allied cause. The foreign soldiers were ready to share food, stories, and money with them. They also did physical work, sometimes a lot of it. Before the war, the people seldom saw whites working physically hard except for miners. Soldiers also brought a staggering volume of cargo to the country. These things all influenced attitudes toward the Europeans.

The group of Europeans with which the people were most closely involved were those who worked for the Australian New Guinea Administrative Unit (ANGAU). ANGAU administered areas out of the actual battle zone, recruited labourers needed to work for the war, and provided interpreters and paymasters. Thus, ANGAU was the successor of the pre-war civil administrations of both territories, and was in charge of almost everything which affected the people.

ANGAU was much bigger than the pre-war civil administrations, and probably it was more efficient, at least so far as getting work done. Its size and the war needs meant that ANGAU affected many more people than the civil administrations had in peacetime. More people than ever before worked for Europeans as ANGAU carriers, workmen, domestic servants, suppliers of food, or in the army or the police. Generally, ANGAU was not popular, although some of its officers were. Even now people tend to associate it with hard times and the many problems of the war. Probably only the Japanese are remembered less favourably.

Attitudes towards the Japanese

It would be difficult to write a detailed view of how the people felt towards the Japanese. However, it is possible to obtain some insight from experiences in several areas where intense fighting took place. Between March 1942 and September 1943 Japanese occupied Finschhafen in Morobe district. The local people categorised the Japanese soldiers according to their insignia and their behaviour. A member of the Infantry Regiment of the Japanese 18th Army, based at Finschhafen, had a star on his helmet, whereas a member of the 5th Sesabo Special Naval Landing Forces had an anchor and a chrysanthemum on his helmet. Patrick Silata recorded the observation of a local villager:

> Those Japanese with star on their helmets were good while those that had anchor on their helmets were brutal ... Defecating and urinating they spoiled our church ... calling buta! buta! they killed and ate our fowls and pigs[13].

That cordial relations existed between the 'good' Japanese and the villagers is demonstrated by the following account of the establishment by the Japanese of a school at Murik Lakes in the Sepik. Between 1943 and 1945, Murik Lakes, at which there were many small ships and landing craft, became a major Japanese base. During this time a Japanese commissioned officer named Yuko Shibata, of the Maritime and Engineering Division of the Akazuke Regiment of the 18th Army, initiated a proposal to establish a school for the local children. With the agreement of a local Karau 'big man' a school teaching Japanese and some simple arithmetic was set up. One of the pupils at this school was the nine-year-old Michael Somare who grew up to become the first prime minister of Papua New Guinea.

New standards of wealth

The war also gave Papua New Guineans new standards of wealth. The Allied soldiers brought in more money than the people had seen before, and gave it to the people, or used it to buy food and souvenirs, or to pay for their assistance against the Japanese. Also, more men earned cash as workers than before the war, so that many areas became more wealthy than anyone had thought possible before 1942.

Men going to work and the increased general wealth intensified the disruption of village life even in areas not directly affected by fighting. While there were more men absent from the villages there were often also more Western goods in them. This increased flow of goods and money into villages changed many people's expectations about the future.

New Australian attitudes to Papua New Guinea

The fighting in Papua New Guinea in 1942 and 1943 brought war closer to Australia than ever before. Many Australians thought a Japanese invasion of their country was imminent, and Australian civilians anxiously followed the course of the fighting. By the time the war ended in 1945 more Australians had died in this country than had lived in it before the war began.

By 1945 Australians were more aware than ever before that Papua New Guinea existed. Newspapers, films, and books talked of the fighting, of the mountains, the jungle, and of the people. Australians learnt about the people through their contact with the soldiers, police and, in particular, the carriers who assisted the troops. They were told of the loyalty, the courage, and kindness of those helping the Allies. In fact, what they were told was often not true, but Australians believed it. Probably the clearest picture of our people that Australians had in the war was of a carrier, probably on the Kokoda Trail, carrying supplies up to the front line, or bringing wounded Australian soldiers to safety. Australians felt grateful that their sons and husbands were being looked after.

However, like the local people's experience of Japanese behaviour, Papua New Guinean experience of Australian behaviour varied. In many areas it was the policy of the Australian 1st Army to hang people who were believed to have collaborated with the Japanese. In 1942, for instance, twenty-eight people were hanged at Higaturu near Popondetta[14]. However, it seems that this policy was opposed by ANGAU and not revealed to the Australian army headquarters in Melbourne or the Australian government until 1945. The Australian government issued orders that this practice should stop. However, there is some evidence that these instructions were ignored by at least some senior army officers.

Because these incidents were not publicised in Australia most Australians continued to believe that the relationship between the army and the people of Papua New Guinea had been good, and the majority of Australians continued to be grateful to Papua New Guineans for their support of the Allied cause. In consequence they felt a sense of obligation to the people, so after the war most Australians were willing to allow their taxes to be spent to help the people and the country towards economic development and eventual independence.

After 1945 there was a general movement of world opinion against colonialism. From 1945 onwards most European colonial powers began to give their African and Asian colonies independence. This was a slow movement, and during the 1940s very few Australians thought of giving Papua New Guinea independence. Indeed, most did not think of Papua New Guinea as a colony or of themselves as colonisers.

In Australia, the governing Labor Party, the party most committed to ending colonialism, embarked on a policy of speeding development towards self-government and eventual independence. In 1945, a period of very rapid development began, although no-one then imagined that an independent Papua New Guinea would emerge only thirty years later. This policy of rapid development seemed radical in 1945, and it was only possible for the Labor government to implement it because of the changes in Australian attitudes caused by the war.

Broader horizons

The war also increased the local people's knowledge of people in other parts of the country. This had been happening to a certain extent before the war, but during the war many people travelled more often and further, even crossing from one territory to the other. There are still communities in parts of Papua New Guinea of people far from their original homes, who settled there during the war.

People's ideas about how they should live and what it was possible to achieve were changed by their wartime experiences. Knowledge and status gained in the war were used to advantage, and new wealth and new ideas were used in new village ventures. Men like Anton of Moseng in the Sepik, Tommy Kabu from the Purari Delta, Yali from Madang and Paliau from Manus brought ideas back to their people. Peter Simongun of Wewak expressed the new attitudes of some of his contemporaries towards Europeans after the war:

> Yes, we have helped you in this war, now we are like cousins, like brothers. We too have won the war. Now whatever knowledge, whatever ideas you have, you can give them to us. Before all the things we did, you gaoled us, and you fined us, all the time. But now. What now?[15]

From 1942 when the Japanese captured Rabaul in East New Britain until their retreat in 1945, parts of New Guinea and Papua became the scene of bitter fighting between the Allied American and Australia troops and the Japanese. The 1 000 000 Americans, 500 000 Australians and 300 000 Japanese made a substantial and often devasting impact on the lives of many indigenous people. Many men were conscripted by both sides, to fight or work as labourers and carriers. The women fled into the jungle or were left in the villages to fend for themselves and their children.

The people were astonished by the vast quantities of goods and weapons brought in by the troops, and some had unrealistic expectations of the availability of these goods in the post war period. While practically no one had any understanding of what the war was about, their attitudes to white men changed, and in many cases improved. However, in the process many lives were lost, much land and property was destroyed, and many societies seriously disrupted. Nonetheless Australians felt grateful that their sons and husbands were being looked after by Papua New Guineans. Bert Bero's popular poem expressed this gratitude:

> Many a mother in Australia
> When a busy day is done
> Sends a prayer to the Almighty
> For the keeping of her son . . .

> Now we see those prayers are answered
> On the Owen Stanley track . . .
> Slow and careful in bad places
> On the awful mountain track,
> The look upon their faces
> Would make you think that Christ was black.

> May the mothers of Australia
> When they offer up a prayer,
> Mention those impromptu angels
> With their fuzzy wuzzy hair[16].

A wind of change 1947–1960

After the war some communities and individual leaders in the country advocated massive economic, social, and political changes. These advocates of rapid change were isolated by moves by the Australian government to centralise power and authority in Canberra. However, in practice, considerable power still resided with the Australian administrators in Port Moresby, Colonel J. K. Murray and Sir Donald Cleland, who helped shape as well as implement post-war policies. They laid the formal structure of government and made a significant contribution towards the goal of independence.

In July 1945, after the Japanese had been driven out of Papua New Guinea, the Australian government passed the Papua New Guinea Provisional Act under which Papua and New Guinea were to be administered as a single territory known as Papua New Guinea. The Act was 'provisional' because of the uncertain status of the Mandated Territory after the collapse of the League of Nations. The situation was formalised with the passing of the Papua New Guinea Act in July 1949. Legislating for a single administration was in fact legitimising the situation which had existed during the war with the formation in 1942 of the Australian New Guinea Administrative Unit (ANGAU) to provide civil administration of all areas in Papua and New Guinea not under military occupation.

'A New Deal'

After the war the Australian Labor Government made a commitment to a 'New Deal' for Papua New Guinea. The Australian grant-in-aid was to be increased greatly. The aim was to provide facilities so that with better health and better education, the Papua New Guineans could take part in the exploitation of their own resources and eventually manage their own affairs. The intention was that the interests of the local population were of major consideration and that priority be given to the educational, economic, and political progress of the people. Policies to be implemented included abolition of the indenture system and repatriation of the labourers to their villages, payment of some compensation for war damage, and better facilities for education, health, and welfare. Under the Minister for External Territories, E. J. Ward, Australia began to fulfil these goals by increasing financial aid and moved to dismantle the legal and administrative barriers between Canberra and Port Moresby. The 'New Deal' was in fact an expression of a 'debt of gratitude' — a form of compensation for the contribution that Papua New Guineans had rendered during the war.

However, the 'New Deal' clouded an 'Old Deal'. From 1884 both the Australians and the Germans plundered the local resources and alienated land. From 1914, when the Australians acquired German plantations and gold was discovered, the wealth flowed into Australian hands. Thus, while the Australians saw the 'New Deal' as compensation for services provided by the people during the war, many Papua New Guineans felt that the 'New Deal' should compensate for services provided and losses incurred in the previous fifty years. It was this perception that was the basis of many of the social movements, or so-called 'cargo cults', in the post-war period. In addition some believed that the 'New Deal' should include provision for the people of Papua New Guinea to run their own affairs, but the Australians appointed their own officials in administrative positions in the colony.

Colonel J. K. Murray, the first post-war administrator, was given only very general ministerial guidelines, and he gave priority to establishing a public service. Two key departments of the service were the Department of Labour and the Department of Education, which were geared towards the social and economic development of Papua New Guinea. Concerning the Department of Labour, Murray was later to reflect:

> An ordinance and ministerial instructions directed that there be improvement in the accommodation of workers, a new ration scale nutritionally balanced and adequate be adopted, improved medical care for workers be provided, an increase in cash wages per month to £15 be made and that hours be reduced to 44 per week. Radical changes in other conditions of employment included reduction in the length of indentures, their replacement as early as possible . . . by an agreement of relatively short duration and the abolition of penal sanctions in relation to employment. Free labour was to be the goal[17].

One effect of this was felt as early as October 1945 when thousands of labourers were sent back to their villages because the Australian Labor government had abolished the indenture system and cancelled all native labour contracts on a single day. This was a radical reform which became unpopular with the expatriate community, but administrator Murray issued a stern warning in 1947:

> It is fair to point out that most dependent and other countries, even those not torn by war, are suffering from these things today and there is no magic which can solve for a handful of Europeans in Papua New Guinea problems which are proving singularly intractable elsewhere; all post-

war governments have to suffer abuse for hardships and difficulties not of their making, and the Administration is no exception.

A new spirit, new ideas, new demands and standards have spread through the native community. I do not propose to attempt, even if I could hope to succeed, to stifle that spirit so that European employers can return to the standards of a vanished world. On the contrary, that spirit will provide energies for new productive activities under administrative guidance. The period of change is not an easy one for any of the parties concerned, and employers cannot be exempted from the need for adjustment[18].

Education

The Department of Education was made responsible for co-ordinating education, including mission education, within the country and determining policy on such matters as standards and the language of instruction. Except in areas where the Japanese or the Allied presence was relatively stable for a long period, education was seriously disrupted by the war.

Post-war educational policy was basically determined by W. C. Groves who was appointed the first Director of Education in 1946 with very limited policy guidelines. Groves' policy was to develop schools which had strong community involvement and had a broad social welfare role as well as an educational role. This gave the indigenous people limited access to western-style education.

In 1955, following criticism of Groves' policies, the Minister for Territories, Paul Hasluck, defined legitimate educational activities more narrowly and initiated the policy of universal primary education with emphasis on English language instruction. Hasluck believed that it was essential to establish a strong network of primary schools before developing a network of post-primary schools. However, the implementation of this policy was hampered by a shortage of qualified teachers, inadequate teacher training facilities and a lack of school buildings and teacher accommodation. As the missions were willing to continue or expand their involvement in the provision of primary education and administrator, Murray, who was particularly committed to the education programme, agreed to subsidise mission education.

Groves pursued a policy of co-operation between the various churches and the administration, particularly over the pooling of resources. However, funding for education was still very limited. Between 1946 and 1949 the missions spent $152 184 and the Education Department only $23 802 on education in the Territory. In 1950 the administration and the missions established forty-one vocational training centres for the purposes of applied education. Administration schools were established only in towns such as Rabaul. However, there was a significant network of church schools in rural areas. By 1951, however, the educational programmes undertaken by both the administration and the missions under the direction of Groves had produced little result.

The failure of this policy led to the administration taking a more active role in providing education. It established more schools, reduced the financial subsidy to church schools, and sought greater control over their activities. The educational programme called for the use of English as a common language because it was believed that this would foster national unity in a country where almost 700 languages were spoken. One concern was that many of the Papua New Guinean teachers could not speak or write accurate English. Colonel E. Taylor, Director of the Department of Native Affairs, once blamed the German presence for the lack of English taught in the mission schools. Often even English-speaking teachers preferred to give instruction in local languages.

The official policy of conducting classes in English had a destructive effect on the culture of the people who received the education. It created a division between the school and the village life. The crucial marker of the cultural gap was the language. One of the students, Nelson Giraure, described his passive learning in this way:

> I remember being completely inhibited during my first years at school. I could no longer make fun through speech. My quick wit was no use to me. I was like a vegetable. I was controlled by the limits of my vocabulary. My days were spent

listening to my teacher. Many questions I wanted to ask remained unasked because I did not have the ability to express them in English. Eventually I found it much easier just to sit and listen rather than attempt to speak. So I sat and listened[19].

In some cases the policy alienated many students from their cultures as Paulias Matane lamented:

Education has made me a foreigner to my own tradition, culture and beliefs . . . I wish that my proud fathers could come back to me now, take me and transform me into one of them so that I would be like them — a colourful, articulate, skilful, proud, confident and brilliant man. But I have lost all these values because I went to school[20].

The drive to establish Western formal education was done to accelerate broader social change. More often than not the system had negative cultural consequences. As P. Smith and G. Guthrie put it:

In providing formal western education, the missionary society and the colonial government saw schools as powerful agents for change. There was never any intention that the schools should serve merely to reproduce the values, beliefs and life-styles of the societies in which they were placed: in fact their explicit intention was the opposite[21].

Educators have already recorded the cultural impact of the colonial education policy which promoted English as a language in the 1950s and 1960s. When the first pilot project of a vernacular school was established in the Buka Island of the North Solomon Province in 1980, the chairman, who had received his education in English, reflected:

When I think about my education I know that there was a very big gap. We were taught in English and so we were moulded to go outside, to leave our villages and go to cities to find jobs. No one taught us about our language, our own place. [The foreigners] trained us to leave not to stay. Australian and American children are taught English for many years, not just so that they can learn the language but so they can learn their history, their values [and] their culture.

The chairman believed that after political independence the new nation should encourage the vernacular schools in order to instill village learning:

> We must train our children in the history, values, and culture of our people. And we must use our language to teach them, for language is culture. If we truly understand our language, we can say that we truly understand our culture. Our language tells us our relationship to everything: to elders, to our parents, even to the sand, the rocks, the sea, and the stars. If my children are divorced from my own language, then I cannot teach them, and then my children will reject both my culture and me[22].

After the administration took control of the education programme and introduced English as the medium of instruction, a considerable change occurred. By 1960, the majority of mission teachers were Anglo-Celts for whom English was a first language. This meant the establishment or expansion of schools and teacher training centres, an increase in school enrolments, and improvement in basic numeracy and English language literacy. Hasluck's policy of attempting to achieve universal primary education continued to be followed under the direction of Groves' successor, G. T. Roscoe. However, this meant that money was spent on primary school education at the expense of secondary school education, and this in turn postponed the emergence of an educated élite.

Public health

The lack of clear guidelines on priorities of funding government departments allowed those departments with strong directors to get the most funds. The Department of Public Health was given priority because of the influence of its director, Dr John Gunther, rather than because of a deliberate policy of the administration.

Gunther's first aim was to eradicate malaria. The disease was widespread in the lowlands and, he believed, not only killed people but also destroyed their morale, capacity, and character. Using many of the drugs that had been developed during the Second World War he also tried to rid the country of yaws, tuberculosis, and leprosy.

Gunther's initiatives included bringing some education, agriculture and manpower responsibilities under the control of the Health Department. For instance, when the lack of basic education made it impossible for some Papua New Guineans to proceed to tertiary education he trained them as laboratory workers and medical assistants in the Health Department. Sir Albert Maori Kiki, Dr Reuben Taureka and Dr Gabriel Gris, all later prominent in public life, owed their initial training to Gunther's initiative.

At the end of the war more than half the population lived in the Central Highlands where there were no Western health services except for some occasional patrols sent to treat epidemic diseases introduced from the coast. However by 1949 sixty village aid posts had been established, and training schools for medical and hygiene assistants were operating at Goroka, Simbu, Kerowagi, Mount Hagen, Kainantu and Wabag. In the same year the medical officer in charge of the region reported:

> The Central Highlands area has been investigated thoroughly . . . The most striking feature is that in this area there is still a large population unexposed to tuberculosis and living under conditions which are such that if tuberculosis were to penetrate it would become almost epidemic . . . It is interesting to note the effect of coastal contact on the natives of the Central Highlands District. This contact dramatically raises the incidence. It is possible to trace the gradient of infection from distant villages. Natives in the Kainanatu Sub-district have always had more contact with the coast than other natives of the Central Highlands and it will be noted that incidence [there] is much higher . . . there is a larger population in danger of becoming infected . . . under conditions where it would be almost impossible to prevent spread of the disease. It is a problem

1 Waisted stone axe blade, Robogara, Sialum area, Morobe Province

2 Stone mortar, Upapa near Aiyura, Kainantu, Eastern Highlands Province

3 Stone pestle, Fergusson Island, Milne Bay Province

4 Obsidian stone tool, Lou Island, Manus Province

5 Hiri Trade: Hanuabada pottery around Port Moresby exchanged with sago from Papuan Gulf, 1880s

6 Duk Duk Dance, Rabaul, about 1900

7 German medical officer and official buildings, early 1900s

8 Manus Island group of men, about 1916

9 Iona Togigi (teacher) and school children and Raluana School near Rabaul, 1920s

10 A Taian Dawari warrior

11 Native house at Kamali, 1885

12 'The latest miracle of the wonder-working white man', 1922

13 Beating tapa cloth, Oro Province, about 1922

14 White missionary woman posing with a group of Papuans, 1920s

15 A war canoe, New Britain, about 1920

16 Bank of Salamoa, Morobe Province, about 1929

18 'Stone Age man of Tari, Western Papua, sees an aeroplane', 1957

17 Woman from the Southern Highlands, n.d.

19 Intelligence gathering, about 1942 — a local policeman draws a map to show Japanese positions, Buna, Oro Province

20 Stretcher bearers, about 1942

21 Displaced by the war — the US moved Nissan Islanders (North Solomon Province) by force to Guadal Canal, Solomon Islands, so that a US base could be constructed, 1944

22 Pacific Island Regiment troops on parade, Port Moresby, 1942

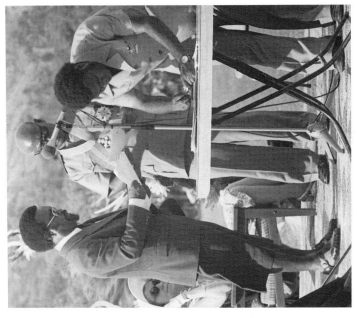

24 Oaths taking at Independence Day, 16 September 1975
— *from left*: Michael Somare (first Prime Minister),
Sir John Guise (first Governor-General), John Haugie

23 Generation gap, about 1970

25 Local government in session, Asaro, Eastern Highlands, 1960s

26 The first graduates of the University of Papua New Guinea, August 1970 —
from left: Renagi Lohia, Rabbie Namaliu, Kas Magari, John Kadiba and John
Pulu

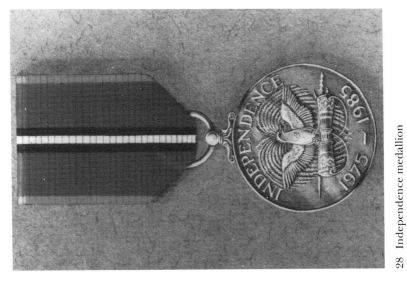

28 Independence medallion

27 PNG Defence Force soldier helps with health
campaign, n.d.

30 Larry Santana, *Self-portrait of Struggle and Pain at the Six-mile Dump*, 1989

29 Wetkin clansmen, Ok Tedi, Star Mountains, 1982

31 Bougainville copper mine at Panguna, North Solomons Province, about 1985

32 Peaceful demonstrators at the national parliament house, 1990

33 Girl with national flag

entirely separate from that of the coastal areas. Owing to its nature, emphasis must be placed on the protection of the highlands area[23].

This warning was taken seriously; Gunther took personal responsibility for organising medical patrols and despatching the supply of medicines. During six months in 1950, for instance, 100 000 people were given anti-tuberculosis treatments as a preventive measure, and later the programme was extended to the rest of the country. Gunther also had very strong moral, political, and financial support from Paul Hasluck, the Minister for Territories in Canberra from 1951 to 1963 and Minister for External Affairs from 1964 to 1969. This is evident from the Hasluck's own commitment:

> Health is a defined, precise and concrete task . . . six years ago in the face of complaints that the Health Department was getting more than its fair share of the budget, I directed that it was to have an even bigger part[24].

Expenditure on public health from 1947 to 1960 was almost twice that of the combined budget for agriculture and education. This evidence indicates clearly that the allocation of resources in the colony was dependent upon the individual influence of heads of departments rather than the implementation of a colonial policy of balanced development.

Missions

Mission stations of churches of all denominations suffered heavy losses of both lives and property during the war. Most foreign missionaries either left or were killed, and where mission activity continued it was through the determined and often heroic efforts of Papua New Guinean Christians.

After the war the missions which had been active in colonial times were re-established. A returning Lutheran missionary found that the area under his pastoral care had changed beyond recognition:

> the first few weeks were a time of bewilderment. Even on the mission station at Ampo I was lost — the old landmarks were gone, almost endless army installations covered the

area which had been so familiar to me, roads had no relations to the old ones, villagers were not seen, all old buildings
destroyed and their old sites entirely overgrown. The distance from Lae to Ampo was the same, but while I used to
tramp over this road on foot — an hour used to be my usual
time — now trucks and jeeps raced through in a few minutes.
I felt like a native of New Guinea might feel if he suddenly
landed in Brisbane. To get my balance again I found the
familiar faces of the natives were helpful[25].

Expatriate missionaries returned or were replaced, and the
mission stations resumed their work of providing health, welfare, and education services, encouraging self-help economic
and social projects, and saving souls. While the administration
was taking more responsibility for health and education, many
societies, particularly in the rural areas, continued to be dependent on missions for these. The missions also provided a
considerable range of informal services and assistance in
establishing plantations, small businesses such as village co-
operatives, and building roads and community centres.

Some people preferred administration schools because in
mission schools they claimed too much emphasis was placed
on the Bible. In the late 1950s, for instance, Buin villagers of
south Bougainville District sent their representatives to meet
Roscoe. They requested an administration school but the
Director of Education refused on the grounds that mission
schools already existed there for the children. The delegation
responded curtly: '*Tok bilong God tasol*', 'only the Word of God'.

Some churches encouraged reading and writing in local languages, mainly so that the people could read the Bible in their
own language. The Anglican mission, for instance, adopted
the Wedau language of Milne Bay District as the 'church
language', and taught the young evangelists who then went to
other areas to preach the Good News. The Lutheran mission
also worked in this way in the Morobe District.

There was great expansion of mission activity in the post-war
period, especially in the newly opened highlands. The Christian churches which had operated in Papua and New Guinea
since early colonial times — the Catholics, Lutherans,

Methodists, Anglicans, and the London Missionary Society — all expanded. However, the pre-war arrangement under which churches had agreed to work within certain territorial boundaries began to crumble after the arrival of a number of other Christian denominations such as the Baptists and Seventh Day Adventists.

Papua New Guinea was, by 1960, a basically Christian country in which there were no non-Christian religions. However, while most people regarded themselves as Christians, many of them retained some traditional spiritual beliefs, so Christianity and traditional beliefs can be said to have co-existed.

The economy

Businesses before the war were mainly only ones to do with the small-scale processing and export of cash crops, timber, and gold. There was also a need for service industries such as repair and maintenance of motor vehicles and boats, and food processing such as bakeries. The Australian government's post-war policy of a 'New Deal' for Papua New Guinea greatly increased spending in the public sector, in particular health, transport, public works, education, and public utilities such as post and telegraphs and the electricity commission. This expansion of the public sector improved the social and economic climate. The Australian government hoped this would make Papua New Guinea more attractive to overseas investors as well as encouraging the development of local business activities.

The funds provided by Australia also improved the marketing of cash crops and assisting such enterprises as fishing and small-scale timber-cutting and mining. In the private sector, foreign investment was far more important than local investment. Before 1960 only foreigners received high salaries and most expatriate money left the country.

After 1945 the pre-war processing industries expanded and there was development in general engineering, electrical machinery, building construction, and small-scale manufacturing such as furniture production. While percentage growth in this area was considerable, the country had started with such a small industrial base that even by 1960 this sector was of little economic significance.

Attempts to stimulate secondary industry and agriculture and encourage the exploitation of natural resources were not particularly successful. There were, however, developments in financial and communication services. The only bank in Papua before the Second World War was the Bank of New South Wales which opened in Port Moresby in 1916. In German New Guinea before 1914, banking was handled by German trading companies. In the Mandated Territory the Commonwealth Bank was established in 1916, and the Bank of New South Wales in 1926. After the Second World War these banks expanded their activities and were joined in the 1950s by several other Australian-based financial institutions. In 1960 the Australian government established a branch of the Reserve Bank in Port Moresby.

Agriculture

Although there was no ministerial policy on agriculture, Murray insisted that a Department of Agriculture be established to co-ordinate the growing of subsistence food and cash crops in the villages, and to redevelop the plantations. The department tried first to restore the cash crops on the existing plantations and the experimental stations, both of which were established before the war. Individual attempts were made by departmental specialists to stimulate new projects in agriculture.

As with John Gunther in the Health Department, the absence of official policy allowed experienced people to take action. In the Department of Agriculture senior staff members encouraged the people to grow new crops. Successful experiments included cocoa, tea, and coffee. Some schemes failed because they were imposed with little or no consultation with the local people or the organisers of the schemes did not have sufficient knowledge of local conditions. William Cottrell-Dormer's rice project in the Central District was one of these.

The Agriculture Department was also expanded to incorporate livestock and fisheries, research, training and marketing, and agricultural extension programmes in the villages. Considerable progress was made in both agricultural extension and research. An experimental tea station was set up at Garaina, Morobe District; livestock breeding stations were established near Port Moresby, at Erap close to Lae, and at Goroka and Baiyer River in the highlands; and an agricultural experimental station for high altitude crops was reopened at Aiyura near Kainantu and another lowlands agricultural station was redeveloped at Kerevat near Rabaul. Many agricultural stations were established in the various districts in the four main regions: at Lae, Madang, Wewak and Aitape, Lorengau, Sohano, Buin, Popondetta, and Sogeri. These stations became the bases for agricultural extension services to the villages. However, in spite of the efforts of the Department of Agriculture growth in the commercial agriculture sector was slow except in the coffee-producing areas of the highlands.

Although the huge coconut plantations owned and managed by foreigners in the islands and parts of the lowlands continued to produce large quantities of copra, cash cropping by the local people developed slowly. Legislation in 1891 made it compulsory for Papuan villagers to plant and tend a given number of coconut palms. Coconuts were grown in small plots, close to villages but set apart from the gardens, and worked communally by villagers. However, most villagers did not take enthusiastically to this attempt to encourage cash cropping, and production in most areas was low.

Cocoa also continued to be produced on foreign-owned plantations, but little was produced by the local people. In the 1950s the Bougainvillean people produced negligible quantities although there had been European contact with this area for more than fifty years. By 1970 they were still producing less than 7000 tons per annum. However, cash cropping was more successful in some lowland areas and in the Gazelle Peninsula the Tolais successfully produced both copra and cocoa in spite of fluctuating prices. The Tolai Cocoa Project owed some of its success to the entrepreneurial nature of the Tolai themselves. However, acknowledgement should also be made of the contribution of David Fenbury and his recognition of the need to respect Tolai land tenure if the project were to be successful.

Cash cropping was most successful in the highlands where consistently high prices paid for coffee in this period provided greater incentives than the unstable market prices of the coastal crops — copra and cocoa. In parts of the highlands cash cropping became an extension of subsistence gardening. Unlike the lowlands where the people had been forced to plant coconut trees, the highlanders planted coffee voluntarily because they could quickly earn money to buy European trade goods. In addition, the success of highland cash cropping depended heavily upon the labour and skill of the women. Women were traditionally the gardeners and they early took a major role in the planting and tending of coffee trees. In some cases this involvement with coffee growing led to their also becoming involved in the preparation of the beans for sale to European buyers from the coast. While this involved women in the cash economy, most of the money from the sale of coffee went to highland village men.

Growth in the rest of the agricultural section was slow. One reason was the lack of adequate transport and marketing systems in most parts of the country. For instance, the growers usually carried bags of produce on their shoulders or by canoes and rafts to the coast for shipment to uncertain marketing outlets in the urban areas. One result of the slow growth of cash crops was that most Papua New Guineans continued to depend on the subsistence economy which, to the extent that it provided for the daily needs of the local people, subsidised the cash economy.

In addition, the growth of the towns created a demand for fruit and vegetables produced by the village women, and markets became well established in such centres as Port Moresby, Rabaul, Lae, Mount Hagen, and Goroka. Women who sold garden produce in the markets were thus drawn into the fringe of the cash economy. However, the cash return was small and transporting the produce to market in *bilums* or string bags on foot or by canoe was very hard work.

Small trade stores and co-operatives

During this period various unsuccessful attempts were made to establish trade stores and marketing co-operatives. The failure of these ventures was due to a lack of local capital and managerial skills. The only exceptions were the trade stores and other businesses owned and managed by the Chinese in the urban areas, particularly in the lowlands.

Natural resources

Before the war the administration allowed foreign companies to explore for gas and oil, particularly in the Papuan region where on-shore and off-shore initial investigation had been done. After the war, the administration organised a detailed topographic, geological and forestry survey of the whole Territory. With the co-operation of the Australian Bureau of Mineral Resources and the Commonwealth Scientific Investigation Research Organization, a wealth of detailed information was collected and made available to the Papua New Guinea government at independence in 1975.

As has been noted earlier, the Australian administration had legislated for significant customary land holdings to be kept by the people. After the war the basic principle of land belonging to the people and not to the state continued to apply. However, the question of indigenous land tenure and the often conflicting demand for land for economic development remained a contentious issue between the traditional owners and those who sought to use the land for foreign developmental purposes.

While mineral exploration continued in this period there were no commercially viable finds. Most gold mining equipment had been destroyed during the war. War-time damage was repaired but world gold prices remained low and gold was not as important to the economy as it had been in the 1930s. Timber production fell below pre-war levels. Production improved in the mid-1950s with the re-establishment of logging and milling at Bulolo. Although attempts were made to establish commercial fishing projects only shell fish became a significant export item in this period. Fish caught was almost entirely consumed locally, and tinned fish imports increased as the local economy expanded and the people changed their traditional ways.

Transport and communication

Construction of transport facilities such as air strips, roads and wharves increased dramatically during the war. Many of these in areas not associated with the cash economy subsequently fell into disrepair. After the war additional airstrips were built by the missions, business enterprises, and the administration. Low-grade roads were often built to link the airstrips with the more populous areas. While air travel was the only rapid means of moving long distances about the country, much cargo continued to be carried by sea and the major ports were upgraded. However, nearly all people still travelled on foot or by canoe.

Postal services were operating in both British Papua and German New Guinea by 1900. In the 1930s air transport allowed these to be extended. In the post-war period postal services and the telephone were the main forms of communication in the commercial sector. Outside urban areas radio-telephone was a valuable means of communication. Personal communication was mainly through verbal or written messages relayed by people travelling between villages, or from villages to towns; there were limited postal and telephone services.

Weekly newspapers had been established in Papua in 1911 and New Guinea in 1925. Several missionary bodies also produced local broadsheets prior to the war and mission presses assisted in the production of the Australian army newspapers. In the 1950s and 1960s several newspapers owned by Australian companies were produced in very limited editions to cater for the foreigners in Papua and New Guinea. Attempts to establish Pidgin English language newspapers in this period were unsuccessful.

Governance

Between 1945 and 1951 Canberra established a body known as the Staff Conference, based in Port Moresby, to provide advice to the Australian government and help implement government policy. This body also provided advice on draft legislation and major decisions concerning the civil service and was responsible for supervising day-to-day administration. The Staff Conference consisted of the administrator as chairman, the heads of departments, and other officials who were added from time to time on an *ad hoc* basis. Below the Staff Conference was a committee system which advised on matters of local concern and also carried out the decisions of the administration at the local level.

In November 1951 the Staff Conference was replaced by a Legislative Council comprising the administrator, sixteen official or administration members, and twelve non-official members. The official members were drawn mainly from the public service and the European planters, and the non-official members came mainly from the missions and European business sector. However the non-official members also included three local men who represented Papua, New Guinea mainland, and the Islands. This excluded the highlands which remained largely beyond administrative control. Although this new body included local representatives this was, as will be shown, only a token involvement. The council membership did not change until 1960, when amendments brought about an expansion in total numbers and significantly increased Papua New Guinean representation.

A 1949 Act allowed for a system of local government through the establishment of village councils and in 1951 village councils were established in Port Moresby and Rabaul where the people had had close European contact since the 1870s. Both men and women were eligible to vote for village councils which, while their authority was very limited, had some control over the collection of local taxes. In 1950 there were four village councils, responsible for a population of 11 900 in the country. A decade later the number of councils elected by the people increased to thirty-nine for a population of 265 352. However, although they were called 'village councils' the councils were, in fact, mainly in the towns so there was hardly any change taking place in the villages during the period under review.

Much of the population was more concerned with coping with the destruction brought about by the war than with anything else. Many villages on the lowlands were destroyed, particularly where the Australians and Japanese had fought each other. As a result these villages had to be resettled and the people put much of their effort towards making gardens to restore the subsistence economy rather than concerning themselves with village councils. By 1960 the rural majority remained under the administration system that was established prior to the war, and village constables and village councillors in Papua or *tultuls* and *luluais* in New Guinea continued to be appointed by the colonial officials.

One of the critical functions of the Australian administration was the creation, staffing, and organisation of the Public Service. Murray believed that some of the Australian commonwealth departments should accept responsibility for the function, management, and appointment of senior officers of the public service within the Territory. This responsibility was accepted by the departments of Civil Aviation, Public Works and Post and Telegraphs. As has been seen, additional departments introduced to implement the Labor government's new policy were the Department of Education and the Department of Labour.

In February 1951, after fifteen months as acting administrator, Colonel D. M. Cleland was appointed to replace Murray, who had retired in 1951. Cleland had been Chief of Staff of the wartime administrative body ANGAU from 1943 to 1945, and occupied senior positions in the post-war administration from 1945 to 1951.

Although the Australian Labor government had been defeated in 1951, Paul Hasluck, Minister for External Territories in the Menzies Liberal-Country Party coalition government from 1951 continued the development begun by his Labor predecessor, Ward, in 1945. Cleland enjoyed the co-operation of both Hasluck and Warwick Smith, Secretary to the Department of External Territories, and was fortunate in having both men remain in these key positions throughout his period of office. The fact that there was one minister, one secretary, and one administrator for over a decade allowed continuity of developing policy and a growing reciprocal trust between the government in Canberra and the colonial administration in Port Moresby.

After the war the colonial administration continued to use the administrative districts established before the war. The district commissioners had very wide powers to impose the white man's law, and the most visible sign of European authority in each district was still the police station and the attached district gaol.

The people in the villages could not understand the motives of the administration and they distrusted the officials.

> To the villager, at first sight, there was no difference between a miner and a missionary, or between a trader and a government official, all of whom were regarded as ruthless intruders from an unknown world, with their peculiar ideas, and the powerful . . . (guns)[26].

Many people resented the administration officials, or *kiaps* as they were commonly known in Tok Pisin or Pidgin English. In a poem entitled 'Bush Kanaka Speaks', Kumalau Tawali used typical Manus Islanders' abusive oratory to attack the colonial domination from a villager's point of view.

> The *kiap* shouts at us
> forcing the veins to stand out in his neck
> nearly forcing excreta out of his bottom.
> he says: you are ignorant.
>
> He says: you are ignorant,
> but can he shape a canoe,
> tie a mask, fix an outrigger?
> Can he steer a canoe through the night
> without losing his way?
> Does he know when a turtle comes ashore
> to lay its eggs?
> . . .
>
> Every white man the government sends to us
> forces his veins out shouting
> nearly forces his excreta out of his bottom
> shouting you bush *kanaka*.
>
> He says: *yu ol les man* (lazy people),
> Yet he sits on soft chair and does nothing
> just shouts, eats, drinks, eats, drinks,
> like a woman with a child in her belly.
>
> These white men have no bones.

If they tried to fight us without their (guns)
they'd surely cover their faces like women[27].

The poet reacted against the officers who, according to the villagers, just sat around in their patrol posts visiting villages from time to time to collect the head tax and to impose his law. The administration established stations in remote parts to extend the white men's influence. From these stations on the coastal districts the colonial administration organised a series of patrols into the central highlands immediately after the war.

Opening of the Highlands

The Japanese invasion of Papua New Guinea did not affect the highland societies. Whilst the lowlanders were concerned with resettling villages and restoring their food gardens, the highlanders were enthusiastic about clearing sites for colonial outposts and linking them with dirt roads which they built by hand. The labourers refused to be paid in cash; they preferred the payment in *kina* shells as there was no trade store in the highlands in 1947. Jim Taylor, the District Commissioner, paid his labourers in cash but some of them 'burst into tears when they got their first pay packets, threw the money on the ground and demanded shell'[28]. This attitude changed within a year as the district commissioner:

> set up display boards and the crowds gathered to stare at the pounds shillings and pence. By 1948 quite a few thousand pounds had spread out into the communities. Asaro Valley men were hoarding nearly three thousand of them for their part in building the road over the mountains separating their valley from the Chimbu[29].

In June 1948 Jim Leahy established the first trade store at the recently-opened Goroka airstrip to take advantage of the cash that was poured into the area. He spent about a thousand pounds sterling to bring in a supply of trade goods including steel axes, knives, and beads. These were flown by air from Lae, as there was no road connecting Goroka and the coast.

> Within five days he had sold the lot. He brought in another thousand pounds' worth. Gorokans were waiting at the

airstrip, cash in hand, when the plane taxied up, and the trade goods went in one day. Word had spread, and ... Asaro Valley men running down the dirt road to Goroka, waving sticks with pound notes stuck in the ends[30].

The trade store exchanged kina shells for cash as well as selling trade goods.

In 1958 the first highlands local government council was established in the Goroka Valley. It imposed a tax of one pound and ten shillings on men and ten shillings on women. In the following year the council taxes raised about 9000 pounds sterling to provide social services such as schools and aid posts. The coastal communities paid their head tax from the money they earned from working for the European planters and miners, but the highlanders obtained their money mainly from growing cash crops and selling the produce to pay the tax.

At the time Donald Cleland was appointed assistant administrator, the Central Highlands District had not been systematically explored by Europeans. However, in the 1950s the number of Europeans based at Goroka, the first administrative headquarters in the highlands, rose from fifteen to 450. The Central Highlands had a population of over half a million who occupied over 26 000 square kilometres from Kainantu in the east to Kopiago in the west and this vast region remained unpatrolled. There were no roads to the coast, and the few vehicles which used the small network of dirt roads in the Eastern Highlands had been flown in from the coast to Goroka. In 1953 Ian Downs, the then District Commissioner based at Goroka, was provided with 9000 shovels and picks with which to construct a road between Goroka and Gussap. It was some years later before the completion of the road from Gussap to Lae finally linked Goroka with the coast. Under Cleland's administration most of the highlands was brought under the administration's control and when he retired in 1966 Europeans estimated that the area unpatrolled had been reduced to 800 square kilometres inhabited by an estimated 10 000 people. However, this was probably an over-optimistic estimate and there were many communities which were very seldom visited by patrols, and others, such as Telefomin in the

Central Highlands, remained outside the colonial administration until the 1950s.

Labour scheme

The newly-opened highlands region was regarded by the administration as a source of unskilled labour to be recruited to work on the plantations of the lowland, mainland, and island areas. Under the Highland Labour Scheme, 2445 men were flown to coastal plantations in 1950, and a decade later over 7000 men were taken to work in the plantations, mainly in the Morobe, Madang, and Sepik districts and on other islands.

The colonial administration's practice of recruiting people from one district to work on plantations in another district as indentured labourers had been going on since 1884. Most of these workers were repatriated to their home districts, while some died, and still others married into the local communities where the plantations were established, such as Koitaki in the Central District, or Kokopo near Rabaul in the East New Britain District. In Rabaul, for instance, some people recruited from the Sepik District remained, some marrying Tolai women, and established a Sepik community. Sometimes the Sepiks clashed with the Tolais, usually over land and women. In other cases there were Kerema people from the Gulf who went to work in Madang where their number increased to establish a Kerema compound in the town. Often in the Mandated Territory one would find a Papua compound such as in Lae and other centres where those people who originally came from Papua lived when they worked for either the public or private sectors. Similarly, in some towns in Papua there were New Guinea compounds whose residents were mainly those people who came from the former German colony. Like the coastal indentured workers, the labourers recruited from the highlands often joined their *wantoks* — people who came from the same community or region — in these compounds and lived there instead of being repatriated to their villages.

The concentration of people from one area tended to breed resentment against individuals or communities who originated from another district. These ill feelings were often expressed in the plantations during working hours or in 'labour compounds' after hours. After the 1960s when Papuans and New Guineans began to play competitive social games such as soccer and rugby football, brawls often disrupted the games. For instance in 1973 there was a rugby match between Papuan and New Guinean teams held in Port Moresby. The spectators were from both parts of the country, and a silly remark from a supporter of one region sparked off violence between the supporters of the two teams and it was several days before the police were able to control the situation.

Because of the longer contact with the outside world, the lowland areas had been introduced to Western education, so the administration recruited skilled and semi-skilled labour from the districts on the coast to work in the highlands. These recruits included local teachers, mechanics, electricians, carpenters, and clerks.

Social change

One very important social change in this post-war period was that steps began to be taken towards the breaking down of the racial discrimination laws and discriminatory practices common before the war. From 1950 the colonial administration was under pressure from three sources: international agencies such as the United Nations, anti-colonialists in Australia, especially those who had war-time contact with Papua New Guineans or were involved in the implementation of the Labor government's post-war 'New Deal', and a very small but increasingly vocal group of Papua New Guineans. While racial equality was not achieved in this period, and discrimination and segregation continued to be practised, it was in the 1950s that the basis was laid for the anti-discrimination legislation of the 1960s and 1970s. However, it should be remembered that many Papua New Guineans had no first-hand experience of racial discrimination because they had had little direct contact with the white colonialists.

Another significant social change was the dramatic response of some societies to the much greater contact with the European world during the war and in the immediate post-war period. For thousands of years the individual communities had existed under a social system which can best be described as small-scale independence. Isolated by deep mountain valleys in the highlands, and by extensive swamps in the lowlands, each community evolved and sustained loose-knit social groups without a central authority. However, one feature common to all these societies has been the ability to adjust to change both before and since contact with European civilisation. These small societies lacked the organisational means or technology to give the people more than a minimal control over their harsh environment. They were constantly threatened by warfare as well as by natural hazards, so they clearly had to be prepared to meet circumstances of drastic change if they were to survive over a long period of time. There were certain ways of coping with social upheavals which some people describe as 'cults'.

Some scholars maintain that cults are responses to social breakdown which results from a clash between Melanesian and introduced cultures. Thus their analyses of cults begin only with the arrival of the white man. Looked at from another angle, a collision of cultures is but one example of a catastrophe, and the reaction of the people was, in some instances, similar to their reaction to natural disasters before and following European contact. As C. A. Valentine argues:

> the age-old instability of land and sea, together with seasonal extremes of weather, are combinations peculiar to the region. This combination is enough to suggest that [Papua New Guinean] cultural responses to crises may have their roots in prehistory ... and that they probably developed their own type of social movement ... to deal with collective crises beyond ordinary everyday forms of human control (and the disasters) stimulated collective adaptation[31].

As has been noted in Chapter 5 the sudden Japanese invasion and Allied counter-attack had a dramatic effect on those people who saw several races of soldiers with overwhelming quantities of goods arrive one after the other. It can be argued that this wartime experience was for many people a catastrophe and that in some cases they responded as they had traditionally responded to natural calamities, that is by the development of cults.

The Paliau Maloat Movement

A striking example of wartime culture contact leading to post-war social change can be seen in the Paliau Movement based on Manus Island in the Admiralty group. While the Paliau Movement exhibited a number of characteristics normally associated with a cult, it was a significant social movement which developed in response to the catastrophe of wartime culture contact. During the war Manus was a major military base and the islanders had seen operations involving 1 000 000 Allied troops which included black and white soldiers working together apparently as equals. The troops had come with planes, ships, cars, and tanks, and had left most of this equipment behind when they retreated in haste ahead of the invading Japanese army. Paliau Maloat, who was born in 1918 on Baluan, a small island close to Manus, was one of the witnesses to these dramatic events. In spite of a lack of formal education Maloat rose to the rank of sergeant in the police force and served in both Rabaul and Morobe. During the war he collaborated with the Japanese and although treated with contempt by the Australians who returned to New Guinea after the Allied victory, he was held in high regard by his own people.

Paliau Maloat formed a new religion based on Christianity in which life revolved around the church built in the centre of the village, and distinctive rituals. He also tried to establish a new social order in which traditional cultural distinctions, including the authority of the 'big men', would be swept aside and the people would live in health, harmony and spiritual cleanliness.

Before the war Paliau gained respect from his people by using his wages to establish a fund to pay taxes on Baluan. After the war Paliau insisted that the money received by the people from the Americans during the war was to be collected into a fund. All marriage payments were to be fixed, and feasts and exchanges were to be abolished. Land was to be held in common by members of the 'new society', and the villages were to be cleaned and well-planned. Nobody would leave the district, but workers would accumulate wages within the district and thus contribute to the fund which would be used to buy European goods.

Paliau was a pragmatic man with a down-to-earth common sense. He realised that his society was undergoing rapid change, and his response was to call for radical social and political reforms in order to adjust to this. He provided the leadership, and in 1947 about 9000 islanders on the south coast of Manus paid money to the Paliau Maloat Fund. The Paliau Movement undermined the authority of the administration and the church alike, and Paliau was arrested and put in prison for six months for an alleged perversion of the Christian religion.

In 1949, because Paliau's prestige grew, the Australian administration introduced a scheme of local government councils for Manus, thereby hoping to isolate Paliau, leaving him as a mere village *luluai* on Baluan island. Paliau's followers, however, boycotted the new institutions and promised allegiance to him. When, in 1950, he was arrested for a second time, their angry protests brought him back from detention in Port Moresby and gave him even greater power and glory. In 1951, Paliau was legally president of the Baluan Local Government Council, yet his following on Manus District persuaded him that he was president of the Manus Local Government Council as well. These councils were among the first in Papua New Guinea to push for schools, aid-posts, and co-operatives for the local people. During 1952–53 there was remarkable growth in Paliau's influence. A giant church was built on Baluan, and Usiai migrants who came down to the southern coast of Manus helped to expand the village of Bunai until it was over a mile long. Representatives from the United Nations visited Manus in 1953 and reported favourably on Paliau's remarkable indigenous movement.

Paliau's power increased considerably when he visited the United States on United Nations funds in the early 1960s. A photograph of Paliau standing under the Statue of Liberty in New York was believed by many of his fellow islanders to be evidence of his encounter with God. By 1967 Paliau was no longer president of a local council, but the crowning of his career came when he was twice elected to the House of

Assembly to represent the Admiralties from 1964 to 1972. Even after 1972, he continued as the single most powerful individual on these islands, trying to preserve his achievements against powerful more-modern forces of change. Paliau discarded some aspects of tradition and adopted new ideas to improve the social conditions of his people. While the Paliau Movement fulfilled some of the functions of a cult it had a greater social purpose and achieved more positive results.

Summary

After the war the Australian government administered Papua and New Guinea as a single territory, known as Papua New Guinea, and Canberra assumed a greater degree of direct control over the affairs of the territory. Under Eddie Ward, Minister for External Territories, the post-war Labor government committed Australia to a 'New Deal' for Papua New Guinea under which substantial funding was made available to accelerate economic development, improve living standards, and greatly expand educational and health services. In addition, plans were made to allow Papua New Guineans a greater degree of involvement in government.

In an attempt to implement this policy Colonel Murray, the first post-war administrator: created a public service; abolished the indenture system and repatriated thousands of labourers to their villages; paid war damage compensation; and allowed significant expansion in education, health, public works, post and telegraph and civil aviation services. The administration also facilitated the exploration of the Territory for mineral and timber resources by organising a detailed topographic, geological and forestry survey. After the war, land which had not already been taken was seen as the property of the people — however, there continued to be conflict between the interests of traditional landowners and foreigners who sought to use the land to expand the cash economy. Copra and cocoa continued to be produced on foreign-owned plantations but the Department of Agriculture's attempts to encourage the local people to grow cash crops in the lowlands were largely unsuccessful. To allow a greater degree of participation in governance the administration established a Legislative Council, which had mainly advisory powers and encouraged the establishment of village councils.

These policies were continued under Cleland, who replaced Murray in 1951 and whose appointment coincided with the appointment of Hasluck as Minister for External Territories in the newly elected Liberal-Country Party coalition government. Under Cleland's administration colonial control was extended to the highlands, a massive labour scheme brought highlanders to work on plantations in the lowlands and the islands, and rapid economic development occurred in highland cash cropping, especially coffee. The success of highland cash cropping was partly due to the relatively high market price of coffee and the labour supplied by the highland women. However, the backbone of the economy continued to be the subsistence sector, in which the vast majority of the people worked and lived.

Christian missionary activity of both established churches and newly introduced sects expanded greatly and by 1960 Papua New Guinea was a basically Christian country.

The substantial social change which accompanied these developments profoundly affected the lives of the people in many Papua New Guinean societies, and some societies, such as Manus, reacted by developing radical new social structures and processes which had some of the characteristics of traditional cults. However, on the whole, the people accepted and adapted to these changes and by 1960 the economic and social changes upon which moves could be made towards independence were in place.

6

Transition to independence 1961–1975

Election lures both young and old,
Like diggers in search of gold,
Win or lose matters not at all
To all but one, who scores the goal.

[M. R. Aoraba, National Election,
unpublished].

From 1945 to 1960 Australia had attempted to insulate Papua New Guinea from the rest of the world. One strategic reason was Australia's fear of the growing power of Indonesia, particularly in view of the latter's claim to Dutch New Guinea. Also it was in Australia's commercial and economic interests to isolate her territory so that if and when she wanted to exploit the natural resources, she could do so without the social and political unrest that had occurred in some other Third World countries. After 1960 this strategy was eroded by significant developments both locally and internationally. Local developments included the establishment of the Bougainville Copper mine by the multi-national company Conzinc Riotinto and the granting of timber concessions in Madang district, while internationally Australia was facing pressure from United Nation agencies and the World Bank to hasten moves towards the country's independence. These pressures led to a change in the relationship between Canberra and the administration in Port Moresby. Decision-making power was gradually devolved to Port Moresby, and greater emphasis was given to indigenous participation in the implementation of policy.

ECONOMIC CHANGE

In 1962 a United Nations mission chaired by Sir Hugh Foot recommended that the World Bank draw up a development plan based on a survey of the economy. The report endorsed the administration's view that the expatriates should be mainly responsible for the provision of capital, technical skills, and marketing of agricultural and livestock products. However, the mission believed that

> Australia should substantially concentrate its efforts on the advancement of the native people. This advancement will come through the native taking a much greater part in expanding production and by accelerating his training and education. The agricultural and livestock program provides for the native farmers to take a major part in increasing production[1].

The mission also addressed the issue of the relationship between cash crop production and land tenure and advised:

> The social institution which affects the organisation of production most profoundly is land tenure. The indigenes own 97 per cent of the land. About 1 per cent is under the control of Europeans either as freehold land or as leasehold from the Administration. The balance of 2 per cent is owned and continues to be held by the Administration. The native commercial farmer needs the assurance of rights to lands upon which perennial crops can be grown and cattle grazed without undue risk of conflicting claims arising under the traditional tenure systems. There is a growing volume of evidence that the indigenes are making progress in arranging with their villages and clans for the continuing use of land upon which perennial tree crops can be planted[2].

The mission suggested that:

> A reasonable approach to the land tenure problem would be to place greater responsibility on the native people, in-

cluding the Local Government Councils, to work out their own solutions adapted to varying circumstances. This approach would not make possible the recording of an individual title but at the same time would be no real disadvantage provided that comparable flexibility in approach could be achieved in regard to security for credits extended for assisting production by the indigenes ... Where the Administration, in the execution of its responsibilities for good government, needs to acquire land, it should not hesitate to do so through legal procedures in the event the owners are reluctant to sell or lease to the Administration[3].

Although there were some misgivings from the expatriates about what they perceived as being 'undue' emphasis on the indigenous population, the administration accepted and implemented the main recommendations of the report during the next decade.

The Five Year Plans and the Eight Point Plan

The First Five Year Plan was designed as an economic guide which was to carry Papua New Guinea through the period 1968–69 to 1972–73. The plan aimed to increase cash crop and livestock production, investigate the possibility of more profitable exploitation of natural resources, and expand the commercial infrastructure of the economy. The plan anticipated a greater involvement by Papua New Guineans in all of these activities as well as an upgrading of subsistence farming. Existing or potential cash crops included copra, cocoa, rubber, coffee, tea, oil palm, rice, peanuts, and sugar cane. Livestock were mainly pigs and cattle. The plan assumed the administration would provide incentives to encourage production in areas which had been identified as being likely to yield greatest profit. The plan emphasised that it was important to seek overseas investment for the exploitation of natural resources such as minerals and timber.

During 1973 the United Nations Development Programme sent a team from the University of East Anglia which prepared a *Report on Development Strategies for Papua New Guinea*. This report became the basis of the Second Five Year Plan for the period 1973 to 1978.

The First Five Year Plan aimed to secure overseas capital investment in the exploitation of natural resources through large mining companies such as Bougainville Copper Limited. In contrast, the Second Five Year Plan proposed an Improvement Programme which gave priority to rural development and self-reliance.

The announcement of the Second Five Year Plan was timely for Michael Somare. He was then Chief Minister in the House of Assembly, which was an elected body established by the administration in preparation for Papua New Guinea's independence. Somare, the single most influential Papua New Guinea politician, used the plan as a basis for his social and economic policy which came to be known as the Eight Point Plan. In February 1973 Somare moved to commit the nation to:

1 a rapid increase in the proportion of the economy under the control of Papua New Guinean individuals and groups and in the proportion of personal and property income that goes to Papua New Guineans;

2 more equal distribution of economic benefits, including movements towards equalisation of income among people and towards equalisation of services, among different areas of the country;

3 decentralisation of economic activity, planning and government spending, with emphasis on agricultural development, village industry, better internal trade and more spending channelled to local and area bodies;

4 an emphasis on small-scale artisan, service and business activity, relying where possible on typically Papua New Guinean forms of activity;

5 a more self-reliant economy, less dependent for its needs on imported goods and services and better able to meet the needs of its people through local production;

6 an increasing capacity for meeting government spending needs from locally raised revenue;

7 a rapid increase in the equal and active participation of

women in all forms of economic and social activity; and

8 government control and investment in those sectors of the economy where control is necessary to achieve the desired kind of development. [PNG House of Assembly, February 1973]

The apparent practicality of this programme, and its emphasis on rural development and improvement of the quality of life for people in the villages, received considerable parliamentary and popular support. However in 1973 the government was already committed to an agreement with Bougainville Copper Ltd to allow mining on Bougainville Island.

Bougainville Copper

In 1964 the trans-national corporation Conzinc Riotinto discovered a large, low-grade copper deposit with significant gold content at Panguna on Bougainville Island in the Bougainville District. Following an economic feasibility report in 1969 the Bougainville Mining Company a subsidiary of Conzinc Riotinto, began operations in the area and production began in 1972. In 1973 the Bougainville Mining Company became Bougainville Copper Pty Limited (BCL).

Under a 1967 agreement between the company and the Australian administration in Port Moresby the Australian government bought 20 per cent of the shares on behalf of the people of Papua New Guinea; 53.6 per cent of shares were to be held by Conzinc Riotinto, and 26.4 per cent by public shareholders, a limited number of whom were Papua New Guineans.

The Bougainvillean people were ambivalent about these agreements. Some opposed all mining while others believed that the project should go ahead if the people were given an adequate share of the profits. Amongst those who believed that the project should proceed there were disagreements as to what proportion of the profits should go to the national government and what proportion should remain with the traditional landowners.

In 1966 Don Grove, Director of Lands and Mines,

introduced a mining bill which included a provision to compensate the traditional owners of the land for being alienated by the company at the rate of 5 per cent of the unimproved value of the land. The bill was opposed by a Bougainvillean member, Paul Lapun, who argued that a greater sum 5 per cent of government receipts, should be given as compensation to the landowners in this and all future mining operations in the country. This was agreed to by the House and incorporated in the *Bougainville Copper Agreement Bill* which was passed in 1967. Although at the time this was regarded by many as a victory for Papua New Guinean interests, it still represented only a token return of profits to the landowners.

Many Bougainvilleans continued to oppose the project and in August 1969 a violent confrontation took place between the people and the police on the construction site. The eye-witness comments of the District Commissioner D. N. Ashton were recorded on audio-tape. The following is taken from a transcript of this recording:

> Minutes past eight and I hear bulldozers coming . . . Now twenty-five past eight and the bulldozer is in the hands of the Police Commissioner. Seven minutes to nine. There is the first gas bomb going off. A beautiful shot. Right in the middle of this group . . . A group of about thirty men have got between the police and the [stake] and are just standing passively on the road . . . Inspector [Clarke] has just ordered a charge and instructions have been issued that it's better to hit them around the legs . . . These people are extremely tough . . . a really tough passive resistance here . . . (Sustained noises of conflict.)
>
> One man has an injured ankle and they claim blood has been spilled and they will now retreat. They feel that honour has been satisfied but I must alert the bulldozer drivers to ensure that no one takes a risk in the way of the dozer[4].

Following this confrontation and the associated publicity, the Australian government, against the advice of the administrators in Port Moresby, obtained greater compensation for the landowners.

Belief that the Bougainvilleans were not receiving a fair

share of the mining profits was one of the main factors which led to a movement for secession of Bougainville District from Papua New Guinea. In 1968 a group of Bougainvilleans living in Port Moresby, including Paul Lapun and some university students, called for a referendum to decide the political future of the province. While this group did not succeed in forcing the government to hold a referendum they did succeed in focusing attention on the need to consider seriously the political future of the province. In 1970 Bougainvilleans did not fully appreciate how much the mining operations would damage their land and disrupt their society.

Nevertheless Bougainville Copper Limited contributed a substantial amount of money to the national government's revenue. In the financial year 1974–75, for instance, of the total of revenue of K180 million, the mine's contribution amounted to K96 million. In this financial year K363 000 was paid to the landowners, and the Bougainville district government was granted over K2 million to fund the capital works programme. In addition K190 000 was granted as the first annual contribution to a non-renewable resource fund.

Timber

There were many difficulties connected with the development of commercial timber projects in Papua New Guinea. These included technical problems associated with climate and terrain, shortage of skilled labour and management, and political and social problems.

A number of overseas companies resolved the main technical, labour, and management problems, and made agreements with the national government and, in some cases, the provincial governments. However, social problems, particularly those associated with land ownership and the entitlements of the local landowners, remained to be resolved. As has already been indicated, land is traditionally owned by clans and not by individuals. A difficulty posed by this situation is accurately identifying the legitimate owners of the land and establishing agreed boundaries. Environmental issues concerned many landowners. Some opposed all logging on the grounds that it would destroy their physical and social environment, while some were prepared to co-operate with a project if they felt they were being sufficiently well–compensated. Amongst the latter group there were inevitably disagreements as to what could be regarded as adequate compensation in terms of royalties, employment and training opportunities, and provision of village facilities such as roads and clinics. Lack of understanding of the cash economy led to some landowners accepting very low returns, while others claimed a level of compensation which would make a project economically unviable.

By 1974, in spite of ongoing difficulties, major timber projects had been established in the Gogol area in Madang, the Kautara region in New Ireland, Mount Giluwe in the Southern Highlands and the Open Bay region in New Britain. Altogether there were seventy projects operating in 1974 of which only four were managed by Papua New Guinean firms, while the national government had an interest in another five. Environmental and social problems associated with the exploitation of timber resources were widespread throughout the country. The following brief description of the Gogol timber project demonstrates some of these problems.

The giant Japanese corporation Mitsu first showed an interest in timber in the Gogol area in Madang province in the early 1960s. In 1971 a timber agreement was signed between Jant Timber Company which had been set up by Honshu Paper Pty Ltd, a subsidiary of Mitsu, and the national government. The administration had first become involved in acquiring timber rights in the area in 1963, and in 1971 the administration identified representatives or agents of the landowners and bought from them rights to all timber in the area except food trees. Jant Timber Company began operations in 1973 and opposition from the local people, who had not been involved in the negotiations with Jant, surfaced in 1974 and led to demonstrations in 1975 and 1976. Opposition was based on several grounds. Some people were concerned about the effect of the project on their physical and social environment. Not only did the removal of trees adversely affect their hunting and gathering activities, but the destruction of the clay from which the people made special pots removed an important item of trade, and disrupted social relationships. This disruption of trading and social relationships based on the exchange of pots particularly affected the women. As it was mainly women who were responsible for the making of pots, their removal as items of value from the exchange system undermined the status of women within their communities.

In addition the villagers were concerned about low royalty payments, lack of employment and training opportunities for local people, and poor working conditions for those who were employed. The situation did not improve with independence in 1975 or the establishment of a provincial government in 1978. Jant Timber Company was still operating and the dispute was continuing in 1991.

Cash crops

Cash cropping and indigenous involvement in cash cropping grew rapidly in the 1960s. About 25 per cent of the 105 972 tons of copra exported in 1963 for $306 million came from Papua New Guinean growers. In the Gazelle Peninsula the Tolai produced the bulk of the 10 014 tons of cocoa which earned more than $2 million in 1962.

However, local cash croppers were most successful in the highlands where 60 per cent of the 3444 tons of coffee worth $3.1 million exported in 1962 was produced by local growers. Less-important crops included rubber which returned $2.4 million for 4680 tons exported in 1962, and small quantities of tea from Garaina in the Morobe District and the Wahgi Valley in the Western Highlands District.

Prior to 1960 Australian government policies had supported expatriate development at the expense of indigenous development. After 1960 increased encouragement was given to local businesses, particularly in the highlands. As has been noted, women took an active part in coffee production in the highlands, but were not officially encouraged by the administration, and the money from the sale of coffee was usually spent by men.

Secondary industry and commerce

At independence in 1975 there were less than five hundred

factories in Papua New Guinea: 25 per cent of these factories were in Port Moresby, and the others were in Lae, Rabaul, Madang, Goroka, Wewak, Samarai, and Lorengau. Partly because of the road to the highlands, the most rapidly growing industrial centre was Lae. Factories associated with the building and service industries were being built more often than others. Development continued to be retarded by the shortage of power, the high cost of transport and labour, and the lack of technical and managerial skills. By 1975 secondary industry accounted for only 5 per cent of the Gross Domestic Product.

There were, however, almost two thousand registered companies by 1975, the majority of which were very small enterprises sometimes run by one or two people. In addition there were approximately two hundred registered foreign companies, almost all branches of overseas companies. Prominent among these were Burns Philp, Steamships, and W. R. Carpenter. These had established connections with both Papua and New Guinea in the early days of colonisation and had developed a wide range of trading and transport interests.

SOCIAL CHANGE

The government's encouragement of urban business interests led to the establishment of a significant group of Papua New Guinean commercial entrepreneurs most of whom were politicians. As a result there developed among the educated élite a group which acquired both political and business interests. However, this group, although socially significant, was still small, and most educated people joined the public service. While the bulk of the commercial activities were owned, managed and controlled by Australians, a significant business sector was in the hands of the locally-born, Australian-educated Chinese who owned wholesaling and small retailing stores that serviced both towns and rural areas. These Chinese entrepreneurs were the section of the business community that exploited the people in the villages, and with whom the emerging group of Papua New Guinean businesses had to compete directly, particularly in the islands and the Momase region.

Commercial activities were supported by improved communications. In 1968 the Post and Telegraphs Department launched a major upgrading of the telecommunication net-work. Half-funded by the World Bank, and heavily supported by Australia, the project made Papua New Guinea's telecommunication system one of the most technically sophisticated on the world. Commercial communication was greatly helped by this project. However, as most houses in the towns did not have telephones, and as most rural villages did not have even one telephone, this technological advance was of little benefit to the vast majority of the people.

At independence, radio broadcasting was the dual responsibility of the Australian Broadcasting Commission and the administration which had established a number of regional radio stations. To the administration, radio was a medium through which its officers could communicate with the people on such matters as current affairs, health, and hygiene. Neither the Australian Broadcasting Commission nor the administration radio stations were instruments of the Australian government or used overtly to publicise Australian government political policy.

From 1969 the *Post–Courier*, published daily in Port Moresby, was available to most other towns within a day or two of publication. It catered for both the expatriate population and the increasing number of literate Papua New Guineans. It was based on Australian newspaper format, uncensored, and independent of government policy. Attempts to establish Pidgin English language newspapers were mainly unsuccessful. An exception was *Wantok*, which first appeared in 1970 as an initiative of an East Sepik Catholic mission. *Wantok*'s editorial policy was secular, and the paper was distributed generally in towns throughout the country.

The labour movement

Because the vast majority of the people were outside the paid workforce, and few within the paid workforce were in industrial organisations, the trade union movement was weak, fragmented, and largely ineffective. In the colonial period the paternalistic indenture system imposed by the administration and supported by the white settlers had inhibited the development of worker organisations. In consequence, there had been no notable organised action apart from the 1929 Rabaul strike. Low wages and poor conditions did not offer enough incentive for adult males to leave subsistence agriculture for paid employment. In addition the small and scattered nature of the workforce made organisation difficult.

Moves towards formalising worker–employer relations modelled on Australian practice had been initiated in response to international pressure and the action of some Port Moresby-based workers in the late 1950s. In 1961, in spite of the fact that trade unions were illegal, a Papua New Guinea Workers' Association was formed and Papua New Guinea's first industrial award brought down. Sir Paul Hasluck, Australia's Minister for Territories, legislated for an industrial relations system which included provision for the establishment of legal trade unions.

As in Australia, the industrial relations system required input from employer organisations, the administration, and the trade unions. The employers and government representatives were organised, but the trade union representatives were not. Between 1963 and independence in 1975, forty-seven unions were formed and registered under an Industrial Organisations Ordinance. However almost all of these were very small, many were regionally based and covered workers in a district rather than an industry, and the majority did not hold properly-constituted elections for officers or keep accurate membership or financial records. In addition, there was a rapid turnover of members even in the larger and more stable unions. Relatively few women were entering the paid workforce, and few women in the private sector joined unions. However, those in teaching and the public service began to play their part in union affairs.

Education

The policy of universal primary education established by the Australian Minister for Territories, Hasluck, in 1955 was actively pursued by G. T. Roscoe when he was appointed the second Director of Education in 1958. As has been indicated, there was, by 1960, a significant improvement in literacy and primary school enrolments, however the secondary sector was weak and the tertiary sector non-existent apart from the understaffed and underfunded teachers colleges.

Hasluck, who remained Minister for Territories until 1963, continued to advocate support for primary education at the expense of secondary and tertiary education. However, local and overseas pressure, in particular that from a visiting mission from the United Nations in 1962, led to a change in policy.

In 1962 the United Nations mission criticised the administration's education policy and urged:

> the expansion of secondary, technical and higher education. Primary education which has advanced rapidly with large numbers of students in the first standards should concentrate on making the full primary course available in existing schools rather than on broadening the primary base by establishing new schools. Secondary and technical training should proceed at the fastest rate which the output of primary students will permit. To achieve the production targets of the development program, secondary level training should concentrate on the development of individuals who can contribute usefully to the agricultural, livestock and forestry programs, to other sectors of the economy, and to administration and the Public Service generally . . .[5].

In 1962 Les Johnson replaced Roscoe as Director of Education and in 1963 Hasluck was replaced as Minister for Territories by C. E. Barnes. The next decade saw a very rapid expansion in both secondary and tertiary education.

Important recommendations of a 1964 commission[6] included the establishment of a university by 1966, the establishment of an institute of higher technical education, and the creation of a preliminary year and an external studies department at the university to assist potential graduates to overcome the disadvantages of inadequate secondary education and geographical isolation. The administration accepted these recommendations. The University of Papua New Guinea (UPNG) with Dr John Gunther as vice-chancellor was established in Port Moresby in 1966 and the Institute of Higher Technical Education, initially established also in Port Moresby, was moved to Lae in the Morobe District following political objections to both major tertiary institutions being in Port Moresby. The Institute of Higher Technical Education subsequently became the Institute of Technology and then, in 1967, Papua New Guinea's University of Technology.

The first intake of students to the University of Papua New Guinea was drawn mostly from those who had completed Grade ten or fourth form in the various high schools throughout the country and were brought to the university to undertake a preliminary year to qualify for undergraduate studies. At the end of 1967 thirty-seven UPNG students, the majority of whom were fully sponsored by the administration, had qualified for matriculation to the university. By 1971 courses which could be taken to bachelor degree level included economics, anthropology and sociology, English language and literature, history, comparative religion, geography, political studies, mathematics, physics, chemistry, earth sciences, biology, science and society, medicine, law, and education. The first graduation was at the end of the first semester 1970 when six male graduands were awarded Bachelor of Arts degrees and four male graduands awarded Bachelor of Science degrees. There were no Papua New Guinean women amongst the first group of graduates. A further eighteen Arts graduands and two Science graduands received degrees at the end of the second semester 1970.

The Papua New Guinea Institute of Technology aimed to provide both professional and para-professional courses at degree and diploma level in a range of technical areas. Courses initially offered included civil engineering, surveying, accountancy, and business studies. In 1969 courses in mechanical and electrical engineering commenced, and architecture and building technology were introduced in 1970. The first diplomats joined the work force in 1971, and the first graduates in 1975.

In 1974, for reasons of political expediency, the government chose not to consider a recommendation by the Gris Inquiry[7] for rationalisation of the system of higher education by establishing a national university under one council with campuses in Port Moresby, Lae, and Goroka.

The dramatic expansion of the tertiary sector had been

made possible by the rapid introduction of secondary education under the guidance of the fourth Director of Education, Dr Ken McKinnon, from 1966 to 1973. Between 1960 and 1970 there was a tenfold increase in secondary school enrolments, The need to provide teachers, buildings, and facilities for these schools, all of which were boarding schools, put a heavy drain on the national budget. Although school fees were charged and much of the gardening (for the provision of vegetables) and cleaning and maintenance was done by the students, most of the funds came through the Department of Education's greatly expanded budget. The supply of teachers was of particular concern and even the substantial increase in the number of students undergoing teacher training failed to keep pace with the increased secondary school enrolments and there was a tendency to sacrifice quality for quantity of teacher graduates.

The curriculum followed closely the basic curriculum of the core subjects of English language and literature, mathematics, general science, history, and geography, that were taught in Australian schools. In some schools practical subjects such as woodwork, agriculture, and commerce were taught, but on the whole little attempt was made to adapt the content of the curriculum to the needs of Papua New Guinea's students, and much of the subject-matter was inappropriate. However, the fact that the secondary system was modelled on the Australian system made it easier for those students who completed secondary schools to cope with the Western-style tertiary institutions which also followed the Australian example.

The Australian apprenticeship system imposed upon the technical education sector was quite inappropriate to Papua New Guinea's needs. Courses were too long, too specialised, and failed to supply a sufficient number of skilled tradesmen. In addition, the technical sector was not adequately funded although technical education, because of the cost of the workshops and equipment required, was more expensive than other forms of post-primary education. Some of the new mission schools established in this period also provided some technical and vocational training as well as the core curriculum and religious studies. However by 1970 the colonial state had accepted that it should bear full responsibility for education at all levels.

In an attempt to link rapid developments in the tertiary sector to the primary and post-primary sectors, the administration also accepted the recommendations of a 1969 report[8] and established a national education system which combined the administration and mission school systems, both primary and secondary, and the teaching service into a national education system.

There were several paths through which Papua New Guineans entered the political and business sectors of the society. These included attendance at administration or mission secondary schools and universities in Papua New Guinea, and overseas secondary or post-secondary education at state or church educational institutions. In addition there were those who moved directly from the secondary schools into the public service and rose to positions of importance without formal tertiary education. The different roads taken led to conflicts between tertiary graduates and those who, although lacking tertiary qualifications, had substantial and practical on-the-job experience.

The majority of Papua New Guineans who received secondary and tertiary education from 1960 to 1975 were the sons, and occasionally the daughters, of parents who had themselves received some education, almost entirely through the mission schools. Many of these parents held low-level administrative positions or were teachers, pastors, policemen, or clerks.

Missions

After 1960 the established churches continued to expand and were joined by a considerable number of minor Christian sects. Many of these sects were fundamentalist and insisted upon their adherents accepting a literal interpretation of the Bible. Their insistence upon the dogma of one God, and the Bible as historical fact, brought them into conflict with many of the people's traditional spiritual beliefs. Thus, there was a significant break with the past amongst those who were converted, often from established Christian denominations, to the fundamentalist sects. This change undermined the established churches and often resulted in conflicts between the fundamentalists sects and the established denominations. On the whole the militant fundamentalists did not regard themselves as having responsibility for the health, education, or physical welfare of the people. Not all the new arrivals were militant fundamentalists. For example, the small but active Salvation Army which had established officers in Port Moresby in the late 1950s undertook extensive welfare work amongst the people by the 1970s.

By independence some churches had a better record of encouraging the appointment of local people to senior positions than others. The Anglicans, the Uniting Church, and the Lutherans, for instance, were almost completely localised, whereas in spite of having the first Papuan priest, most Catholic priests were still expatriates. While the Papua New Guineans in the mission service were almost entirely men, some girls educated in the mission schools remained with the missions as missionaries, as teachers, health or clerical workers, or domestic servants.

In the decade before independence several of the churches decided to advance the cause of Christianity generally by forming co-operative organisations such as the Melanesian Council of Churches, in which the Catholics, the Lutherans, the Anglicans, the Baptists, the Uniting Church, and the Salvation Army were represented. Co-operation amongst these and other churches whose congregations included Papua New Guineans from many parts of the country contributed to the development of the concept of nationalism so important in the decade after independence. The consolidation of the power of the churches hastened the disintegration of the traditional customs and value systems and increasingly traditional ceremonies were replaced by Christian ceremonies. While many of the older generation lamented the passing of their traditional ceremonies and values, by 1975 the vast majority of the population accepted the churches, and most Papua New Guineans regarded themselves as practising Christians. In addition most leading politicians were practising Christians through whom the established churches could exercise political influence. Some churches such as the Catholic and

Lutheran churches, which had alienated land on which they established plantations, exercised economic as well as social and political influence in the society.

Health

A massive campaign was mounted by the colonial administration after the war against endemic diseases, and medical services were extended to the highlands. When Dr John Gunther moved from the Department of Health in 1957, some of the impetus behind these campaigns waned, and health was no longer the administration's first budget priority. In this period the Australian government's priority, supported and implemented by the administration, was the development of secondary and tertiary education. This was an attempt to encourage the emergence of an educated élite which could take over the management of the affairs of the country.

Preventive measures against such diseases as tuberculosis, and projects to improve standards of hygiene and nutrition continued, and family planning programmes which operated through rural and urban health centres were formally established. Improved health services had reduced the infant mortality rate, and family planning programmes also promoted the use of contraceptives, and offered free contraceptives and contraceptive advice in an attempt to slow the rapid expansion in population which was putting a serious strain on health, education, and other services.

Those districts in which most money and effort had been spent in the immediate post-war period continued to be provided with better medical services. This was partly because staff trained in the earlier period passed on their expertise to those entering the service. While most of these trainees were men, the health department began, in this period, to train some women as nurses or nursing assistants. In spite of the inequality amongst the regions, Papua New Guineans were basically healthy people. Nutritionally, subsistence agriculture provided a balanced diet in most districts, and the introduced foods of tinned fish, rice, and large quantities of locally-produced green leafy vegetables also contributed towards a balanced diet in both towns and villages.

Other social changes

A most significant development in this period was the creation of an educated Papua New Guinean élite of men who were being prepared to take over the reins of political power and administration. This élite group grew rapidly once the Australian government bowed to pressure from international agencies and vocal groups within Australia itself and rapidly expanded secondary and tertiary education. It also actively promoted the training of Papua New Guineans in the Public Service and private industry, and allowed greater local participation in government. This process was assisted by the beginnings of a nationalist movement amongst a section of the educated Papua New Guineans.

In this climate it was inevitable that there should be a further breaking down of the colonial segregation practices prevalent before the war. Following a recommendation of a committee set up in 1958 to identify discriminatory provisions in legislation, the *White Women's Protection Ordinance* and the *New Guinea Criminal Code* which had, amongst other things, made it illegal for a Papua New Guinean to have sexual intercourse with a white woman, were repealed. In 1962 the term *native* was removed from legislation, and in 1969 the terms *boi*, *meri*, *kanaka*, and *masta* were banned. In 1963 the restrictions on the sale of alcohol to Papua New Guineans were removed. However, full legal equality was not achieved until after the passage of the Discriminatory Practices Ordinance which made discrimination on the grounds of race or colour a punishable offence. In 1969 the House of Assembly amended this ordinance to broaden the definition of discrimination to include ethnic, tribal, or national differences. The amendment included provisions for severe penalties for anyone who publicly used words or behaved with intent to stir up hatred, ridicule, or contempt against individuals or groups distinguished by colour, race, ethnic, tribal, or national origin.

One effect of this legislation was to end the publication of *Black and White*, a racist magazine produced in Port Moresby and widely circulated amongst Papua New Guinea's white community. The readership of this magazine, which has been described as 'a promoter of racial hatred'[9], has been estimated at 4000.

In 1972 the House of Assembly passed a Human Rights Ordinance which declared every person to be entitled to the fundamental rights and freedoms of the individual, whatever his or her race, tribe, place of origin, political opinion, colour, creed, or sex. Each person could exercise these rights subject to respect for the rights and freedom of others. In 1975 this concept of human rights was enshrined in the national constitution.

The purpose of including 'sex' in the Human Rights legislation was an attempt to prevent discrimination against women. However, as women were frequently discriminated against in traditional society, and continued to be discriminated against by Europeans and Papua New Guinean men in the emerging national élite, this provision of the legislation was almost impossible to enforce. In February 1973 Michael Somare had attempted to promote the cause of women by advocating in his Eight Point Plan a rapid increase in the equal and active participation of women in all forms of economic and social activity. As women were already actively participating in economic and social activity in the villages, the intention was presumably to try to ensure that they were allowed to participate equally. While this idea was accepted in theory, little was done to translate this policy into practice, and women continued to be discriminated against in most sections of society. However, during this period more girls received schooling, a handful even received tertiary education, and more women entered the paid workforce, usually into occupations in which women were mostly found in the introduced Western employment such as nursing, teaching, secretarial duties, and domestic service. When the educated and working women developed non-traditional ideas about the role and status of women in society they provided models which some girls were to follow in the decade after independence.

The creative arts

Relatively few Papua New Guineans were conscious of how much their society and the lives of people were being effected by the rapid pace of social change. Amongst those who were aware of the impact of change were a group of writers — biographers, novelists, playwrights, poets, and short story writers — painters, sculptors, and musicians who expressed some of their concerns through a creative arts movement which developed in the years immediately before independence.

In this period, 'the twilight of colonialism'[10], their work showed concern for the damaging effects of colonialism, the rising tide of nationalism, the impact of both cultures, and the need to search for personal identity in a changing society. While this movement expressed some of the concerns of the few women in the educated élite and some of the village women, it did not, at this stage, include any Papua New Guinean women except in the screen printing of local designs onto cloth.

Amongst the first of the writers were Albert Maori Kiki, and later Vincent Eri. In *Ten Thousand Years in a Lifetime,* Kiki described his experience of growing up in a village and his introduction to the Western world of work as a 'tea boy' under the colonial administration. In *The Crocodile* Eri described his introduction to Western values and beliefs at his local primary school. Both books have been translated and published in several major languages as well as in English.

In 1967, Ulli Beier, a German who had been working in Nigeria, introduced a creative writing course at the University of Papua New Guinea. The writers then at the University owe much of their inspiration to Ulli Beier who created a climate that enabled Papua New Guineans to bring to the surface their literary talents, and facilitated the publication of their work.

Amongst the most articulate of the writers were the playwrights both inside and outside the University. Kirsty Powell believed that the playwrights derived their inspiration from

> . . . the heat of the emotion of the political ferment of the day; from the experience of everyday life in a complex cultural environment; from the ancient Papua New Guinean oral literary tradition; and from the thoughtful, personal identity[11].

She also felt that:

> What was most notable in those first plays was the serious-
> ness, the intensity of the feeling they expressed, along with
> the humour that is part of Papua New Guinea tradition[12].

Leo Hannett's *Em Rod Bilong Kago* is a good example to illustrate this point. In *The Sun* and *The Victim of Death* Arthur
Javodimbari drew on oral tradition to write about the sun and
a myth about the origins of death.

Other plays took up other themes. Some of the plays written
by staff and students at Goroka Teachers' College concerned
the clash of Western and Melanesian cultures. In *The Cry of the
Cassowary*, John Kaniku describes the conflicts of values between village and town, traditional custom and Western ways.
In *The Unexpected Hawk* John Waiko explores the manner in
which the village people reacted against the colonial intrusion
into their lives.

Other writers chose the medium of the short story or the
novel. For instance, a novel in which the writer is seeking to
establish personal identity is *Wanpis*, in which Russel Soaba is
concerned with his personal life experiences. A popular short
story, *The Old Man and the Balus*, by John Waiko, is concerned
with a villager's introduction to Western technology, especially
his first experience of flying in aeroplane.

While the emerging educated Papua New Guinean élite
used literary skills to express their political, social and
economic views, experiences and feelings, those among the
grassroots who were unable to read and write chose the visual
media to make subtle comments on social change. In 1972
the Department of Education, encouraged by the work of
Georgina Beier, provided funds to set up a Creative Arts Centre
near the university in Port Moresby. Tom Craig was appointed
first director with Kambau Nameleu as his assistant, and the
Centre quickly attracted fine and prolific artists such as Akis,
Ruki Fame, Kauage, and Jakupa.

Akis worked with the themes of the magical domain of
animals, birds, people, and spirit beings that inhabited his village and the nearby forest of the Simbai Valley to show with

modern techniques the richness of traditional culture. Ruki Fame used decorative screens and sculptures of village people from various parts of Papua New Guinea to demonstrate the need for national unity. Jakupa also used the village and the grassroots theme, and his work reflects the changing life-styles as well as the diversity of cultures in Papua New Guinea. Kauage's fascination with modern technology, trucks, cars, aeroplanes, and helicopters is depicted in highly-coloured paintings, woodcuts, and aluminium and copper sculptures.

By 1974 these and other artists had made the Centre a national focus for contemporary visual art. In 1976 the Centre became the National Arts School, and textiles, sculpture, photography, drama, dance, and music were added to the curriculum.

Like the Constitutional Planning Committee which was concerned to draft a 'home grown' constitution, the National Arts School was interested in creating a 'home grown' contemporary music style. The first well-known contemporary musical group to come from the School was the highly popular Sanguma band which wrote and arranged songs in Tok Pisin, Pidgin English, and some local languages. The Sanguma blend of traditional and contemporary music attracted an international audience.

As has been shown in Chapter 1, the people's artistic heritage goes back at least 20 000 years. Developments in the creative arts in the late 1960s and early 1970s tried to link the old to the new, and tried to respond to the challenge posed by social change. Much of the work produced in this period conjures up the image of the newly-emerging state as a figure with one leg rooted in the Stone Age culture while the other leg is plunging into the Space Age.

Some creative artists expressed anti-colonial feelings. John Kasaipwalova, in his poem 'The Reluctant Flame', first published in 1971, demonstrates his rage against the colonialist:

> Look how orderly fat and silent they float this earth
> With their guns, their aeroplanes,
> their cyclone heels and their bishops . . .[13]

In the last stanza he urges his brothers to cast aside the colonial yoke of subservience, despair, and humiliation and adopt a position of confidence and vision:

> Reluctant flame open your volcano
> Take your pulse and your fuel
> Burn burn burn burn
> Burn away my weighty ice
> Burn into my heart a dancing flame.[14]

John Kasaipwalova was one of those who saw literature as a political weapon against colonialism.

POLITICAL CHANGE

Local government councils

An avenue through which some Papua New Guineans achieved a measure of political awareness was the local government councils. Some local government councils were established following the enactment of the Native Village Council Ordinance at the end of 1949. The main role of local government councils was to provide a link between the villagers and the administration in Port Moresby and to attempt to enforce European law. In Hasluck's view an expansion of the system of local government would help the village people understand basic Western democratic processes. The implementation of this policy was hampered by the fact that the majority of the population was illiterate. Nevertheless, as the following table shows, 109 local councils were established between 1950 and 1965. However, as can also be seen, most of these councils were established after 1960.

It would appear that the failure to make progress in establishing effective local government councils before 1960 was due partly to lack of funds and partly to local opposition amongst the coastal and island people, particularly the Tolai, who distrusted earlier administration attempts to establish multi-racial local government bodies. The rapid expansion of local government councils after 1960 was associated with the opening up of the highlands.

Table 6.1: Local government councils

Year	Papua	New Guinea	Total	Population
1950	1	3	4	11 900
1951	1	4	5	17 900
1952	2	4	6	19 000
1953	2	6	8	29 449
1954	2	6	8	29 449
1955	3	6	9	38 124
1956	4	6	10	49 400
1957	6	10	16	76 655
1958	9	15	24	146 436
1959	10	18	28	187 421
1960	16	23	39	265 352
1961	16	27	43	309 597
1962	21	38	59	501 664
1963	27	50	77	696 845
1964	34	55	89	911 396
1965	37	72	109	1 188 165

Source: *Report of the Committee of Enquiry into Local Government Finance and Borrowing* (1972) A. W. McCasker (Chairman)

The eighty-nine councils which were in place at the time of the first general election to the House of Assembly in 1964 covered approximately one million people to some of whom the councils had demonstrated the operation of some basic Western democratic processes.

The Legislative Council and House of Assembly

From 1951 to 1961 the contribution of Papua New Guinean members to the Legislative Council debates was very limited because they lacked Western education and skill in speaking the English language, and the debates were conducted only in English. By the end of the decade, however, changes began to appear. A very good example is that the administration was forced in the early 1960s, by the minority local members, to shelve a Land Bill, although the official members had the numbers to pass it without any difficulty. At the end of 1962 a Select Committee under John Guise recommended the establishment of a national House of Assembly of sixty-four members, the majority of whom were to be elected representatives of the indigenous people. A United Nations Visiting Mission led by Sir Hugh Foot also recommended the establishment of an elected national legislature with substantial indigenous representation and pressured the Australian government to bring about this proposal.

In Australia there were mixed reactions to these proposals. Prime Minister Menzies believed that it was better for Australia to get out sooner than later; the Ministers for External Territories, in particular Paul Hasluck and Charles Barnes, believed that the people of the Territory had the right to choose self government or independence at any time; while others, particularly those with strong economic interests in the Territory, argued that change should occur very slowly. As a consequence of this debate, and in response to international and internal pressure, Australia gradually loosened political control until, in 1975, the Territory became the independent state of Papua New Guinea. However, it should be noted that political separation from Australia was not accompanied by economic separation.

The process of political separation began with the first general election to the House of Assembly in 1964. The House of Assembly replaced the Legislative Council and the Administrator's Council with which some indigenous members were becoming increasingly dissatisfied. John Guise, a prominent member of the Legislative Council, expressed the frustration of many when he told an Australian Broadcasting Corporation interviewer in 1961:

> I sat in the new Legislative Council and in the Administrator's Council since they were founded and I can tell you that important policy matters still don't originate with us. Most of them originate in Canberra with the Ministers and the Department of Territories . . . Members have no power to initiate matters in the Council itself or in the Legislative Council. They have no power to review matters which may be introduced by the Administrator or anybody else into the Administrator's Council . . . The Administrator has the

power to disallow Ordinances passed by the House of Assembly[15].

However, one purpose that these bodies served was to help create in people such as Guise an awareness of the potential power of a properly constituted parliamentary body, and they exerted pressure on Australia to increase local participation in running the affairs of the country.

While most of the members of the 1964 House of Assembly had little experience in parliamentary procedure, they at least had a mandate from their people and in theory the power to legislate. However, in practice the exercise of this power was severely curtailed because all legislative decisions were subject to the colonial administrator's assent or the Australian governor general's approval. In May 1965 John Guise successfully moved in the House of Assembly for the establishment of a Select Committee to draft proposals to guide constitutional development in the Territory. This committee, chaired by Guise, toured the country seeking public response to their proposals. Also in 1965 a ministerial system was introduced in order to allow selected members of the House of Assembly chosen by the Australian administration to gain experience in running the government.

In 1968 elections were held for members of the second House of Assembly and the number of members increased.

Until 1968 constitutional change had preceded popular demand. However, in 1968 six political parties contested the election. The most important of these was the Pangu party with ten elected members led by Michael Somare. The administrator had intended to appoint some Pangu members to the ministry, however the party refused to accept positions in the ministry and chose to go into opposition under its young outspoken leader. John Guise, who had been closely involved in the development of the constitution, was elected the first indigenous Speaker of the House of Assembly. The emergence of a strong opposition in the House of Assembly hastened the process of political decolonisation. The Australian government could not afford to ignore the newly emerging voice of the people, particularly when the House of Assembly's demands for increased independence were supported by a vocal Labor Party opposition within the Australian parliament, and by a 1968 United Nations Visiting Mission. While the political decolonisation process was well under way, Australia had not committed itself to an actual date for independence.

Self-government

Self-government meant the transfer from Australia to an elected Papua New Guinean government of all powers except those concerning foreign affairs, defence, and the legal system which were to be handed over when Papua New Guinea achieved complete independence.

There was controversy both in Papua New Guinea and in Australia on the timing of each of these stages. The most immediate issue in 1970 was the timing of self-government. Amongst the lowlanders, views ranged from demands for immediate self-government to self-government by 1980. However, many highlanders, represented by the United Party which also included expatriates with plantation interests, advocated postponing self-government indefinitely. One reason many highlanders opposed self-government was their fear that following self-government the country would be dominated by the better-educated lowland élite. In spite of highlands opposition the move towards self-government gathered momentum. Following a 1971 report of a Select Committee on Constitutional Development, the name Territory of Papua and New Guinea was changed to Papua New Guinea, and the House adopted a national flag and emblem, and proclaimed a national day.

In Australia, Gough Whitlam, leader of the Labor Party, championed the cause of self-government and independence. Realising that he needed up-to-date political, social, and economic information, he visited the Territory in December 1969 as part of a fact-finding mission. He exploited both the Australian Liberal-Country Party coalition government's conservative attitudes and the growing Papua New Guinean nationalism with perceptive skill to his utmost advantage. On arrival, Whitlam announced his target dates: self-government in 1972 and independence in 1976. Outlining Labor's policy, Whitlam declared:

> An Australian election must be held by the end of 1972 at the latest . . . It is our belief that a Labor Government will emerge from those elections . . . Papua New Guinea will have [self-government] as soon as the Labor Government can make the necessary arrangement with the House of Assembly which will also be elected in 1972.
>
> . . . [Papua New Guinea] is not unique in its economy, in the difference of economic standards between sections of the country, its educational or social standards, its needs for economic aid from abroad, its needs for advisers, the diversity of local customs, or even the multiplicity of its languages . . . None of these problems require colonial rule for their solution or easing. In fact many of them will worsen if foreign techniques, methods, laws and customs continue to exclude local custom, knowledge and experience. An outside administration cannot teach or impose unity. It can by its errors unite a people against it. This is the very situation which Australians at home will not permit[16].

This declaration, together with the resignation of the Australian administrator Johnson, whose efforts to promote the devolution of power from Canberra to Port Moresby had been constantly frustrated by the Canberra bureaucracy, greatly embarrassed the Australian government. Whitlam's visit and Johnson's resignation were coincidental, but Johnson's resignation indicated a growing tension between Canberra and Port Moresby.

In order to save face, Prime Minister J. G. Gorton had to reshuffle the Canberra-based bureaucrats associated with devolution of powers to Papua New Guinea. In May 1970 David Hay replaced Warwick Smith as Secretary for the Department of External Territories. Les Johnson was recalled to Port Moresby as administrator, and he skilfully masterminded and helped the transfer of power from Canberra to Port Moresby.

The final report of the Select Committee on Constitutional Development, accepted by the House of Assembly, recommended a centralised single-house Westminster system rather than a presidential system advocated by John Guise at the time. Other Select Committee recommendations included provision for an expansion of regional electorates from fifteen to eighteen, and open constituencies from sixty-nine to eighty-two; reduction of the number of official members from ten to four; and the addition of three nominated members. Thus, by the end of 1971, Papua New Guinea was ready for the election of the third House of Assembly. And Johnson had the last word which he delivered in Pidgin English:

> As I look around the House I am proud to say that I can see many friends from all parts of Papua New Guinea. There are New Guineans and Papuans and Australians and some from other countries too, but we have all worked together for the good of Papua New Guinea. The second House of Assembly has brought Papua New Guinea to the door of nationhood, the Third House may well open that door so that we may enter[17].

In February 1972 the election for the third House of Assembly attracted a very large field of candidates. There were 553 candidates for the open constituencies, and fifty-eight contestants for regional seats. Of the three major parties, the United Party represented the highlands conservative elements, the People's Progress Party was committed to supporting business, mainly lowland business enterprise, and the Pangu Party claimed to represent the interests of the people as a whole. Josephine Abaijah, the only woman elected in 1972, did not belong to any of these three parties but represented the interests of Papua Besena, a pressure group based in the Central District. As a visiting United Nations Mission noted, the dominant issue in the election was the timing of self-government.

In April 1972 a national coalition government was formed with the People's Progress Party and Pangu as senior partners. As the national coalition was in favour of early self-government, one of its first tasks was to establish a timetable for self-government.

In June 1972 Chief Minister Michael Somare gave notice in the House of Assembly that constitutional change was neces-

sary if the country was to have full internal self-government by
1 December 1973 or as soon as possible thereafter. The United
Party continued to prefer to delay self-government and
proposed December 1975 as a target date. When Somare put
the motion on self-government to the September 1972 sitting
of the House of Assembly, Anton Parao, a young highlander,
led the United Party attack on the proposed earlier date of
self-government:

> I do not want to see the white colonial government handed
> to a black colonial government just for the sake of a minority
> group such as Michael Somare's government.

Somare's reply was direct and simple:

> It is high time that the people of this country held their
> heads high . . . and have pride in their country. If not now,
> when?[18]

When the motion was put, fifty-two members voted in favour
of early self-government and thirty-four voted against it. As the
following table shows, voting was on regional lines with the
highlands being the only area voting overwhelming
against the motion.

Table 6.2: Voting on self-government

	Ayes	Noes	Absent
Islands	13	2	2
Momase	20	6	2
Papua	12	3	3
Highlands	7	23	6
Total	52	34	13

Source: Johnson, L., *Colonial Sunset: Australia and Papua New Guinea
1970–74* (1983)

The House then agreed to a target date of December 1973 for
self-government.

At the end of 1972 there was a change of government in
Australia. The Liberal-Country Party coalition, led by Billy Mc-
Mahon, lost to the Labor Party, whose leader Gough Whitlam
became prime minister. Whitlam was committed to granting

independence within two years but Chief Minister Somare and his coalition government insisted that the decision to set the independence date had to be reached by Papua New Guineans. On 17 January 1973 the Australian prime minister and Papua New Guinea's chief minister met to discuss the dates of both self-government and complete independence. During these discussions Whitlam argued that Papua New Guinea should become self-governing as soon as possible and should be independent by the end of 1974. However he accepted Somare's position that the timing should be a matter for consultation between the Australian and Papua New Guinea governments and that the decision should be endorsed by the Papua New Guinea House of Assembly. Whitlam further agreed that negotiations should continue on moving the border between Papua New Guinea and Australia.

A 'home grown' constitution

Somare introduced the issue of the development of a constitution in characteristic nationalistic style:

> It is important that the fullest consideration be given to the type of future government we shall have. It is for our people that a constitution will be made. It is our people who shall have to live under the system of government that is established. We must ensure, therefore, that the constitution is suited to the needs and circumstances of Papua New Guinea and is not imposed from outside. In short it should be a home-grown constitution[19].

In 1972 the House established a Constitutional Planning Committee (CPC) with very wide terms of reference. Michael Somare was nominally chairman, however his deputy Father John Momis soon took control of the committee of fourteen members. As Johnson put it:

> Somare thought there was unlikely to be sufficient unity among the members to obstruct his own objective, a quick and controversy-free movement to self-government and independence; but, in fact the Committee escaped his control entirely in the face of an alliance between Momis and

Kaputin, the two best educated and most radical members of the team. The lack of interest of Guise and the death of Arek, the Chairman of the two previous Constitutional Committees, both men who could have influenced the direction of events, left leadership in the hands of the radicals[20].

In August the committee members visited a number of provincial centres to gauge the views of the people. In many centres regional autonomy and local government were discussed and proposals which reflected these concerns were made. In a number of areas there were people who sought a measure of local autonomy in the form of associations as the transition to independence gathered momentum. Some of these developed into break-away movements or pressure groups throughout the country. The most important of these were in Bougainville, the Mataungan Association in East New Britain, Papua Besena based in the Central District, and the Kabisawali Association in the Trobriand Islands. Some people in the Bougainville District had violently opposed the exploitation of their natural resources and as early as 1964 threatened to break away if the Australian administration ignored their warning. From 1950 onwards Tolais in East New Britain rejected a multi-racial council which was imposed by the administration, and in the 1960s they established the Mataungan Association and broadened their opposition to include restoration of their land that had been alienated to establish European-owned plantations. These conflicts died down after independence as the Tolais began to get their land back with the existing plantations. Papua Besena was a separatist movement around which the people in Papua sought to protect their identity, and they, too, opposed union with New Guinea. The Kabisawali Association opposed the local government council which, in turn, led to rivalry amongst the clans and between the chiefs. Both the Kabisawali and Besena movements faded from the political scene as Papua New Guinea approached independence.

While most women in Papua New Guinea played little part in Western political affairs, it is interesting to note there were women of influence in three of these separatist movements.

In Bougainville women were heavily involved in violent protests against mining activities; in East New Britain some Tolai women were vocal in their support for independence for the region; and the Papua Besena movement was led by a woman, Josephine Abaijah, who organised strong local support and in 1972 became the first woman to be elected to the House of Assembly.

The Constitutional Planning Committee's concern about the timing of the transfer of powers from Australia was noted in an Interim Report presented to the September 1973 sitting of the House of Assembly. In its second Interim Report, tabled in the House of Assembly, in November 1973, the CPC proposed an alternative to the Westminster system which included a complex arrangement under which the powers of head of state would be shared amongst the prime minister, the ministers for foreign affairs and justice, the speaker of the House of Assembly, and the chief justice. This proposal was decisively rejected by Somare, and the then speaker of the House, Guise, on the grounds that it was administratively completely unworkable. On the question of citizenship, the report proposed that resident foreigners be required to redistribute their financial assets before being eligible for citizenship.

The proceedings of the Constitutional Planning Committee uncovered ideological and personality problems which were to delay independence for a further twelve months. With Somare busy on other major problems, the deputy chairman, Father John Momis, became by default de facto chairman of the CPC.

The Constitutional Planning Committee had wide terms of reference and interpreted its role as including involvement with the dates of self-government and independence, and the question of regional autonomy. Somare's desire to hasten the process of self-government and independence led to Momis accusing him of giving in to 'colonial pressure' and engaging in negotiations with Prime Minister Whitlam in Australia which pre-empted the final recommendations of the CPC. In spite of the strength of the Constitutional Planning Committee, Somare demonstrated that he was capable of taking decisive action and had emerged as a young and articulate leader who was able to lead Papua New Guinea to self-government and eventual independence. Somare provided a rallying point for national support.

Although Michael Somare was emerging as the undoubted leader, he had a most difficult task in holding together a fragile coalition which was formed as a result of political expediency rather than as a cohesive group with a set of comprehensive policies. Pangu's policies, which were most like those of Western Social Democratic parties, emphasised rural development and the welfare of the people, and the party was suspicious of the motives of foreign investors, whereas Pangu's coalition partner, the People's Progress Party, advocated unrestricted capitalist development and welcomed foreign investors. The Pangu Party was unable to translate into social and economic action its aim of harnessing the human and financial resources of the nation to benefit the people in the rural areas, and gradually lost control of its policy to the People's Progress Party. For instance, when Julius Chan, leader of the People's Progress Party and Minister for Finance in the coalition government, announced the 1973 national budget, the two universities were allocated $11 million while a mere $3 million was allocated to rural development, and urban business interests were favoured at the expense of the interests of the people in the villages.

In November 1973 the House of Assembly approved the transfer of power from the Commonwealth of Australia to the self-governing nation of Papua New Guinea. To avoid the possibility of regional conflicts no official arrangements were made to celebrate the day. To discourage violence, riot squads were dispatched on stand-by to Port Moresby, Mount Hagen, Rabaul, and Kieta, and a national ban was placed on the sale of liquor.

The self-government weekend was quiet and trouble-free. At the only official function, the ex-administrator, Les Johnson, was sworn in as Australian High Commissioner by the Chief Justice, John Minogue, and the High Commissioner then administered the Executive Council oath of secrecy to Chief Minister Somare and his Cabinet colleagues. Johnson made a short speech to mark the occasion:

> We are fortunate to be here on ... [this] occasion when Michael Somare makes his mark as the Leader of his people, on the day that Papua New Guinea becomes self-governing ... Today Papua New Guinea begins to make its ways from the colonial womb to independent nationhood. Chief Minister, you bear the hopes and the fears of all of your people. May the fears be banished and the hopes be realised[21].

Somare's response was even shorter and quite simple: 'My government and my people take up our responsibility with confidence.'[22]

Thus, the co-operation between the colonial power and the local leaders allowed for a smooth transition to self-government unaccompanied by the physical violence that some Papua New Guineans and Australians had feared.

Independence

In the next eighteen months, parliamentary and public debate was mainly concerned with the finalisation of the constitution and the legal and administrative processes associated with complete independence.

Controversial issues in these debates were the timing of the adoption of the constitution and the date of independence; eligibility for citizenship; the powers of the head of state, the legislature, parliamentary committees, and provincial governments; and control over foreign investment. The main protagonists were those grouped around Somare and Guise on the one hand, and Momis and Kaputin on the other hand.

On the question of timing, Somare believed it necessary that the constitution should be adopted by June 1974 and that 1 December 1974 be set as the date for independence. However, Somare lost this argument and Momis's view prevailed that the completion of the constitution should be delayed and independence postponed for a further twelve months.

The question of who should be eligible for citizenship of the new nation aroused strong emotions. The CPC, which was dominated by Momis, proposed to the House that all Europeans, Asians, and those of mixed race should be excluded from citizenship, and that the right to vote, to serve in

Parliament, and be appointed to senior positions in the public service should be restricted to those with both parents and grandparents born in Papua New Guinea. This proposal threatened to split the government when the People's Progress Party realised that its leader, Finance Minister Julius Chan, who was of Chinese origin, would become one of the first casualties of such a policy. By April the People's Progress Party, the National Party, the United Party, and many independents rallied behind Somare in support of the concept of a multi-racial society.

On the question of the powers of the legislature and head of state, the House agreed with Somare that a Westminster-style government was to be preferred to the complex proposal of the CPC for a five-way division of power. The House also considered that the CPC was mistaken in urging the estab-lishment of a network of parliamentary standing committees, and that it would be more appropriate to appoint *ad hoc* special-purpose select committees as the need arose. The issue of the establishment and powers of provincial governments was one of the most difficult and contentious matters to be faced in this period. In fact this issue proved so difficult to resolve that the decision was postponed until after independence.

The Somare and Momis factions also disagreed about the extent of control that should be exercised over foreign invest-ment. Somare had come to believe that it was in the best interests of the country to promote economic growth by en-couraging foreign investment. Momis and Kaputin were behind a national pressure group formed in September 1974 to sway public opinion and parliamentary parties against foreign investment so natural resources could be protected. The issue was partially resolved when the House agreed to a certain measure of control over companies seeking to exploit natural resources.

In June 1975 the House chose 16 September 1975 as independence day, and on 15 August the constitution was finally adopted. The constitution sets out national goals and directive principles. It provides for a national parliament elected by universal suffrage with a minimum of 100 and a maximum of 107 members, the Queen of the United Kingdom as Head of State represented by a Governor General and the Prime Minister, as the chief executive officer of the government, as the head of a National Executive Council which is composed of cabinet ministers and controls the armed forces. The constitution also allows for citizenship to be granted to anyone with two indigenous grandparents, and to aliens with eight years residence in the country if they revoke citizenship of any other country, the operation of an independent national judicial system, and an Ombudsman Commission. In addition the constitution guarantees equal opportunity and the right to life and freedom of expression to citizens of Papua New Guinea.

Power over foreign affairs and defence was transferred from the Australian government to the Papua New Guinean government after the adoption of the constitution. The fact that the process of the transfer of power had occurred in stages over a considerable period of time and that all powers were effectively handed over prior to independence day was partly responsible for there being little popular celebration and no disturbances on the day itself. The celebrations of the formal granting of independence in Port Moresby and other main urban centres are recorded in the film *Yu Mi Yet* (*Independence*). In the rural areas some local people gathered in the schools or patrol posts to participate in the dancing and other activities, but the majority of the villagers went about their daily routines as though no important event was taking place at all, and the day of independence came and went almost unnoticed in most of the villages in the remote areas.

The constitution required that at the independence ceremony, oaths of allegiance and declarations of loyalty be made to Her Majesty Queen Elizabeth II, and to the independent state of Papua New Guinea.

At 5.15 p.m. on 15 September 1975 the Australian flag was lowered, and at 10.25 a.m. on 16 September the Bird of Paradise flag of the independent state of Papua New Guinea was raised on Independence Hill at Waigani, Port Moresby. The ceremonies of the day and the flag itself symbolised the people's aspirations for a united egalitarian nation.

SUMMARY

By 1961 the Australian government was under pressure from international agencies, the Australian parliamentary opposition and groups within Papua New Guinea to prepare the country for independence.

In 1962 a United Nations Mission addressed the issues of economic development, the 'advancement of the native people' and land tenure. The first Five Year Plan emphasised the importance of overseas investment in the exploitation of natural resources and the second Five Year Plan emphasised the importance of development of the rural sector. In 1973 Chief Minister Somare's Eight Point Plan aimed to equalise economic benefits, decentralise economic activity, encourage small enterprises and assist rural areas. However, these goals were not supported by the Pangu Party's coalition partner, the People's Progress Party, and they remained largely unrealised.

The most important single economic development was the establishment, despite some opposition from the landowners, of the Bougainville Copper mine by a subsidiary of the transnational Conzinc Riotinto. Other overseas companies such as the Jant Timber Company were involved in commercial timber projects. Cash cropping in copra, cocoa and coffee, and indigenous involvement in cash cropping grew rapidly in the 1960s. In spite of an extension of supporting activities, such as banking, secondary industry grew slowly. The very small trade union movement was fragmented and ineffective except insofar as it provided a base from which several important political leaders emerged.

The administration took over from the missions greater responsibility for the provision of education and health services — however, the established churches extended their influence and fundamentalist sects came to compete with the established denominations.

The emergence of an educated élite to take over the management of the country and establish business interests was made possible by the rapid expansion of secondary and tertiary education. The educated élite included very few women, and those women who entered the paid workforce were usually in the health and teaching services, clerks, shop assistants or domestic servants. In the 1960s racially discriminatory legislation was repealed and in 1972 a Human Rights Ordinance banned discrimination on the grounds of race, tribe, political opinion, colour, creed or sex.

One response to social change was the development of a group of creative artists — writers, painters and musicians — who tried to link traditional concepts and values with the newly emerging Westernised society.

There were a number of significant political developments in this period. An avenue through which some Papua New Guineans achieved political awareness was the local government councils. The first House of Assembly, elected in 1964, established a committee to draft a constitution. Six political parties contested the 1968 election and Canberra began to devolve powers to the national parliament. Devolution occurred in two stages: self-government, under which Canberra handed over all powers except those relating to foreign affairs, defence and the legal system; and complete independence, under which all powers resided with the national parliament.

Not everyone in Papua New Guinea supported early self-government and independence. Expatriates who were concerned with protecting their commercial interests and highland groups who were afraid that an independent country would be dominated by the lowlands sought to keep the Australian presence. However, Michael Somare, the leader of the largest and most influential political party, the Pangu Party, persuaded the House to move rapidly towards freeing the colony from Australian control. After 1972 he was assisted by the newly elected Labor government in Australia, which was committed to early self-government and independence.

Conservative elements were not the only ones advocating delaying independence. Radical members of Parliament who came to dominate the Constitutional Planning Committee argued that more time was needed to develop a fully 'home-grown' constitution. The provisions of the constitution were the subject of considerable debate which was resolved by compromise. Separatist movements in Bougainville, East New Britain and Papua were unsuccessful. The country won self-government in December 1973 and complete independence in September 1975.

In spite of the expansion of the cash economy and the extension of Western social, cultural and political influence, the great majority of the people still lived outside the cash economy, were mainly dependent upon subsistence agriculture, followed many traditional customs, and were not directly affected by the economic, social, cultural and political changes of these fifteen years.

7

A decade of nationhood 1975–1985

Papua New Guinea
We are one
Divided, we fall
United, we stand
The national flag
A symbol of unity.

[Anon].

For Papua New Guinea the decade after independence was one of profound significance. This chapter deals with some of the issues which confronted the country during those ten years and then describes the government structure which was established to deal with these issues.

As Papua New Guinea is a small and in many ways vulnerable country its relationships with other, usually more powerful, countries is of great importance. Relationships with other countries in this period were mainly peaceful and mostly concerned with establishing diplomatic relations, aid, trade, and investment. However, Papua New Guinea did maintain a defence force. In 1975 when the independent state undertook responsibility for its own defence it established the Papua New Guinea Defence Force, directly responsible to the national parliament. Following a recommendation of a 1982 Defence

Policy Review Committee, the government decided that priority should be given to developing the army to the strength of two infantry battalions and an engineer battalion. This meant that Papua New Guinea would rely on a land force supported by a few naval ships and airforce planes.

PAPUA NEW GUINEA'S RELATIONSHIP WITH OTHER COUNTRIES

Papua New Guinea's foreign policy during this period can be seen as operating in five zones: Australia, neighbouring island states in the south-western Pacific, Indonesia, other countries in East Asia, and the rest of the world.

Australia

Of these five zones, the most important single relationship was that with Australia, the ex-colonial power. The delicate nature of Australia's relationship with Indonesia made Australia's strategic interest in Papua New Guinea a prime concern. A foreign policy issue which required early resolution was the position of the border between Australia and Papua New Guinea. While in practice the matter was resolved between the two governments in June 1976, there was disagreement within Australia arising from concern by some members of the Liberal Party and business interests over the control of off-shore minerals. This dispute stalled the signing of the agreement until the end of the year.

Other than the border issue, Papua New Guinea continued to enjoy what became known as a 'unique' relationship with Australia which resulted mainly from historical factors, including nostalgia based on the experiences of World War Two, and geographical location. The Australian government was conscious of the strategic importance of Papua New Guinea for its defence policy, and recognised the importance of having a politically stable neighbour. Australian business interests were anxious to be involved in the exploitation of natural resources. Also, Papua New Guinea needed Australian financial aid and hoped that Australia would provide military support if asked to do so.

Australian foreign policy was closely linked to Australia's aid commitment to Papua New Guinea. At independence 40 per cent of Papua New Guinea's budget came from Australian aid. In late 1975 Papua New Guinea was concerned that Australia might drastically reduce this aid contribution. However, in March 1976 Prime Minister Somare announced that Australia had guaranteed to provide K930 million for the following five-year period. This assistance prompted Donald Denoon to say that 'Papua New Guinea and Australia have, in this respect, created a new world record for direct financial dependence'[1]. Over the next five months both countries tried to agree on an appropriate formula through which to reduce Papua New Guinea's reliance on Australian aid. In 1981 a formula was agreed upon which would lead to a 5 per cent per annum reduction in real terms. It was assumed at this stage that the shortfall would be made up from revenue from the exploitation of natural resources. However, it soon became evident that this was too ambitious a target, and in 1983 a new formula under which Australia's aid contribution was to decline by 1 per cent in 1982–1984, 2 per cent in 1984–1985 and 3 per cent in 1985–1986 was agreed upon. By the middle of 1985 it was clear that Papua New Guinea would be forced to negotiate for a further aid package for the period 1986–1991. Prior to this, in 1984, an official Australian report known as the Jackson Report recommended that Australia's aid should be reduced more rapidly and that aid should be tied to specific projects rather than given as a grant to the national budget[2]. Papua New Guinea strongly opposed this recommended policy, and talks between the two countries came to a deadlock. Negotiations were resumed on the understanding that a large amount of Australian aid would be tied to specific projects after full discussion between both countries. Australian-based companies or Australian components of transnational corporations became more actively involved in the Papua New Guinea economy in the decade after independence, and Australian companies increased their investment in the commercial and transport sectors as well as in plantations. However, more Australian capital was linked with transnational investment, especially in mining, and the extent of this involvement will be considered later.

Australia continued to be Papua New Guinea's main trading partner. Prior to independence Australia had been the destination for almost a quarter of Papua New Guinea's exports. This figure declined after 1975 with the increasing interest of other countries in the exploitation of Papua New Guinea's natural resources. At independence 50 per cent of Papua New Guinea's imports came from Australia. This figure was also reduced in the following decade when Papua New Guinea became more dependent on Asian sources for the supply of consumer goods such as food, clothing, and electrical equipment.

South Pacific island countries

New Zealand, the second-largest country in the south Pacific region, was interested in Papua New Guinea mainly for strategic reasons. Relations between the two countries had always been good. New Zealanders formed an important part of the expatriate population, and New Zealand exported a range of manufactured goods to Papua New Guinea.

In the south Pacific, Papua New Guinea confirmed its solidarity with other island states by opposing French nuclear testing on Mururoa Atoll and supporting moves to declare the area a nuclear-free zone. In July 1975, during the sixth South Pacific Forum, Papua New Guinea agreed to a plan for pooling resources for common purposes such as shipping and the protection of territorial and economic zones. Also at the meeting Papua New Guinea and Fiji successfully moved to oppose United States' entry into the Pacific Regional Fishery Pact.

In 1980 Papua New Guinea troops were engaged in combat for the first time when the government agreed to a request from the properly constituted government of Vanuatu for assistance in suppressing a rebel attempt to capture government. Papua New Guinea's agreement to provide this support stemmed from its concern that a successful coup by the rebel leader, Jimmy Stephens, and the overthrow of the Melanesian Prime Minister, Father Walter Lini, would have had a destabilising political effect in the South Pacific region. Following a direct request from Father Lini in June 1980, Prime Minister Julius Chan agreed to commit Papua New Guinean troops to assist the Vanuatu government in this armed conflict. This exercise was thoroughly planned and effectively executed, and within three months the one battalion of Papua New Guinean troops successfully crushed the rebellion. At independence Australia had left behind a well-trained and well-equipped defence force. The army, under the command of Brigadier General Ted Diro, had maintained these standards and thus had little difficulty in overcoming the rebel forces. The combat skills of the defence force were of such high calibre that they succeeded in this enterprise without any casualties and in September the troops returned to Port Moresby in triumph under the command of the Chief of Operations, Anthony Huai.

Apart from New Zealand and Vanuatu, Papua New Guinea's relationships with countries in this region were almost entirely diplomatic and political. There were no significant trade relationships, and no aid relationships except to the extent that these countries might be seen as being in competition for money from international agencies.

Indonesia

A particularly sensitive area of Papua New Guinea's foreign policy was its relationship with Indonesia. An ongoing concern was the existence in Irian Jaya of a Melanesian population opposed to the Indonesian presence. For many of these Irian Jayan Melanesians, opposition took the form of armed conflict, and these rebels formed a guerilla movement known as The Organisasi Papua Merdeka (OPM). A specific problem this situation posed for Papua New Guinea was that the Irian Jayan guerillas did not recognise the Irian Jaya–Papua New Guinea border imposed by colonial powers in an earlier period; they sometimes crossed into Papua New Guinea to evade Indonesian troops.

Although the Papua New Guinean government's official position was that the rebel movement was an Indonesian domestic problem, the government could not ignore incidents such as occurred in June 1978 when Indonesian troops crossed the border into Papua New Guinea in pursuit of rebels. The government response was to send troops and police to patrol the border in an attempt to prevent the Irianese using Papua

New Guinea soil for sanctuary, and thus to avoid further incursions by Indonesian troops. The tensions on the border may have prompted President Soeharto's visit to Port Moresby in June 1979 under the tightest security ever mounted in Papua New Guinea. At this meeting the two governments reaffirmed that Irian Jaya was a province of Indonesia and the OPM was an Indonesian internal problem. It was also agreed that both countries should establish a way of dealing with the rebels. In December Papua New Guinea and Indonesia signed a new treaty to strengthen their relations. However, in spite of the apparent restoration of harmony between the two countries, many Papua New Guineans in the tertiary institutions and churches strongly opposed what they saw as a policy of capitulation to Indonesian interests.

When Indonesian activity along the border intensified, many Irianese began to come across to Papua New Guinea. Between February and June 1984 the number of these border crossers increased from 400 to 7000. This influx of Irianese created serious security and resource problems for Papua New Guinea. Following a series of incidents which included the abduction by the rebels and subsequent return of a Swiss pilot, and the deportation by Papua New Guinea of an Australian Broadcasting Corporation correspondent on the grounds of biased reporting, the two governments arranged to review the border agreement. Despite Indonesia's refusal to allow supervision of the operation by the United Nations High Commission for Refugees (UNHCR), Papua New Guinea agreed to repatriate the border-crossers and accept Indonesia's unilateral guarantee of their safety.

The next dramatic event which occurred on the border was in October 1984 when an estimated 11 000 Irianese walked over the border to Papua New Guinea, and the Department of Foreign Affairs announced that it intended to escort the crossers back to Irian Jaya. University students again spearheaded internal opposition against repatriation. Also at that time, it was reported that Indonesian troops had burnt down Papua New Guinean villages in search of rebels. However, by the end of December 1984, relations between the two countries was warmer. Indonesia agreed to allow UNHCR to participate in the repatriation exercise and to let Papua New Guinean officials accompany border-crossers returning to their home villages, and make follow-up checks at later times. In return, Papua New Guinea granted political refugee status to 500 Irianese, mostly academics, government officials, and army deserters, who refused to go back to Irian Jaya. At this time it is estimated that more than 1000 had already voluntarily returned to their villages, leaving about 9300 in camps on the border.

Papua New Guinea's relationship with Indonesia was almost entirely political and diplomatic. There was no significant trade between the countries. Indonesia had no financial investment in Papua New Guinea, and it did not supply any form of aid.

Other Asian countries

It was also necessary for Papua New Guinea to establish a policy towards other Asian countries, in particular China and Japan. In 1975 the People's Republic of China offered to buy a large amount of raw materials including copper and cocoa worth K33 million, as well as timber, palm oil, and coconut oil. In November 1975 a Papua New Guinea delegation went to China and exactly a year later Prime Minister Somare visited the country. However, it was reported that he was unimpressed with Chinese ideology and had been impressed with capitalist overtures in the Philippines on the return journey. A month earlier Somare's Minister for Finance, Julius Chan, had visited Hong Kong to woo investors, and a Hong Kong trade mission visited Papua New Guinea in December.

During this decade Japan came to dominate investment and trade with Papua New Guinea. The rapid expansion of the Japanese economy in the 1960s and early 1970s led to a greatly increased need for raw materials, and Japan became the major buyer of Papua New Guinea's copper. However the Japanese economy reacted strongly to the 1974 world recession, particularly in response to a sharp rise in oil prices, and she greatly reduced her copper orders in 1975. This provided the Papua New Guinea government with an early lesson in the dangers of the economy being too heavily dependent upon the export of a few natural resources to a very limited number of buyers. With the recovery of the Japanese economy in the second half of the 1970s and the 1980s, Japanese policy moved from the purchase of raw materials through transnational corporations to direct investment, and Japan established several major timber and fishing projects, and expressed interest in copper exploration. While this was perceived by many people as being beneficial to the Papua New Guinean economy, others were concerned that, given its poor record of protection of the environment, such as the Trans-Golgol timber project, Japanese companies might evade the environmental clauses which the Papua New Guinean government insisted should be included in their contracts.

In spite of Japanese legislation in 1972 allowing the government to give untied aid, the little aid offered to Papua New Guinea was tied to projects which would benefit Japanese interests. Relations deteriorated in 1976 when Japan, perhaps taking advantage of what it perceived to be the weakness of the young country, threatened to cancel all aid unless a palm oil project at Bialla in West New Britain was undertaken by Japanese contractors using Japanese consultants. The Papua New Guinean government did not approve the project.

Japan was also interested in Papua New Guinea as a market for manufactured goods. At independence 20 per cent of Papua New Guinea's imports of manufactured goods came from Japan, and the value and variety of these goods increased greatly during the decade.

Other Asian countries, in particular Taiwan, South Korea, Malaysia, and Singapore also wanted to invest in the country's natural resources and in trade. The involvement of these countries in this decade was mainly through capital contributed to some of the transnational enterprises.

Other regions

Of the countries in other regions the most important were the United States of America, the Soviet Union, and the countries of the European Economic Community.

The United States government's interest was mainly strategic, and the United States Embassy maintained a high profile in Port Moresby. Direct trade between the two countries was negligible, however the United States-based transnational corporations showed interest in the potential of Papua New Guinea's natural resources, in particular copper and oil. In the early 1980s the United States provided military training to the Papua New Guinea Defence Force, and various government and private United States agencies such as the Peace Corps volunteers were involved in aid projects.

At the end of 1975 the Minister for Foreign Affairs and Trade, Sir Albert Maori Kiki, visited Europe to make arrangements for Papua New Guinea to join the European Economic Community aid programme, and set up an office in Brussels. Exports to the European Economic Community increased to approximately 40 per cent of total exports, with Germany taking the major share. Germany was involved in transnational investment, and Germany, and to a lesser extent other European countries, sponsored aid projects.

The Soviet Union invited Papua New Guinea to set up an office in Moscow, offered to buy limited quantities of primary products and help build the fishing industry, and provided favourable long-term loans.

International organisations and transnational corporations

International organisations with which Papua New Guinea was concerned included aid and monetary agencies such as the World Bank, the Asian Development Bank, and the International Labour Organisation. Papua New Guinea was represented at the Commonwealth Secretariat, the South Pacific Bureau of Economic Co-operation, the associations of African, Caribbean and Pacific nations, international coffee and cocoa organisations, the European Economic Community, and the United Nations. Previous chapters have shown how the colonial powers exploited local labour and natural resources for their own gain. In this process they effectively tied the colony into the world capitalist system[3].

Major investment in the exploitation of natural resources came from transnational corporations. However the national government found that negotiating with transnationals presented special difficulties. As shown in Chapter 6, the first transnational to invest in Papua New Guinea was Conzinc Riotinto which began copper mining operations on Bougainville under an agreement reached with the Australian colonial administration in 1967. A Conzinc Riotinto subsidiary, the Bougainville Copper Company Limited (BCL), expanded its activities greatly and by 1983 BCL was one of the most profitable copper operations in the world.

At the end of this period another major transnational enterprise involving Australian, United States, and German capital began operation at the gold and copper mine at Ok Tedi in the Star Mountains in the Western Province of Papua New Guinea near the border with Indonesia. Minerals had been discovered in the area in the early 1970s, however negotiations concerning the terms under which foreign investors would be allowed to operate were influenced by the renegotiation of the BCL agreement in 1976. Discussions were protracted, and production was delayed for a number of years. Under the agreement reached with Ok Tedi it was anticipated that the company would make a substantial contribution to the national budget in the second half of the 1980s. As is shown below these projects seriously affected the physical environment and created major social disruption.

Universalism versus selective engagement

In 1975 Papua New Guinea adopted a Universalist foreign policy. Apart from those countries which pursued racial or social policies which were offensive to Papua New Guinea, the government recognised all countries which would recognise Papua New Guinea, unless recognition involved taking sides in regional or domestic conflicts.

In September 1976 Kiki attended a United Nations meeting at which he defined his government's foreign policy: 'Universalism to Papua New Guinea means taking the middle path without veering to either side on questions relating to political ideologies, creeds or governmental systems.'[4] Kiki gave, as an example, Papua New Guinea's recognition of both communist North Korea and capitalist South Korea. In July 1980, however, in a significant foreign policy shift, the government abandoned 'universalism' in favour of a policy of 'selective engagement'. In practice this meant that the government's broad foreign policy objectives were to strengthen links with the South Pacific Commission's regional organisations; establish closer ties with the Association of South East Asian Nations (ASEAN) member states; co-operate with Indonesia on border development programmes; oppose colonial powers and racist regimes; seek to diversify trade relations with Japan, China, and Korea; and maintain and consolidate strong bonds with Australia.

THE ECONOMY

During the decade the country moved further into the Western cash economy. However, in 1985 80 per cent of the population was still engaged in subsistence agriculture supplemented by hunting, fishing, and gathering, and small amounts of cash from the sale of excess produce and fish. The most important means into the Western cash economy were the exploitation of natural resources and the expansion of plantation and cash crop activities. Of the natural resources, the mining of copper and gold provided 25 per cent of internal revenue, and a number of major timber and fishing projects were established. All major projects required input of foreign capital, although the government attempted to keep an equity interest wherever possible.

The government had hoped that revenue from the Ok Tedi copper mine would assist the national budget when the Five Year Aid agreement with Australia ran out in 1986. However, relationships between the government and Ok Tedi progressively deteriorated. Ok Tedi had failed to build a permanent tailings dam to process the poisonous waste, so environmental concerns led to the government taking the extreme step of closing the mine in August 1984. The government took this strong action despite the company's claim that shareholders would withdraw their capital if Ok Tedi had to comply with these government attempts to protect the environment. This conflict was resolved in March 1985 with an agreement which committed the Ok Tedi Company to building a permanent tailings dam. In spite of this environmental concession by the company, the people of the Western Province continued to be concerned about other adverse effects of the mining project. For instance, in 1985 the boat which was carrying a consignment of 200 forty-four gallon drums of highly toxic cyanide to the mining site capsized, and the cyanide was released into the sea at the mouth of the Fly River. As a result marine resources which were an important part of the people's diet were poisoned. Both physical and social effects of the mining project continued to be a concern.

In Bougainville also, some of the people were worried about the operation of Bougainville Copper Limited. As discussed earlier, in 1967, in spite of the violent opposition of the local landowners, the Australian administration reached an agreement with Bougainville Copper Limited to mine copper and gold at Panguna on Bougainville Island. Bedford and Mamak have noted the concerns of local villagers at the alienation of their land:

> Land is our life. Land is our physical life, food and sustenance. Land is our social life; it is marriage; it is status; it is security; it is politics, in fact it is our only world. When you (colonial officials) take our land, you cut away the very heart of our existence. We have little or no experience of social survival detached from the land. For us to be completely landless is a nightmare which no dollar in the pocket or dollar in the bank will allay; we are a threatened people[5].

Despite this resistance the project was established and some of the hidden costs such as environmental degradation and social disruption began to emerge. A company official who was given the task of liaising between the company and the landowners reported:

> I have been asked to explain to Bougainville Copper that the harvesting of the smaller streams was peculiarly the job of the women and that apart from the loss of variety in the local diet, the loss of the streams has affected the social life of the women and children in that small cooperative fishing parties are no longer possible. As well as bringing about social changes at the village level, the mine has affected the religious practices of the people as a few examples will show.

Prior to the coming of the Bougainville Copper it was the custom to take a newborn child to a particular pool just downstream from the concentration for a ritual wash[6].

As early as 1975, concerned by what they saw to be the national government's capitulation to BCL, a group of Bougainville leaders made a unilateral declaration of independence, thus decisively signalling their unwillingness to join the proposed independent state of Papua New Guinea. When the Prime Minister, Michael Somare, responded by abolishing the provincial government and freezing its assets, violence broke out, and airstrips and government property were damaged. Somare resisted pressure to use troops to restore order in the area and used his contacts with Bougainville leaders such as Leo Hannett, Father John Momis and Dr Alexis Sarei to negotiate a form of statehood by March 1976. These negotiations were not immediately successful, and riot police were despatched to Bougainville to quell ongoing violent protests. Nevertheless, by August 1976 Somare was able to guarantee the Bougainville people an effective role in running their own affairs within the framework of the national government. The mine continued operations.

During this decade BCL provided the single most important source of internally generated revenue to the national budget. While the amount and the percentage varied from year to year, BCL contributions amounted to an average of 30 per cent of the budget during this period. From its first year of operation in 1972, to 1985, the end of the first decade of independence, BCL paid an average of K55 000 000 a year to the Papua New Guinean government or government bodies, and provided 46 per cent of Papua New Guinea's export earnings. In addition it was the nation's largest single employer, and over 80 per cent of its 3700 workers were Papua New Guineans.

Cash cropping and the people's involvement in the growing and marketing of crops continued to expand. While the largest plantations continued to be owned and operated by foreigners, some Papua New Guineans developed substantial businesses growing and marketing coffee, cocoa, and copra. In spite of a sharp decline in export earnings in 1981, coffee remained, throughout this period, by far the most important cash crop export earner. Coffee was followed by cocoa, and then copra. No other cash crops generated significant export earnings, however the total value of cash crop exports, including tea, rubber, and palm oil, trebled within the decade.

Natural resources and agricultural products are very vulnerable to fluctuations in world market prices, and all export items were heavily hit by the world-wide economic recession of 1974. The effects of this depressed the Papua New Guinean economy at independence in 1975. While the situation improved during the decade, Papua New Guinea's economy was not strong enough or diversified enough for it to be protected from the downturn in world demand. Attempts to establish secondary industries during this period failed to attract overseas or local capital. This was mainly due to problems associated with the transport of raw and processed materials, and the relatively high wage structure of the country.

By 1975 imported tinned fish had become a staple item in the diet of many Papua New Guineans. In an attempt to replace tinned fish with fresh fish, or fish tinned locally, the government set up several fisheries projects. However these were mostly unsuccessful, and Papua New Guineans continued to eat tinned fish imported mainly from Asian countries, in particular Japan. In many cases these countries had caught the fish in Papua New Guinean waters, taken it to their own countries for processing, and exported it back to Papua New Guinea. Even in villages where people traditionally caught fresh fish, many came to prefer eating tinned fish to fishing for it themselves.

The nation was far from being self-sufficient, and the national government relied heavily upon overseas aid and revenue from the export of natural resources and agricultural products — all unstable forms of income.

Immediately following independence, the government established a National Planning Office to advise on the development of financial planning policy. On the authority of the National Executive Council the National Planning Office established a list of priorities of government expenditure which was published in a document known as the National

Public Expenditure Plan (NPEP). These priorities covered the areas of industrial and agricultural production, training, environmental management, administration, and law. The NPEP was to recommend to the government the allocation of funds to each of these areas over a four-year period and subsequently produce annual four-year rolling plans. The original aim of the NPEP was to translate into practical policies the aspirations of the Eight Point Plan. However, this policy was reversed by the 1980 Chan government. Both Prime Minister Chan and his deputy, Okuk, supported foreign investment and exploitation of natural resources rather than priorities based on rural development as in Somare's Eight Point Plan. In addition there were concerns about the effectiveness of this planning process. In January 1984 the National Executive Council approved a revised system which became known as the National Development Plan. Under this system priorities were to be identified in specific categories such as education, health, defence, and urban development, and the planning cycle was to be increased from four to five years.

Systematic planning was required to monitor the spending of public monies, and measures were needed to deal with the worsening international economic situation. From 1982 onwards the national budget expenditure figures show that the government had abandoned the comprehensive set of Acts aimed at enforcing and promoting the goals of sound environmental management; it had embarked upon an almost unrestricted exploitation of natural resources.

TRADE UNIONS

The relatively high wage structure in the country was not a response to a highly organised trade union movement. In an attempt to create a functioning industrial relations system, the administration had established, in 1972, a Bureau of Industrial Organisations (BIO) which turned out to be ineffective. There were four effective unions: the Public Service Association, the Teachers' Association, the Bougainville Copper Union, and the Waterside Workers' Union. Of these, the Waterside Workers' Union was probably the most effective organisation at the time of independence[7]. In addition, there were some largely ineffective workers associations. This situation did not change significantly after independence. While the number of registered unions rose to fifty-four in 1985, covering approximately a quarter of the paid workforce, many unions still failed to hold elections, keep adequate records, and most had small memberships. With the exception of the unions referred to earlier, and the Seamen Union which joined the Waterside Workers' Union in 1980, the industrial organisations had little power to influence the wages and conditions of their members. The wage scales in Papua New Guinea were high in comparison with other developing countries was due not to workers' industrial activity but to the scarcity of skilled labour. A government policy of restricting the immigration of expatriate labour meant that the country was not flooded with Asian unskilled labour to the disadvantage of the local workforce.

In spite of the weakness of most trade unions, Papua New Guinea inherited from the colonial period a limited but stable and relatively efficient infrastructure, with a relatively well-paid workforce, with some sectors such as health, education, transport, and communication considerably in advance of those in most developing countries.

HEALTH SERVICES

During the 1950s and 1960s the administration had developed a health service designed to combat a wide range of endemic and introduced diseases. The post-independence government maintained — but was not able to expand — the services in the decade after independence in spite of the injection of aid from Australia and international agencies for special projects. However, Papua New Guinea still had a more extensive Western-style medical service, and spent more per capita on medical services, than most developing countries, and the overall health of the people remained relatively good. The national government was still aware of the special needs of the rural areas and attempted to provide for these needs through the maintenance and establishment of aid posts covering communities of up to 5000 people, and health centres which catered for communities up to 20 000 people, staffed by paraprofessionals. There was still only one national hospital, the Port Moresby General Hospital, which was staffed by qualified medical doctors, nurses, and orderlies. Although the number of Western-trained professional and para-professional Papua New Guineans in health services increased, these were mainly concentrated in the urban centres. This is because in many cases better-qualified people were, mainly for financial reasons, unwilling to work in the rural areas.

The health problems of greatest concern continued to be malaria, gastric and respiratory infections, pneumonia, venereal disease, and malnutrition. National and provincial governments kept diseases such as measles and whooping cough under control through the effective organisation of massive vaccination programmes. An unfortunate consequence of the mass vaccination programme was that many village people came to believe that injections (or as the villagers call them, 'shoots') could cure all diseases. A further effect of this dependence on Western medicine led to the decline of the use of traditional remedies, many of which were very effective.

One of the difficulties in extending health services was the increase in the country's population. During the decade, the population increased rapidly, and by 1985 over 40 per cent of the total population of approximately three and a half million people was under the age of fifteen, and a further 20 per cent were aged between fifteen and twenty-five. In an attempt to slow the population growth, the national government embarked upon a birth control campaign which advocated, amongst other things, the use of contraception. However, as contraception was discouraged by some on religious grounds, and as the campaign was mostly directed towards the literate section of the population, and suffered seriously from lack of funds, it had little real effect.

Thus, in spite of the government policy, these health and contraceptive services reached only a limited section of the population. In areas not covered by these government services the people continue to rely solely upon traditional remedies. Even in places where Western medicines were available, many communities combined traditional with Western remedies.

EDUCATION

In the decade after independence, education continued to be the national governments' single most important budgetary item, and by 1984 absorbed 20 per cent of the national budget. The immediate post-independence policy was threefold: to provide a primary school system which would result in all children between seven and twelve receiving formal schooling by the year 2000; to promote adult literacy; and to expand the post-primary and tertiary education systems. In practice, priority continued to be given to secondary and tertiary education in an attempt to expand the national élite who could take over positions still held by foreigners in key areas of the administration. The implementation of this policy required an increase in funding to the universities and other tertiary institutions such as the teachers' colleges, and to post-primary schools. While the long-term goal was still universal primary education as rapidly as possible, the expansion of the post-primary and tertiary sectors was inevitably at the expense of the primary or community school system and the adult literacy programmes. At the end of the period under review over two-thirds of the adult population were still illiterate, and only 60 per cent of seven- to twelve-year-olds were enrolled in primary schools, although some children over the age of twelve were also receiving primary education.

There was, however, progress in the provision of primary education. At independence the national government believed that providing basic literacy and numeracy skills was necessary for national development both economically and politically, and the 500 new primary schools which were established between 1975 and 1985 greatly increased primary school enrolments. However within this period Papua New Guinea's school-age population grew more rapidly than had been predicted and it is doubtful whether these increased enrolments greatly changed the proportion of children receiving formal education.

A switch in colonial government policy in the 1960s had meant that the secondary education sector was already expanding rapidly by 1975. Between 1975 and 1985 thirty-five new secondary schools, mainly provincial high schools, covering years seven to ten were built, three national high schools covering years eleven and twelve were established, and the existing senior national high school at Sogeri expanded. This expenditure almost doubled the number of high schools and increased enrolments by almost 70 per cent. Even so, less than a third of students who completed grade six could be given a place at a secondary school.

Following the establishment of provincial governments in 1977 the Education Department moved to decentralise policy making and administration. While the national government continued to provide the funds for salaries and most school buildings, the provincial authorities were given power to make decisions on a whole range of important matters. During this period too, the national government undertook responsibility for the salaries of teaching staff in the missions, which still controlled almost 50 per cent of the community schools, and conducted several post-primary schools. In 1980 North Solomons Province was not only a pace-setter in the decentralisation of power, but also the first provincial government to support village Tok Ples (local language) schools, the first of which was established in 1980. Ruth Kovoho, the first assistant co-ordinator of the project, summarised the aims of the Tok Ples school as providing:

(i)   A cultural benefit, by allowing the children to receive the foundations of their education in the language, culture, and custom of their community, and giving Tok Ples equal status in their minds with the English language.

(ii) A social benefit, by giving them a basis of knowledge, skills, and values which would prepare them for participation in the life of their community after leaving school . . .

(iii) An educational benefit, by letting them acquire literacy in their mother tongue before proceeding to learn English, a second language.

According to Graham Kemelfield the North Solomons pilot project was a great success, as the parents approved of their children learning to read and write in the vernacular.

Of the 10 per cent of students who completed secondary schooling and went on to tertiary institutions, approximately 35 per cent attended universities, including the secondary teachers' college which was attached to the University of Papua New Guinea; 25 per cent attended secretarial colleges, and less than 10 per cent attended the primary teachers' colleges. Very small groups of other students attended a wide variety of other tertiary institutions and completed occupational training to certificate or diploma level. In spite of a substantial expansion of the tertiary sector, which absorbed over 20 per cent of the total education budget in the decade after independence, there were not enough appropriately trained national staff for all the professional positions, and it was still necessary to continue to employ contract officers from overseas.

CHURCHES

In the decade 1975 to 1985 it is more appropriate to speak of churches than missions when considering the role and influence of organised Christianity in Papua New Guinea. Churches in Papua New Guinea during this period performed much the same spiritual and social function as they did in industrial Western societies. As the state accepted almost complete responsibility for education, health, and welfare, these aspects of the activity of the established churches waned, and churches concentrated on the task for which the missionaries had originally come to the country — the conversion of the people to Christianity.

Encouraged by the government, the churches significantly extended their influence in this decade. By 1985 Papua New Guinea was a more apparently religious country than Australia, Britain, or Germany, the colonial powers who had introduced Christianity into the country. It is difficult to estimate figures of the number of adherents or members of each denomination. According to the 1980 census it appears that almost all adults professed belief in a Christian denomination. What proportion of these people were practising Christians is, of course, very difficult to determine. However, it is evident from the high public profile of the churches in this period that many of them had many followers.

TRANSPORT AND COMMUNICATION

During this decade the maintenance and development of the transport system continued to be largely determined by the geography of the country. The ruggedness of the terrain in many regions meant that the nation was still dependent mainly on sea and air transport. Limited road networks which had been established near the towns of Mount Hagen and Goroka were extended, but the highlands highway between Mount Hagen and Lae was still the only road between the densely-populated highlands and the coast. There were no railways or plans to develop a railway system. In the rural areas of Papua New Guinea most people who needed to move between villages or from the village to the town still travelled by foot, or in canoes. This method of transport made it difficult for people to remain in touch with relatives who had moved away from their original settlements, or to get their produce to markets.

Water transport, traditionally important amongst coastal and island people, expanded and the number of commercial vessels engaged in local and overseas trade increased. Canoes and other small craft were still used extensively to transport people and goods both at sea and on the major rivers. Water transport was faster with the introduction of outboard motors attached to traditional style canoes, and the introduction of Western-style dinghies.

Air travel was particularly important to the economy in this decade. Increased commercial activity and, in particular, the new projects associated with the exploitation of natural resources such as copper and timber, led to a significant expansion of air traffic for both people and freight. However the expansion of these services was mainly an increase in the number of flights between towns, or between towns and natural resource projects. There was little increase in the services to the people in the villages. One of the problems of extending rural services was the cost of building airstrips in difficult country, and an increase in air fares.

The national government maintained the highly sophisticated telephone system which it had inherited at independence. And while the radio network was extended, there were few newspapers outside the urban areas. In urban areas also, a limited satellite video system was available, however, there was no local television broadcasting station.

The concentration of transport and communication systems in the main towns, in particular Port Moresby and Lae, was in part a cause of, and in part a response to, the concentration of the small manufacturing sector and service facilities such as banking, legal, and administrative institutions in the urban areas. Exceptions were the mining and timber projects which developed specific-purpose settlements in some rural areas.

CREATIVE ARTS

After 1975 the creative protest literature that had flourished in the decade before independence declined, and literary magazines such as *Kovave, Papua Pocket Poets Series*, and *New Guinea Writing* ceased publication. Exceptions were some of the entries to the nationwide annual literature competition conducted by the Institute of Papua New Guinea Studies. Entries were published both in English and the vernacular in new literary journals like *Ondobondo* and *Bikmaus*.

After a decade of independence, Vincent Warakai's poem 'Dancing Yet to the Dim Dim's [white men's] Beat' pointed out that colonial forces continue to call the tune, and Papua New Guineans continue to dance to it.

> We are dancing
> Yes, but without leaping
> For the fetters of dominance
> still persist
> Yes, still insist
> On dominating
> Holding us down
>
> We have been dancing
> Yes, but not for our own tune
> For we are not immune
> Yes, for our truly, our own truly
> Music of life is eroding
> Yes, the mystic tune holds
> Us spellbound

Our Independence is abused
. . .
We have been dancing
Yes, but the euphoria has died
It is now the dull drumming
Yes, of the flat drums
Thud dada thud da thud dada thud
Yes, it is signalling not the bliss
But the impending crisis[8].

While literature declined, the visual arts of painting, print-making, sculpture, and architecture, and the performing arts, including theatre, dance/drama performances, and band music, flourished. These creative artists continued, after 1975, to make social comment about the ongoing changes within the society. In the visual arts individual artists came to the National Arts School and used their natural talents to produce some of the best contemporary images. Gickmai Kundun, a villager from Simbu Province, for instance, used metal scraps such as car bumpers and hub caps and transformed them into new sculptural forms. Kundun contributed his artistic imagination to murals which adorn the national parliament, national museum, city offices, hotels, and churches. Gickmai, like many other contemporary artists, was concerned at the passing of traditional ways of life, and used his work to try to link the old and the new.

In the performing arts, the National Theatre Company, Raun Raun and Dua Dua Theatres produced dramatic performances throughout Papua New Guinea, and at international arts festivals around the world. In music, the Sanguma Band won international recognition for its skill in blending traditional and Western sounds.

J. A. Fishman once said, 'The quest is for modernity . . . and authenticity simultaneously, for seeing the world, but "through our own eyes", for going to the world, but in our own way'[9]. Or, in the words of playwright, politician and strong advocate of Melanesian identity, Bernard Narokobi:

The contemporary arts depicted by artists are our national treasures, the world's treasures, for in a very real sense they express what lies deep in our hearts, a longing to be new, yet rooted in our rich and ancient past[10].

Thus, in the eyes of many Papua New Guineans, the country found a national identity through blending the ancient and modern in the expressive arts.

LAW AND ORDER

One of the social issues with which creative artists and others were concerned was the growing lawlessness in society, particularly in the urban areas. The traditional social order began to break down during the colonial period when the Europeans imposed their own law. By imposing their own law they undermined the traditionally accepted systems of social control such as decisions being made by village elders, and tribal fighting conducted according to traditionally recognised rules. After independence Papua New Guinea to a large extent adopted the white man's law. However, the police and government officials did not have sufficient power and resources to impose this law, and at times tribal fighting resumed outside the customary accepted rules, often with the use of home-made fire-arms.

As village society broke down more and more, villagers moved to the urban areas in the hope of employment and greater access to Western goods. As there was no housing for most of these people, they built shanties out of any available materials and created squatter settlements. As there was very often no employment for them, many turned to crime. Frustration caused by this way of life also led to an increase in rape and domestic violence. The undertrained, understaffed, and underpaid police force was unable to deal with the rapidly rising crime rate. When the police did manage to catch criminals, the courts and the gaols lacked people and facilities to handle them.

There was also a serious increase in crime amongst the élite, with politicians openly breaking the Leadership Code, and businessmen engaging in illegal financial activities. This criminal activity on the part of those who were supposed to provide examples of good conduct and give leadership to society, further encouraged lawlessness at the lower levels of society.

GOVERNMENT

At independence, legislative power was vested in the national parliament. Executive power was vested in the National Executive Council, which consisted of the prime minister as its head and a maximum of twenty-seven ministers chosen by him, all of whom had to be elected members of parliament. In order to govern, however, the prime minister needed the support of a majority of the votes in parliament. This Westminster-style democracy survived the many political storms of the 1970s and 1980s.

Certainly Papua New Guinea was evolving its own version of Westminster democracy. A conflict between the executive and the judiciary is illustrated by the 'Rooney Affair' in 1979. Mrs Nahau Rooney was the Minister of Justice. She wrote two letters: one to the chief justice on a case involving an academic advisor who was issued a deportation order by the government; the other letter went to the public prosecutor, and it concerned the Minister for Planning and Development, John Kaputin, who failed to comply with a court order to submit taxation returns. This correspondence was interpreted by the judges as state interference with the administration of justice. As a result Mrs Rooney was tried in the Supreme Court and sentenced to eight months gaol. Prime Minister Michael Somare assumed the Justice Ministry, overturned the decision, and released Mrs Rooney. This action led to mass outbreaks from prisoners, student demonstrations, and the resignation of five judges, including the chief justice from the National and Supreme Courts. The government brought in a new chief justice and appointed Mari Kapi as the first Papua New Guinean judge. The constitutional crisis came to an end. However, this was an extraordinary and unusual situation; on the whole, the independent state of Papua New Guinea had established and maintained an independent judicial system.

From 1975 there was even less party political activity than there had been before independence. This was partly because most of the issues on which the parties had disagreed had been resolved. The timing of independence was obviously no longer an issue, and, as the Pangu Party abandoned its more-radical economic proposals and quietly dropped the reformist social democratic programmes embodied in the Eight Point Plan, there was no basic disagreement over economic and social policy. The policy of rapidly appointing local people to positions in the public and private sector was accepted by all except a handful of whites in the United Party and the National Party, who recognised that they had lost on the issue.

The personal interests of parliamentarians of all parties began to coincide as they developed or expanded their business interests. The Pangu Party joined other parties in the concern to keep down local wages and encourage foreign investment, and in so doing, distanced itself from the fledgling trade union movement. In an effort to fund political organisations, each party acquired interests in local businesses, a practice which encouraged a conflict of interest and corruption. Through both individual enterprises and the business arms of political parties parliamentarians became increasingly entangled with foreign business interests.

Changing allegiances of members of parties and changing alliances amongst the parties created political instability. The instability was particularly significant because it affected the governing coalition partners. In addition, there emerged, in this period, a series of allegations of corrupt practices involving parliamentarians. The instability within and amongst parties, and the corrupt practices of politicians, inevitably affected the operation and the morale of all parties.

There was disagreement within the executive of the Pangu Party on major issues including citizenship and the interpretation of some of the provisions of the constitution. The government appeared to be losing its grip on the country when, during the first year of office, it failed to meet expectations of providing policies in the national interest which would give the country leadership and direction.

The first national election, 1977

During the first half of 1977 the parliament was preoccupied with the first national election since independence. A coalition government consisting of the Pangu and People's Progress parties was returned to power with an increased majority. The United Party became the opposition, with its organisation in considerable disarray. Somare claimed victory, announcing that the people had given his coalition the mandate to govern again. However, by this time, the majority of Pangu Party branches were no longer active. As one commentator put it:

> elections in Papua New Guinea are not about 'mandates' in the sense that they are tests of public opinion on government performance and policy issues. Elections remain essentially electorate level contests between competing clan candidates and personalities, with the government being pulled together in the legislative arena[11].

The 1977 election had 879 candidates fighting for 109 seats, compared with 611 candidates competing for 100 seats in 1972. Candidates now needed to have both money and organisation for success, and a core of leaders and officials had already invested in real estate and other business interests to generate funds. Before the second election all parties produced platforms which amounted to a bland mass of documents which promised all things to all people. Pangu had an advantage over other parties in that the party's campaign was based on the popularity of Prime Minister Somare.

The result of the election was that out of ninety-four members of parliament who sought re-election, only thirty-five were returned, and nine of the eighteen ministers in the former government lost their seats. The turnover of politicians was partly due to members' failure to keep in touch with their electorates, and their inability to deliver goods and services. It was also partly the result of the preferential voting system. The 1977 election also indicated a rise in strength of the Pangu and People's Progress Party coalition and the decline of the United Party. One result of the success of the return of the government was that Somare, who again became the prime minister, stood unchallenged as the most adroit politician in the country.

Leadership code

Michael Somare was worried by the growing tendency of politicians and bureaucrats to become involved with foreign business interests. In the March sitting of the national parliament he proposed a stringent Leadership Code:

> For some time now . . . I have been increasingly disturbed by some of the trends I see in our country. I have become convinced that there are dangerous tendencies at work in our society and that if allowed to continue these tendencies will corrupt our policies, subvert our efforts at national development, and set us on the wrong road[12].

He went further to give notice of the introduction of a law dealing with the funding of political parties and their activities. He said:

> If we do not take these steps, history will record that I was a Prime Minister of a government of empty words — a government which entrenched the interest of a small élite and let the national goals of a fair, honest and equal society sink into the Waigani swamps[13].

However, Somare had not consulted his coalition partner about this proposal, and opposition to the Leadership Code was spearheaded by the leader of the People's Progress Party, Julius Chan. Thus the Leadership Code threatened the survival of the coalition government. The Code was also attacked by Iambakey Okuk, at the time a young, influential, and ambitious highlander. Shortly after, Michael Somare shelved the proposal because of the 'volatility of parliament and the desire to avoid instability'. The shelving of the Code only placed a temporary lid on hot soup.

When Okuk captured the leadership of the opposition he exploited the division and the personal animosity within the government coalition, consolidated opposition numbers, and mounted a sustained attack on the government's performance. By the August session the first motion of no-confidence was moved, and Okuk was nominated as alternative prime minister. Michael Somare again attempted to introduce the legislation on the Leadership Code but again retreated in response to solid opposition. During the debate the opposition leader was accused of 'being hungry for power politics' to which the colourful Okuk replied, 'If you are not hungry for power then you should be working for the missions and reading the Bible all the day'[14].

A government in turmoil

Nineteen-seventy-nine was a most difficult year for the Somare government. The government was plagued by industrial strikes, rural neglect, and allegations of mal-administration. Law and order had broken down in June when a state of emergency was declared in the five highland provinces. There were problems with ineffectiveness in the public service and apparent lack of solidarity in the National Executive Council. The government approached these problems on an *ad hoc* basis and frequently employed delaying tactics instead of meeting the challenges with decisive leadership. Many of the problems were referred to committees of which no less than ten were set up during the year. However, with the defeat of two motions of no-confidence it was clear that the opposition failed at that stage to provide an alternative government.

Change of government

Michael Somare's reign of eight years came to an end in 1980 when Okuk, the leader of the opposition, moved the fourth motion of no-confidence, nominating Julius Chan as prime minister. The vote of no-confidence was passed and Julius Chan was sworn in as prime minister on 11 March 1980.

From the outset Chan had little control over his newly-created ministry, given that each party in his coalition bargained both for the number of ministries per party and for the right to allocate portfolios among their own members. The coalition parties had little in common. As in the previous government the coalition parties disagreed on major issues such as the leadership code, decentralisation, and foreign affairs.

The government was held together by the prime minister and his deputy: a combination of Chan as 'manager' and Okuk as 'action man'. An example of the style of the dynamic pair concerned Okuk's deal to purchase the Canadian Dash-7 aircraft for the national airline, Air Niugini, at a cost of K27 million. Okuk, supported by Chan, completed the purchase before authorisation had been given by the National Executive Council. While the National Executive Council failed to reverse this decision, Okuk's action brought allegations of corruption. Corruption was becoming apparent in other areas also, and the Ombudsman Commission *Annual Report* of 1980 stated:

> Many leaders have got themselves involved in private businesses by instigating business groups or family business. Some leaders obtained loans from the Banks which were guaranteed to be repaid from funds to be made available from the Village Economic Development Fund (VEDF). Some people jokingly stated that the name Village Economic Development Fund is a misnomer, it should be called 'Leader's Economic Development Fund'[15].

The national election, 1982

By the 1982 elections, it was evident that Papua New Guinea had moved a long way from a conventional Westminster two-party system. There were eight major parties contesting the election: Pangu, People's Progress, National, United, Melanesian Alliance, Papua Besena, Papua Action, and the PNG Independent Group.

Although women were entitled to vote and comprised slightly over half of the voting population, very few women sought to enter parliament, even amongst those who had acquired some prominence in society. One of the reasons for the lack of female candidates appears to be that even those women who had become highly successful in the Western sector of Papua New Guinean society assumed that men were so prejudiced, and women so uninformed, that they would inevitably be defeated. The only women to enter the national parliament were Josephine Abaijah (1972 to 1982), Waliyato Clowes (1977 to 1982), and Nahau Rooney (1977 to 1987) who was the only Papua New Guinean woman to be included in

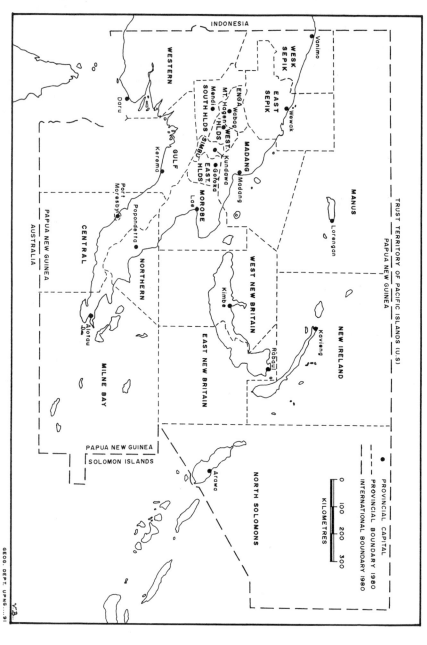

Provincial boundaries

INDONESIA

TRUST TERRITORY OF PACIFIC ISLANDS (U.S.)
PAPUA NEW GUINEA

WESK SEPIK
EAST SEPIK
Vanimo
Wewak
WESTERN
Daru
ENGA
Wabag
MT. Hagen
WEST HLDS
SOUTH HLDS
Mendi
SIMBU
HLDS
EAST HLDS
Goroka
Kundawa
MADANG
Madang
Lorengau
MANUS
GULF
Kerema
EAST
MOROBE
Lae
Port Moresby
CENTRAL
Popondetta
NORTHERN
WEST NEW BRITAIN
Kimbe
Kavieng
NEW IRELAND
Rabaul
EAST NEW BRITAIN
PAPUA NEW GUINEA
AUSTRALIA
Alotau
MILNE BAY
PAPUA NEW GUINEA
SOLOMON ISLANDS
Arawa
NORTH SOLOMONS

● PROVINCIAL CAPITAL
‒‒‒ PROVINCIAL BOUNDARY 1980
— INTERNATIONAL BOUNDARY 1980

0   100   200   300
KILOMETRES

the cabinet. The success of Josephine Abaijah was at least partly based on her leadership of Papua Besena, and Nahau Rooney came from Manus province in which the majority of people were better-educated than in other provinces.

Pangu, the best-organised and best-funded party, won fifty of the 108 seats, and thus became the senior partner in the coalition government. As the decade unrolled, it became increasingly evident that political processes were becoming dangerously fragmented, and there was still no evidence of the emergence of clearly identifiable ideological trends among the major political parties.

It would also appear that members of the smaller parties were motivated by self-interest, or the expectations of benefits and services which would accrue to the voters to whom the members were responsible. This situation seriously contributed towards political instability in Papua New Guinea which had seen five votes of no-confidence in the government in the first decade after independence. By 1985 national politics can best be described as being extremely formless, and politicians demonstrated an impressive ability to make 180-degree turns if this would help them gain government.

National Party politics absorbed the attention of the educated élite in both the public and private sectors. It should be remembered that those people constituted a very small percentage of the population. The daily lives of the rural majority continued to remain unaffected by changes in the party alliances and the associated instability at the national level.

Provincial government

In the colonial period Australia had imposed a highly centralised system of administration. Towards the end of the colonial period some regions tried to acquire some policy-making and administrative powers. These pressures led, immediately after Independence, to a commitment by the national government to a policy of devolution of power through the establishment of nineteen provincial governments.

The loudest regional voice was that of Bougainville, which had made a unilateral declaration of independence on 1 September 1975. This desire was undoubtedly connected with the

Bougainvilleans' desire to benefit from the well-established and successful Bougainville Copper project.

The central government's concern about Bougainville having a measure of autonomy was its fear of provoking similar developments in other parts of the country, so it took a particularly cautious approach to the situation in order to avoid setting an undesirable precedent. At the same time the government tried to establish a mechanism to harness the enthusiasm generated from other regions regarding devolution of power to the provinces. There were mixed reactions to the national government's decentralisation policy. While it was accepted in Bougainville as a compromise with Bougainvillean separatist demands, it was less well-received in other parts of the country. In some areas the response was at best lukewarm, and only in East New Britain and the Eastern Highlands did the leaders respond enthusiastically to the government's invitation to draft a provincial constitution.

Inevitably, Bougainville was the pace-setter, and established precedents for the devolution of power to provinces throughout the country. The Organic Law of 1977 divided powers between the national and provincial governments, and created a tier of semi-autonomous governments within the unitary state. However, the national government retained the overall power to intervene, suspend, or even abolish the provincial governments. The political consequences of decentralisation can be summed up at national, provincial, and local levels.

The national government regarded provincial governments as having complicated legal, administrative, and staffing arrangements which created potential conflict between the provinces and the centre, and which weakened the ability of the centre to plan, co-ordinate, and control an integrated development strategy. Some of these problems were highlighted in November 1977 when the provincial premiers demanded more power, including power to control public service salaries, foreign investment, citizenship, the police, and internal migration.

At the provincial level, those from the less-developed provinces began to fear, that the system of provincial governments would entrench regional inequalities. Also at the provincial level, a new arena of political conflict and patronage had been opened. A new stage had been set for traditional rivalries between provincial and national parliamentarians seeking either to build or safeguard their support base. For unsuccessful national-level candidates, the provincial governments had opened up a new power and patronage base for both politicians and bureaucrats. There was also a widespread feeling that provincial politicians should not align themselves with political parties.

At the local level there were disputes over the representation of certain groups in the provincial government, and the delineation of boundaries for planned local governments. Indeed, both the national politicians and ordinary villagers pointed their fingers at provincial politicians for what they perceived to be growing signs of extravagance, waste, corruption, and nepotism.

At the insistence of Bougainville's Father John Momis, the Ministry of Provincial Affairs was renamed the Ministry of Decentralisation in 1977 as a strategy for nation building. In the following year John Momis, who was also the de facto Chairman of the Constitutional Planning Committee, was appointed the first Minister of Decentralisation. Provincial governments continued to be established, and by July 1980 eighteen provinces had held democratic elections. However, only four of the provincial governments, Bougainville, East and West New Britain, and Eastern Highlands had achieved some measure of financial autonomy.

During the implementation of the decentralisation policy the administration of provinces was reorganised so that all public servants in the field came under the umbrella of a provincial department run by a secretary with the same status as a head of department in Port Moresby. Father Momis expressed serious concerns over rip-off attitudes and an excessive interest in the perks of office by provincial politicians, administrative overlap between the two tiers of government, lack of liaison between national and provincial members, financial mismanagement, and the reluctance of provinces to devolve powers to the local community governments. Towards the end of 1980 the national government had to come to the aid of four provinces in debt. The minister took steps to impose tighter financial controls by requiring forward budget estimates and monthly reports from all provinces.

Father Momis continued to champion the devolution of power, and in 1981 all the nineteen provinces had elected provincial governments. But by the end of 1983 corruption and financial incompetence were said to be widespread throughout the nineteen provinces. This forced the government to persuade parliament to adopt a simpler procedure for suspending provincial governments. Instead of the parliamentary vote to suspend them, now the National Executive Council was given a 'right to provisional suspension'. During 1984 the Enga, Manus, and Simbu provincial governments were suspended for financial mismanagement. Numerous motions of no-confidence, both successful and unsuccessful, disrupted the decentralisation system, and the national government was forced to impose certain minimum standards of performance and accountability.

However, in spite of the problems associated with the decentralisation process, all agreed on the principle of devolution of a certain measure of power to the provinces, and leaders of goodwill at both national and provincial levels co-operated in seeking better decentralisation processes. In spite of the heat generated by the decentralisation debate amongst the politicians, most of the people in the villages remained unconcerned by the changes in provincial politics. To most villagers the provincial politicians, like the national parliamentarians, were mainly concerned with their perks, powers, and privileges rather than with the well-being of the people whom they represented.

It is clear from Table 7.1 that the majority of the provincial governments were reluctant to devolve power further down to the village level. These provinces often retained, by default, the somewhat ineffective colonial local government system. A minority of the provinces have established effective community governments. The most successful province has been the North Solomons, where forty community governments were operating before the crisis began in November 1988. By then

Table 7.1 Local level government councils between 1974 and 1988

Province	1974 Local government councils (a)	1985 Local government councils (b)	Community governments	Total 1988
Central	11	11	—	11
East New Britain	05	—	20	20
East Sepik	11	22	—	22
Eastern Highlands	08	08	—	08
Enga	06	07	—	07
Gulf	07	08	—	08
Madang	15	16	—	16
Manus	01	—	16	16
Milne Bay	14	14	01	15
Morobe	14	03	17	20
New Ireland	05	05	—	05
North Solomons (B'vil)	09	01	40	41
Northern (Oro)	06	08	—	08
Simbu	09	09	—	09
Southern Highlands	14	14	—	14
West New Britain	06	10	—	10
West Sepik (Sandaun)	09	11	—	11
West (Fly River)	08	11	—	11
Western Highlands	07	12	—	12
Total (1988)	—	170	94	264
Total (1974 & 1988)	165	—	—	264

Notes: (a) Figures include interim councils and town commissions/authorities but not Port Moresby/National Capital District. (b) Figures include interim/preparatory governments.
Source: Peasah, J., *Discussion Paper No. 63*, National Research Institute, 1991, Appendix 1, p. 31.

two types of community government emerged: one followed the example of East New Britain and the other was based on the North Solomons model. There has been very little change from the colonial local government system in the first model, except appointing women representatives and making politicians at both national and provincial levels ex-officio members of the community governments. According to Joseph Peasah

> the provincial governments have not found it necessary to give traditional leadership structures or local political cultures any role in the community government system, despite rhetoric to contrary; nor are the local peoples given any significant freedom to determine their own forms of community government. The manner of composing the councils and determining their powers and functions are all provided for in the relevant provincial Acts.[16]

By contrast, however, the North Solomons model allows the local communities to devise the form and the content of the constitutional structures which are suitable to the various localities. Legal provisions allow for the appointment of some traditional leaders, or any other persons as members of the Councils, and accommodate various local political cultures.

> Let the people at the Community Government level do what is meant by the term 'government' by themselves provided that certain minimum standards are observed and certain common sets of rules are followed and a certain amount of control is recognised and the rights of people at the village level are not left unprotected.[17]

Thus, the community government system aims

> to promote and recognise traditional leadership and authority while merging these concepts with those of the modern government ideals and structures.[18]

In both models the community government areas are smaller than those of the local government councils established in the colonial period. The smaller size allows greater participation and accountability; preserves the territorial autonomy and integrity of the traditional ethnic and/or linguistic groups; consolidates internal cohesion and solidarity; absorbs the existing political changes and moulds the group as a viable entity for the community government. The basic distinction between the two models lies in the extent to which each model is prepared to allow the local village people to determine the forms of their community governments.

At the time of independence in 1975 there were 165 local government councils. Thirteen years later five more new councils were added under the old system in majority of the provinces whereas during the same period only ninety-four community governments were established in four provinces. Nevertheless, the most successful democratic and liberal types of community governments have been established in the rich province of the North Solomons, where the tragic conflict has been going on since November 1988. It is too early to assess the impact of the crisis on the local-level forms of government. Recent history informs us that the North Solomons Provincial Government facilitated the drafting of the constitutions of the various community governments

> so as to fit the law into the existing structure of the de facto community governments in operation in the provinces; [and the] local traditional, political culture had a substantial impact on the composition and operation of the community and village governments which were spontaneously and unofficially established by the people in the 1970s to replace the unpopular local government councils.[19]

This being the case, there is no reason to believe that the community governments collapsed under the weight of the current crisis. On the contrary the early success clearly demonstrates that the self-styled Bougainville Revolutionary Army (BRA) mobilised and utilised the existing village governments. Since September 1990, when the national security forces regained control over Buka Island, and given the rapid speed at which the government has been restoring normal social services in most parts of the province, there is no doubt that the national government has been imposing an interim authority over the existing community governments — or, rather, regaining the latter from the hands of the BRA. After the crisis is resolved the various community governments are likely to be strengthened rather than weakened. And this will lead to devolving further powers to the villages. Ultimately, as was the case with the secessionist threat in 1976 when the province became the pacesetter in the decentralisation process, the North Solomons Province will, after the current crisis, become the exemplar of the community governments in Papua New Guinea.

SUMMARY

Establishing or consolidating diplomatic, trade, investment and aid relationships with overseas countries was very important to the newly independent state of Papua New Guinea. During the decade the government changed from a Universalist foreign policy to a policy of Selective Engagement in which it attempted to concentrate attention on those countries most directly important to the progress of the nation. These countries included: Australia, which made the single most important contribution to the national budget; New Zealand and South Pacific island states; Indonesia and other South East Asian countries; China; Japan; the United States and the countries of the European Economic Community. Except for a period in 1980 when Papua New Guinea sent troops to assist the elected government of Vanuatu suppress a rebel attempt to capture government, relations were peaceful. The country also had important relationships with a number of international monetary and aid organisations and several transnational corporations.

In the economy the main development was in the exploitation of copper, gold, timber and fish resources. The most important single project was the copper mine operated by the trans-national Bougainville Copper Limited, which made a substantial contribution to the national budget but generated very serious environmental and social problems. Cash crops, of which coffee was the most important, trebled the value of their export earnings during the decade but did not make a significant contribution to the national economy. The secondary industry sector could not overcome the problems of high transport, power and labour costs and most consumer goods continued to be imported.

The national government maintained but could not expand

the health and education services inherited from the colonial period. This was in part due to a rapid population growth. Infrastructure facilities, such as telecommunications, electricity and transport, continued to provide efficient services to the urban areas.

Papua New Guinea showed itself to be in a unique position to choose the best aspects of both traditional and Western cultures as amply illustrated in the contemporary artistic forms, images and styles which blended the values of the old with the new.

Papua New Guinea's Westminster-style parliamentary system survived the many political storms of the post-independence decade. However, no party attracted a substantial membership or developed a clear ideological position. The differences which had existed among the leading parties prior to independence subsided in the post-independence decade. Many parliamentarians changed party allegiance according to individual or regional interests. The changing party alliances in the government was a source of political instability. However, as no one party had a monopoly of talent, changes in the party composition of the government did little to affect the course of events in the country. And as a number of talented citizens had joined the public service the affairs of the nation continued to be conducted by much the same group of educated Papua New Guineans who had participated in the negotiations which had preceded independence. However, as has been noted, this group was almost entirely composed of men.

An issue over which the national government had difficulty in exercising control was the aspiration of some regional leaders for greater autonomy for their regions. As has been seen, Bougainville, the Mataungan Association of East New Britain and Papua Besena had made strong moves for a measure of autonomy, or in the case of Bougainville complete separation, at the time of independence. While the growth of Port Moresby dampened the Papua movement, the East New Britain and Bougainville movements strengthened and several other regions made bids for a greater degree of power. In 1977 the national government legislated to establish nineteen provinces to which certain powers previously held by the national government would be devolved. However, by 1985 serious flaws had emerged in the provincial government system and the decentralisation processes again came under review.

One of the major social problems with which the country had to deal in this post-independence period was a rapid increase in serious crime some amongst corrupt members of the élite and villagers who had moved into towns but failed to find employment. The under-resourced police, courts and goals were unable to cope with this marked increase in criminal activity.

Thus, by 1985 the nation had a functioning national and provincial government system, non-aggressive relations with overseas countries, and an economy which operated at both monetary-sector and subsistence-sector levels. The monetary sector was heavily dependent upon the exploitation of natural resources and, to a lesser extent, the export of cash crops, and international aid — all of which were unstable sources of income. While many of the country's processes were based on highly sophisticated Western industrial models, the vast majority of the people lived in the subsistence agriculture sector and had only a marginal connection with the cash economy.

8

From Stone Age
to Space Age

National identity
Rooted in the Stone Age
Unique art forms
Display the dynamic change,
Expressive arts
Ushers in the Space Age.

[Anon].

As has been emphasised throughout the book the majority of the people live in the subsistence sector, and some communities are only marginally affected by the cash economy. In the rural areas the land group is still small in area and small in population and each society is made up of a number of families and relatives who own land. The membership of the household is based on kinship through blood, marriage, or adoption. In ethical terms, whatever helps the group maintain itself and the land is right, and whatever goes against the group is wrong; the welfare — food, family, work, safety, housing, and proper burial — of every individual member is guaranteed by custom. Leaders are chosen by the people by consensus on the grounds of ability and performance; the security of the land group household is the responsibility of every member under the guidance of the leaders, and the alliances of land groups form the foundation of defence. Many aspects of group life reflected in cults relate to land, fertility, ancestors, food, and defence. The economy is almost completely self-sufficient with some trading for specialised goods, and all natural resources are owned by the group. Almost all communication is face to face, and all knowledge of the past learnt from oral traditions is passed on to each succeeding generation by word of mouth.

By contrast, the modern independent state of Papua New Guinea has features which have evolved between 1884 and 1992. The size of the new nation is large, with a population of over three million people, and each individual within the national borders is a citizen, either automatic or naturalised, or a foreign resident in the country. All land and sea inside the national borders is under the 'control' of the state. Whereas the distinct ethnic land groups have particular ethical concern for the resources within the confines of the land group, the new state has ethical principles and rules by constitutional statute law that embraces all the people within the national borders. The state attempts to provide work but relies mainly upon individual groups in the subsistence sector to provide basic welfare. The political leaders are chosen by adult citizens through democratic election. The state has responsibility for both internal and external security as well as diplomatic and trading relations with foreign countries. In the modern state there is a distinction between the sacred world of the Christian religion and the secular world of economic and political activity. In addition the modern state is dependent upon the cash economy to provide the Western goods which many individuals now increasingly want. There is limited face-to-face communication, an increasing reliance on writing and electronic mass media, and some attempt to find common languages — English, *Pisin* and *Motu.* Among the young generation, oral history has been replaced by history heavily dependent upon documents produced by the colonial powers or, since 1975, Western-trained Papua New Guineans. Whereas in the past, members of each land group had limited opportunity for travel due to terrain, hostilities, and language barriers, nowadays travel is possible throughout the nation and beyond, on roads, ships, and aircraft. In terms of maturity, the various land groups have been weathered by hundreds of years and have a very stable character, whereas the independent state of Papua New Guinea has existed for only seventeen years, and the modern institutions as well as the system of government are still changing.

Nowadays the most important single distinction between traditional society and the modern state concerns land and resource use. The basic social unit is the land group as is well-recognised by a nationalistic lawyer, Peter Donigi.

> There is only one legitimate Papua New Guinea social, political and economic organisation in all villages and societies in this country. That organisation is the land group. Many battles and wars have been fought, won and lost over land throughout the length and breadth of Papua New Guinea. The land groups are a social and political unit. It is therefore imperative that land groups all over Papua New Guinea are registered at all costs and a system of customary land registration be brought into force as soon as possible.[1]

This is a prophetic warning, and the national government should take heed and assist land groups all over the country to begin the learning process of transition from customary management based on oral traditions to customary management assisted by the literate and electronic technologies of the modern world. To ignore the message is to ignite a bomb that might catch fire among hundreds of land groups who are extremely reluctant to give up the customary ownership of their land and other resources to the state.

Land is life, which means that villagers have a very strong emotional and spiritual relationship with land. In the modern state land is usually regarded solely as something to be exploited for material gain — to support buildings or yield resources which can be sold for cash.

There are several factors destabilising the modern state. Conflicts arise because traditional and modern societies have different concepts of land ownership and resource use. Whereas in traditional society land and the resources of the land are owned by clans, the modern state refuses to recognise clan ownership, but seeks to impose individual ownership under which individuals have rights to clearly demarcated areas of land. The modern state also refuses to accept that the resources such as minerals which lie below the surface of the land belong to the people who own the land — a problem which did not arise in traditional society. Moreover, there are water rights that include marine and fresh-water resources, whose ownership is claimed along the same principle as land.

The different concepts of ownership of land and water and the use of resources have been one of the reasons for the disputes between the villagers and the state in recent years. Amongst the most publicised and tragic of these are the forestry resource exploitation in the Golgol area, illegal transnational fishing in the 200 kilometres of the territorial zones. Ok Tedi mining activity and, the most disruptive of all, the Bougainville Copper Limited mine at Panguna. In each of these projects transnational corporations have aggressively exploited the Papua New Guinea élite's acceptance of the modern state's concept of land and resource use to the disadvantage of the villagers. In many instances landowners have agreed to a project without understanding the environmental implications of the project.

To date the most evidence of corruption comes from the exploitation of forest resources. For instance, the Barnett Forest Enquiry in 1989 revealed that there was a widespread practice of bribery in the granting of timber leases and transfer pricing (an illegal practice under which corrupt officials and politicians prevent the landowners, as well as the provincial and national governments, receiving the share to which they are legally entitled). There was also evidence that corrupt leaders had allowed timber firms to ignore the environmental clauses in their contracts, and that this had resulted in major irreparable damage to the land in areas under lease. The Forest Inquiry made recommendations aimed at curbing these practices. One of these recommendations was the establishment of a Tribunal to investigate allegations of corruption against the Deputy Prime Minister, Ted Diro. Following constitutional and legal wrangling, Ted Diro left the national parliament. Some of the major destabilising factors have to do with the exploitation of natural resources by transnational corporations whose impact includes social disruption, damage to the physical environment, regional and national disunity and political corruption.

There is a complex relationship between what are regarded as acceptable practices in traditional society and what are considered to be corrupt practices in modern society. In the traditional 'big man' system, leaders acquired and distributed wealth in order to establish and maintain status and power within their local communities. Nowadays politicians and public servants attempt to emulate the 'big man' by developing modern commercial business interests in order to accumulate wealth. To accumulate this wealth they often resort to illegal practices and taking lavish bribes offered by many transnational companies. Having accumulated wealth they are, in turn, expected to reward those who helped them acquire it, which means, in the case of politicians, rewarding their constituents. In addition, politicians with business interests often have a conflict between their parliamentary role and their business role which can result in their abusing their political power for personal gain.

A striking and tragic example of a transnational corporation's destabilising impact is the Bougainville Copper Ltd project at Panguna in the North Solomons. Because this crisis had repercussions throughout the nation it is worth examining in some detail. The main causes of the Bougainville crisis appear to be the alienation of the Panguna land on which the mine stands, and a rift between the younger and the older generations of Panguna landowners concerning the distribution of the benefits derived from the mine, and compensation payments for the environmental damage resulting from the mining operation. Between 1987 and 1988 Francis Ona provided leadership around which the younger generation rallied support to take control of a landowner corporation. They effectively took advantage of the people's resentment against the social and environmental impact of the mine to demand K10 billion from the mining company to clean up the mess.

In July 1988 the Namaliu government took over the reins of power and promised to give a better deal to landowners in all provinces with major mining operations, and to look into the grievances of the Panguna landowners in particular. In November, a meeting between Ona and the national government was held. Ona walked out of the meeting into the bush and attacked the sources of the company power supply and other mine facilities. The national government moved in to protect its major revenue earner by despatching police force riot squads to the island. This led to killings on both sides and, in early 1989, Ona included secession as an integral part of his demands. When the clashes escalated the government ordered the defence force to assist the police, but the conflict worsened and by May 1989 the mine was forced to close. By the end of the year the government's military option to solve the Bougainville crisis had clearly failed. A cease-fire agreement was signed between the two parties in February 1990, the national government's forces withdrew in haste, and the self-proclaimed Bougainville Revolutionary Army (BRA) took control of the mine and the entire province. This obviously provided a big boost for the BRA's demand for secession. The government imposed economic sanctions and offered to negotiate a peaceful settlement that included greater political autonomy and increased revenue for the province. The BRA rejected the offer and unilaterally declared the North Solomons province the Republic of Meekamui on 17 May 1990. The national government rejected the declaration and maintained its previous stance that the province remained an integral part of Papua New Guinea.

By July all the government and commercial services in the province had ceased, and the government suspended the North Solomons provincial government. However, the Premier James Kabui supported the BRA which had offered him a ministry in its self-proclaimed government. In early August both parties agreed to negotiate on HMS *Endeavour*, a ship provided by the New Zealand government. The agreement signed by representatives of both parties became known as the Endeavour Accord. This agreement contained, among other things, the provision that the national government restore social services to the province and that both sides meet in the immediate future to review the situation. In its efforts to implement the Accord the national government despatched the defence force to deliver food and medical supplies. According to the BRA the involvement of troops had not been agreed upon, and the government's attempts to restore services were hampered by the armed resistance of a hard-core of BRA rebels still on the island. Allegations of bad faith were exchanged between the BRA and the national government, with each side accusing the other of breaking the Endeavour Accord. However, there is evidence that there was also genuine misunderstanding by each side on the interpretation of the Accord.

The situation changed significantly in October 1990 when a BRA faction on Buka Island, an economically and socially important part of the North Solomons, broke away from Francis Ona and invited the national government to restore welfare and commercial services to the island.

However, the return of national government services to Buka did not resolve the situation, and BRA rebel activity continued. This North Solomons crisis was far more complex than the earlier threat of secession which Michael Somare was able to solve with his personal diplomacy and some assistance from leaders in the province.

Unlike the breakaway threat in 1976, when the secessionist call was confined to the towns, the current crisis had also affected the villages. Many people in the villages have experienced social and technological changes. An important social change concerns education. In 1992 many people believed that the national government school curriculum failed to provide sufficient and relevant rural education. In some schools a new syllabus has been proposed to include topics such as land management and crop rotation. Even within the established education system the crisis has created serious problems. Between 1985 and 1990, for example, only 18 per cent of Grade 6 leavers were selected to go to high schools and only 35 per cent of the students who entered high schools came from rural areas. Many village parents wish to reverse this trend. When the crisis is resolved pressure is likely to be exerted on the next provincial government to reduce the funding of urban schools in favour of rural schools.

An important technological change concerns the production of sago. Before 1988 the men pounded sago using adzes. Since then many men have been involved in the government's conflict with the BRA and women have been left to fend for themselves and feed their families. This has led to their taking over the responsibility of making sago. The men's ways of making sago produced noise, which attracted the attention of the BRA and the national government's security forces; the women have invented a quiet sago-making tool based on the principle of a pit-saw, which enables them to make sago without being detected. Furthermore, the sago that the women produce by this method is better ground and of better quality than that previously produced. These two examples highlight the fact that the current crisis has brought about some fundamental changes in the villages in addition to disrupting the flow of revenue from the copper mine to the national budget during the last three years. The impact of these changes is likely to set, as well as to influence, the future social, economic and political agenda for the North Solomons province and the national government.

In the present crisis there are various courses of action which could be taken in an attempt to solve the situation. These include the possibility that the national government comes to a compromise with the BRA and offers the North Solomons Province the status of an autonomous provincial government, as recommended by a joint national and provincial working party in March 1990. If this happens it will also be necessary to offer both the provincial government and the Panguna landowners an increased share in the mining project's profits. Another possibility is that the national government could decide to centralise all powers in Port Moresby and abolish the provincial government structure entirely. The second course of action would probably involve the occupation by the national defence force of the North Solomons Province for the forseeable future to enforce central government authority. A total military solution has already been unsuccessful, and it is unlikely that it would be successful in the future. In addition such a course of action would inevitably lead to an adverse reaction from some other provinces which could create further political and social unrest in other parts of the country.

In the interests of the people of the North Solomons Province and the Papua New Guinea state as a whole, it is to be hoped that the national government takes the compromise course of action, because under the current situation whichever side 'wins' the regional conflict, in the end the people of both the province and the nation are the losers.

In 1991 Papua New Guinea celebrated its sixteenth year of independence. At the ceremonies all national leaders, whether in government or in opposition, strongly emphasised the theme of national unity. In doing so they echoed the voice of the father of Papua New Guinea's independence. Michael Somare said in 1976 when he solved the first major Bougainville crisis:

> While the rest of the twentieth century is impatient, violent and insensitive, we are building a nation prepared to be patient and determined to peacefully resolve our differences ... In Papua New Guinea our ability to seek compromise, and our patience to seek peaceful solutions is something we can show the rest of the world with pride ... I believe we have shown this twentieth century ... what nationhood really means within the first year of our Independence[2].

Michael Somare was the leader of the government team in the Endeavour Accord and continues to enjoy the nation's respect as the founding father of independence and the fountain of Papua New Guinea's national unity. The current Bougainville crisis must also be solved so that Papua New Guinea enters the twenty-first century as a united nation. It is now generally accepted that even when people acted in good faith, tremendous mistakes in handling this tragic Bougainville situation have been made by all concerned: the Australian colonial administration, the successive national governments, Bougainville Copper Limited, and the Panguna landowners. The Bougainville crisis has been presented in detail to demonstrate the broader political, economic, and social implications of the exploitation of the country's natural

resources. This example also shows the difficulty in the inter-
face between what Sean Dorney calls the thousands of 'tiny
independent society states'[3] of land groups in the villages, and
the independent state of Papua New Guinea, particularly in
the last five years. The government must take notice of the
people's strong desire to take part in the cash economy
through the registration of customary land on a group rather
than an individual basis. A good beginning has been made in
the East Sepik Province where the provincial government has
introduced legislation to register land under group ownership.
This pilot project needs to be applied in other provinces, perhaps with slight variations, and it is in the national
government's interest to support such legislation.

Papua New Guinea is fortunate in having been endowed
with rich natural resources. All provinces have something to
share with the nation: gold, copper, oil, timber, fish, or fertile
land for growing crops. In this situation we can learn from the
experience of our traditional societies in which those who had
material wealth shared with others. A system of delayed
reciprocity operated in traditional societies. If someone was
short of food or bride price, other members of the clan would
provide it, and he or she would return the food or bride price
when able to do so. In the meantime he or she was under an
obligation to the relatives who had helped. This principle of
reciprocity often extended beyond the land group to adjacent
friendly or allied clans, which built up a network of reciprocal
obligations over time and space.

Given that Papua New Guinea is a nation made up of a number of provinces, we need to apply to this nation the principle
of reciprocity amongst the nineteen provinces. If each
province will share its wealth through contributing to the national purse as the North Solomons Province has done, the
nation, as a whole, will prosper. However, in order for this to
occur it is important that we work out ways in which this aim
can be achieved so that the landowners and the province from
which the resources come are the first but not the only ones
to benefit from the wealth of the region. If we can devise a
national profit-sharing natural resources policy which also
protects the environment, we will have learnt from the tragedy

of Bougainville. Papua New Guinea benefited from the substantial revenue from the North Solomons Province through
BCL in the past, and it must remain within the nation in order
to be reciprocated by the revenues generated from other
provinces. If the North Solomons Province secedes it will miss
out on the riches that will flow from such projects as Ok Tedi,
Misima, Porgera, Lihir gold mines, and the Iagifu oil field.
Papua New Guinea must learn from the mistakes of Bougainville and work out a viable sharing formula before it is too late.

While the revenue from the exploitation of the natural
resources has brought some benefits to some of the people,
the wealth acquired by some local people from alluvial gold
mining or royalties has created some difficulties. Some people
understand and use the money wisely, while others cannot
comprehend the cash economy, and do not realise that the
income from the sale of natural resources is limited and can
dry up any time. Some people are simply unable to grasp the
basic idea of how a cash economy works, and their sense of a
reasonable share is not in proportion. In an attempt to resolve
this problem, the national parliament has legislated that there
will be a limit of K5000 compensation for any single claim.
Compensation demands, both realistic and unrealistic, claims
over the use of land and other resources, damage to the environment, and killings are rife throughout Papua New
Guinea. The K10 billion demand by the Bougainvilleans, the
various compensation claims to the national government over
land on which towns and plantations were established, and the
claim of K2 million plus a thousand pigs as compensation for
the murder of the national Minister for Communication,
Geoffrey Balakau, are examples of these mounting problems.

In addition, the rapid expansion of the cash economy is
accompanied by an accelerating disintegration of traditional
society. An extreme instance of the social impact of acquiring
too much money too quickly comes from an elderly highland
woman who had a sweet potato garden on the other side of
the valley. Usually it took many hours or even a day to walk
across the ravine to collect the garden produce for daily meals
and some to sell in the market for cash. After a mining corporation was established she was given a lot of money from

the royalty payments. One rainy afternoon, wearing a traditional *pulpul* or a carefully woven and matted set of strings that covered her back and front private parts, and an old *bilum*, a string bag, hanging down from her head, she walked to a helicopter company official and hired a helicopter to go to her garden. She returned with a string bag of sweet potato and a bunch of neatly-chopped firewood in the helicopter, and saved herself a long, wet walk. The rapid transition that some villagers are forced to make from traditional society has a destabilising effect on village life.

Between 1985 and 1992 Papua New Guinea appeared to be on a threshold between traditional and modern ways of life. On the one hand, individual members from each land group throughout the country have been obliged, by custom, to retain their identity with the village groups, and on the other hand, the same individuals have become citizens of the modern state. New personal and group identities have been forged in order to relate to the new institutions established in different places: political groupings, commercial ventures, trade unions, and recreational and professional associations.

Many people are caught between the traditional and modern societies, and in some cases people have difficulty in coping with the demands and obligations of the receding traditional society, and the demands and expectations of the emerging society. This creates a situation of divided loyalties. Many people find it difficult to continue to identify with village society and at the same time become members of modern institutions.

These interactions pose challenges and create stresses which have resulted in a struggle to establish the legitimacy of the new groups, including the state itself. Individuals have struggled to have their identities recognised as competent citizens by the state and at the same time the independent state of Papua New Guinea is struggling to have its identity and authority recognised and accepted by its own citizens. Very strong district and provincial identities have also emerged at the expense of the traditional identity of the village land group. This group has been weakened and the village people are often unable to resist the state's attempts to use their land and resources. This situation has created particular difficulties for women who are, in many cases, getting the worst aspects of both the Stone Age and the Space Age cultures. On the one hand the breakdown of village society has undermined their status in that certain significant traditional roles performed by women are no longer recognised or encouraged. On the other hand when women wish to enter the modern market economy they are expected to maintain their domestic responsibilities as well as meeting the demands of paid employment in the modern society. In addition the women are discriminated against by black and white men in both the public and private sectors. However, in spite of these problems, Papua New Guinean women are emerging as a significant force in the new society.

One of the most disturbing destabilising factors has been the increase in urban violence. Hardly a day goes by without theft and break-and-enter crimes involving both people and property. Some crimes are committed by organised gangs of professional criminals, and some, mainly robbery and rape, by unemployed and frustrated youth. In addition there is now more domestic violence which often results in the breakdown of marriages as shown in the film 'Stap Isi'. In the last five years the country has witnessed an unprecented urban drift that has resulted in a rising tide of unemployment in the towns, where there is no social welfare system. This situation is made worse because of the increased affluence of the urban élite. This creates greater frustration, particularly among the educated youth, who often expect to secure employment in the cash economy. This expectation cannot always be met.

Larry Santana, one of Papua New Guinea's youngest contemporary graphic artists, lives in the nation's capital where, like hundreds of those without money, he has to beg or sift for food scraps in the discarded refuse. His drawings show poverty, hunger, and loss of traditional pride and dignity in city life. In describing a drawing entitled 'Self portrait: Struggle and Pain at the Six Mile Dump' the artist tells of how he scavenges from one of Port Moresby's dumps:

This is an image of myself, and the little settlement house

which I built is under me. There are my hands and my brush. Tears and blood are in my eyes. The silhouette of the people in the back are people coming back from the dump. They are my inlaws coming from the dump where they have collected scraps of food and material waste from the city. The background carving represents the traditional culture we have lost. The wash of red is the pain of living in the city — all those highrise buildings. The blue washing down below shows my little kids playing around the house. This is the struggle and pain that I face when I have no job and run out of money. I can't stand it. Life is not worth living but I have my family to care for. As an artist, I work with my brush to make money. But I can't paint. How can I live with only a few *kina*? How can I save money to make my work and yet still feed my family. I see the kids sick. It is such a struggle to keep us all together. I feel so down. Also how can I paint when these problems come into my mind. I can't hold the brush steady to do anything. These problems have gotten worse and so I wanted to put them down on paper. As you can see, the sketch is not too neatly done. But it is painting with feeling — from my heart to let the world know what is happening to artists like myself as we struggle to survive on the garbage dump[4].

This is a typical example of the pain, hunger, and loss of self-esteem experienced by many of those people who drift to the urban areas. Rapes, domestic violence, and urban crime occur as a direct result of drastic social change associated with the general breakdown of traditional values. The sad part of it is that the successive governments have failed to resolve the problem. An underpaid and frequently undisciplined police force has been unable to cope with the increasing crime, which is now also spreading quickly into many rural areas.

This problem is made worse by the fact that Papua New Guinea has one of the fastest growing populations in the world. This increase in population leads to conflicts which result from competing demands for land and other resources, particularly in the highlands and the Gazelle Peninsula. Sometimes this conflict erupts into group or 'tribal' warfare. Warfare was endemic to most traditional societies. The administration forcibly suppressed tribal warfare during the colonial period, but after the colonial authority was removed at Independence, tribal wars flared up, particularly in the highlands. Mainly as a result of the breakdown of the traditional sanctions, alternative means of resolving these problems no longer exists.

Tribal warfare also contributes greatly to the chronic law and order problems in the urban areas. When a killing occurs, especially in the highlands, the relatives sometimes attempt to avenge the death by killing a relative of the killer in a town. A good example of this widespread payback practice is the 1990 conflict between the Simbu of the Western Highlands Province over the killing of a Simbu businessman, allegedly by the Engans of the Enga Province. It was believed that the killing of an Engan student at the University of Papua New Guinea campus was done in retaliation by students from the Western Highlands Province. In some areas sorcery has replaced warfare as a means of avenging deaths. Although sorcery is illegal, many people continue to practise it, sometimes using chemicals, such as insecticides, under the cover of the traditional rituals. Most local, provincial, and national leaders, and the churches, speak out against crime and sorcery. However, in spite of the opposition of the leaders and the churches, crimes are becoming more violent, and sorcery is still common even in areas where all the people are practising Christians.

It is difficult to identify the cause of the current law and order problem. It is clearly not because a substantial number of people are starving or even hungry, as the strength of the subsistence sector makes it possible for the vast majority of the population to be adequately fed. One apparent cause, the failure of the society to meet the employment expectation of school leavers, has already been mentioned. A further cause seems to be that people want to acquire Western goods faster than society can provide them. That is, some people steal, not to meet real 'needs', but to buy introduced goods such as cars, beer, and tobacco. In addition, some take to random violence in reaction to a society which has lost many traditional values without replacing them with any positive alternatives.

So far I have emphasised the destabilising factors which have been operating within the society, and it is important to put them in the context of many of the positive factors that greatly contribute towards the stability of Papua New Guinea.

The most important stabilising factor in Papua New Guinean society is the strength of the subsistence sector which provides food, housing, and, in some cases, clothing, for the majority of the population. The continued existence of a functioning subsistence sector, combined with the social and family ties which most people in the towns have maintained with their villages, means that most urban dwellers can, if necessary, return to their villages where they can be provided with food, shelter, and a proper burial in the case of the bodies of the dead relatives. This is because most rural communities are not yet dependent on the cash economy, and so far do not consider themselves as being dependent upon government-sponsored services such as health and communication. This situation, however, is changing rapidly in areas where people are most affected by the cash economy. For instance, in the North Solomons Province when mining and mine-related employment ceased and the national government services were withdrawn, many people suffered considerable hardship.

Secondly, the diversified nature of Papua New Guinea's natural resources — minerals, timber, fish, and fertile land — means that the national economy is not dependent upon a single source of revenue. For instance, when world copra prices drop, the economy can be boosted by the export of copper; or the economic effects of a decline in the price of gold can be cushioned by an increase in the production of timber.

Thirdly, the sustained financial support from Australian and international aid and monetary agencies has contributed to economic stability. For example, when the Bougainville Copper Ltd mine was closed at Panguna in May 1989, Australia increased her aid, and the International Monetary Fund increased its loan to help account for the shortfall in Papua New Guinea's revenue. Often this kind of overseas assistance includes the construction and maintenance of the country's infrastructure, such as roads, and there are now plans to investigate the construction of a railway network. Given that road transport is limited by the difficult terrain, Papua New Guinea relies heavily on air transport. In 1990, however, the increase in the price of fuel for air and boats has set back the expansion of the transport system. This effect is most felt by operators of small airlines and the small boats such as dinghys and vessels with outboard motors which serve the people in the rural coastal areas. This difficulty could be overcome when Papua New Guinea successfully exploits its known oil resources and becomes less dependent on overseas aid.

Fourthly, a further factor which promotes stability and enhances national unity is the increasing tendency for Papua New Guineans to marry someone born in another province. As has been seen, the exchange of women in marriage in the traditional society, and the accompanying exchange of material wealth such as food and shell money, was one way of establishing or restoring peaceful relationships with neighbouring groups. While this custom continues to a limited extent, many people, especially in towns, marry someone born in another province. This modern practice serves much the same purpose by promoting harmonious relationships between the people from different regions. Thus, a social practice once common in small-scale societies between immediate neighbours now operates at the provincial and national levels.

Fifthly, the general acceptance by Papua New Guineans of the presence of the expatriate population also assists national unity. On the whole, the white expatriates, including those from Australia — the ex-colonial power — are usually well-regarded if they are working in the interests of Papua New Guinea, and there is little anti-white racism. Most Papua New Guineans recognise that the vast majority of whites return to their own countries. Apart from the local-born Chinese, no identifiable non-Melanesian ethnic group has emerged. On the whole the local-born Chinese are accepted as Papua New Guinean citizens, and there are not enough other Asians in Papua New Guinea to constitute significant ethnic groups, and a very few have become naturalised citizens. This absence of ethnic conflict contributes to national harmony.

The sixth stabilising factor is that the national leaders in 1992 were mainly those who led Papua New Guinea to independence in 1975. Whether in government or in opposition, the continuity of political leadership at the national level has been relatively stable. The democratic state has survived the political storms of its seventeen years of political independence and has at no stage been threatened with the likelihood of a military dictatorship. Whichever political parties have been in power, the government has pursued a workable and consistent foreign policy, successfully handled relationships with Australia, the major world powers, and the extremely delicate issues associated with Melanesian Irianese on the Indonesia–Papua New Guinea border. The continued existence of a relatively independent judicial system and an uncensored press, radio, and television service is further evidence of the strength of the young democracy.

There are some social factors which produce both stabilising and destabilising effects. Amongst these are: the role played by churches, the communication networks, and the education system.

On the whole, the various Christian denominations, particularly the established churches, encourage peaceful relationships amongst people from the various regions. In particular, the ecumenical movement which encouraged cooperation between the established churches from the mid 1970s promoted national unity. An exception to this is the behaviour of the expatriate and the Papua New Guinean Catholic church leaders in the North Solomons Province. Although the clergymen have advocated national unity in public, most of the bishops and priests have, in practice, supported the Bougainville Revolutionary Army and its secessionist movement. Support of Bougainville secessionists by some Catholic leaders has been a destabilising influence. A further destabilising factor has been the tendency for some of the more recently introduced fundamentalist Christian sects to undermine the authority of the established churches. In some areas these activities have led to violent physical conflicts.

Papua New Guinea has over 700 languages. However, English, *Tok Pisin* (also called Pidgin English), and *Motu* languages are now used across the country. Although English is the language of instruction in schools, *Tok Pisin* is gaining much currency among the younger generation, and *Motu* is used mainly by the older generation in the Papuan region. The Papua New Guinean parents from different ethnic groups in the society are no longer communicating in their mother tongues to their children. One result is that their children, especially in towns, are learning to read and write and speak English, and speak in *Pisin* or, in limited areas, *Motu.*

After 1987, television broadcasting stations were established in Port Moresby, Lae, and other major centres. Sophisticated methods of communication such as facsimile machines allow Papua New Guinea to transmit information on trade and commerce to other parts of the world. However, some of the destabilising factors presented earlier, such as law and order, are attributed by some people to the electronic media. In particular, most of the commercial TV programmes are of Western origin and have adverse effects on Papua New Guinean cultures. It is a national disgrace to allow programmes that corrupt the cultural tradition, while many of the excellent locally produced films such as *Shark Callers of Kontu, Cowboy and Maria Come to Town, First Contact, Man Without Pigs,* and *Tin Pis Run,* which portray Papua New Guinean identity and the current social problems, are not shown.

On the whole, Papua New Guineans being able to communicate throughout the country in *Pisin* is a stabilising factor, but because it is accompanied by a breakdown in traditional *Tok Ples* and other values, it is a destabilising factor. On the other hand, the widespread radio network has helped to spread English and, *Pisin* throughout the country.

By 1992 the system of education had produced both stabilising and destabilising effects. The common curriculum that runs through primary, secondary, and tertiary levels means that the system produces an educated élite with common basic values, and this encourages national unity. As indicated above, *Tok Ples* schools encourage cultural values and contribute towards the stability of the local community. On the other hand, the system has also created a high degree of expectation for further education that the national government has been unable to meet. Secondary school places, for instance, were available for only a very small proportion of the students who successfully completed primary schooling in 1990, and the remainder, estimated at around 50 000 were 'pushed' out of the school system. One of the consequences of the failure of these students to secure places in secondary and tertiary education is that the teenage youth are still not sufficiently qualified to be eligible for the jobs that are available in the increasingly sophisticated cash economy, and they are often unwilling to return to the village life and subsistence agriculture. As a result these youngsters frequently drift into the urban centres and join the criminal or 'rascal' gangs and become part of the growing law and order problem that threatens stability throughout Papua New Guinea. However in July 1992, the Wingti-led government abolished school fees in the primary schools and introduced free education.

On balance, the stabilising factors outweigh the destabilising factors in this period of transition. Most Papua New Guineans still live in societies which have many of the characteristics of the Stone Age. On the other hand, much of the population has been exposed to a Western society which has many of the features of the Space Age. Papua New Guineans often experience the best and the worst characteristics of each type of society. However, this situation puts the country in a unique position to take advantage of the best of both types of society and adapt traditional ideas and values to improve the modern society. In addition to the diversity of peoples and cultures, Papua New Guinea is blessed with rich natural resources in gold, copper, oil, timber, fish, and fertile land. The rapid population growth is a serious social concern, however the reasonably well-functioning subsistence sector still feeds 80 per cent of the population. This means that the country has neither beggars nor people starving to death in the villages or urban streets. This subsistence sector, in which the majority of the people have direct access to traditionally owned land and food sources, provides the basis for a substantial measure of economic and social security.

Few countries in the world have undergone such rapid changes as Papua New Guinea has experienced during the nine decades of Australian colonial rule, and over one-and-a-half decades of political independence. Papua New Guineans are now living through a period of considerable stress and change. It is amazing that most societies tolerate the country's cultural diversity and have so far successfully adapted to economic and social change. This gives confidence to the people and their leaders at the local, provincial and national levels — those who are determined to resolve the considerable internal and external problems and take Papua New Guinea into the twenty-first century as a united nation.

Notes

Chapter 1

[1] Powell, K., The First Papua New Guinea Playwrights and their Plays, MA thesis, University of Papua New Guinea, Port Moresby, n.d., n. 99.

[2] Whittaker, J. L., Gash, N. G., Hookey, J. F. and Lacey, R. J., eds, *Documents and Readings in New Guinea: Pre-History to 1889*, Queensland University Press, Milton, 1971, p. 189.

[3] Ibid., p. 189–90.

Chapter 2

[1] Monckton, C. A. W., *Some Experiences of a New Guinea Resident Magistrate*, Lane & Co, London, 1920, p. 228.

[2] Quoted in Joyce, R. B., *Sir William MacGregor*, Melbourne University Press, 1971, p. 132.

[3] Quoted in Joyce, ibid, p. 129.

[4] Jackson, C. F., *Native Labour Law and Practice in Papua New Guinea*, Law Book Company, Sydney, 1924, p. 1.

[5] Hess, M., 'In the long, run . . .: Australian Colonial Labour Policy in the Territory of Papua and New Guinea.' *Journal of Industralian Relations*, Vol. 25, No. 1, (1983).

[6] Wolfers, E., *Race Relations and Colonial Rule in Papua New Guinea*, Angus and Robertson, Sydney, 1975, p. 14.

[7] Neumann, K., Not the way it really was: Constructing the Tolai Past, PhD thesis, Australian National University, Canberra, 1988, pp. 1–6.

[8] Ibid., p. 27.

[9] Ibid., p. 1–2.

Chapter 3

[1] *Report of the Royal Commission on Papua*, 1907, p. 166.

[2] Hess, p. 68.

[3] Jackson, p. 1.

[4] Hess, p. 69.

[5] Jinks, B., Biskup, P., Nelson, H., eds, *Readings in New Guinea History*, Angus and Robertson, Sydney, 1973, p. 139.

[6] Lapi, T., The First Contact in My Village, unpublished, 1987.

[7] Ibid., p. 128.

[8] Native Regulation 1/1897, *Supplement to the British New Guinea Government Gazette*, Vol. X, No. 8, 1897.

[9] Native Crown Ordinance, *Supplement to the British New Guinea Government Gazette*, Vol. X, No. 8, 1897.

[10] Nelson, H. and Bowden T., Australian Broadcasting Commission, *Taim Bilong Masta: The Australian involvement with Papua New Guinea*, based on an ABC radio series, Sydney, Australian Broadcasting Commission, 1982, p. 20.

[11] Hess, p. 69.

[12] Jinks, et al., pp. 150–1.

Chapter 4

[1] Firth, S., *New Guinea under the Germans*, republished by WEB Books, Port Moresby, 1986, p. 187.

[2] Connolly, B. and Anderson, R., *First Contact: New Guinea Highlanders Encounter the Outside World*, Penguin Books, New York, 1987, p. 278.

[3] Hughes, I., 'Good Money and Bad: Inflation and Devaluation in the Colonial Process', *Mankind*, Vol. 11, 1978, p. 313.

[4] Gitlow, A. L., *Economics of the Mount Hagen Tribes, New Guinea*, University of Washington Press, Seattle, 1947 p. 16.

[5] Connolly and Anderson, p. 280.

[6] Ibid, p. 241.

[7] *Rabaul Times*, 5 November 1939, p. 3.

[8] Reed, S. W., *The Making of Modern New Guinea*, American Philosophical Society, Philadelphia, 1943, p. 416.

[9] *Pacific Island Monthly*, Vol. 6, No. 3, 1935, p. 75.

[10] Willis, I., *Lae, Village and City*, Melbourne University Press, Melbourne, 1974 p. 93.

[11] Gammage, B., 'The Rabaul Strike, 1929', *Journal of Pacific History*, Vol. 10, Nos 3–4, 1975, p. 3–29.

[12] Ibid., p. 10.

[13] Ibid., p. 12.

[14] Ibid., p. 18–19.

[15] Ibid., p. 20.

[16] Ibid., p. 26.

[17] Ibid., p. 20–1.

[18] Ibid., p. 24.

[19] Ibid., p. 28.

[20] Laracy, H., *Marists and Melanesians: A History of Catholic Missions in the North Solomons*, Australian National University Press, Canberra, 1976, p. 46.

Chapter 5

[1] Waiko, J., 'Binandere Songs', *Bikmaus: A Journal of Papua New Guinea Affairs, Ideas and the Arts*, Vol. 5, No. 3, 1984, p. 23.

[2] Waiko, J., 'The damp soil my bed, rotten log my pillow', *Journal of Solomon Island Studies*, No. 4. 1988, p. 45.

3   Ryan, P., 'The Australian New Guinea Administrative Unit (ANGAU)' in *The History of Melanesia: Second Waigani Seminar*, ed. K. S. Inglis, Australian National University Press, Canberra and the University of Papua New Guinea Press, Port Moresby, first published 1969, reprinted 1971, p. 540.

4   Ibid., p. 542.

5   Ibid., p. 504.

6   Ibid., p. 502.

7   Waiko, p. 46.

8   Waiko, J., 'Oral History and the War: in White, G., *Remembering the Pacific War, Occasional Paper Series*, University of Hawaii, Honolulu 1991, p. 3.

9   Reed, p. 261.

10   Hogbin, H. I., *Transformation Scene: the Changing Culture of a New Guinea Village*, Routledge and Kegan Paul, London, 1951, p. 278.

11   Barrett, D., 'The Pacific Islands Regiment', in *The History of Melanesia: Second Waigani Seminar*, ed. K. S. Inglis, Australian National University Press, Canberra and the University of Papua New Guinea Press, Port Moresby, 1971, p. 501.

12   Waiko, p. 12.

13   Silata, W. P. B., The Oral History and Historical Archaeology of the Pacific War on Huon Peninsula, Moroke Province, BA Honours thesis, University of Papua New Guinea, Port Moresby, 1986, p. 65.

14   Chalk, A. J., The King's Reward: the Australian army's execution of Papua New Guinean 'natives' 1942–1945, BA Honours thesis, University of New South Wales, 1986.

15   Allen, B. J., Information Flow and Innovation Diffusion in the East Sepik District, Papua New Guinea, PhD thesis, Australian National University, Canberra, 1976, p. 380.

16   Inglis, K. S., 'War, Race and Loyalty in New Guinea 1939–1945', *The History of Melanesia: Second Waigani Seminar*, ed. K. S. Inglis, Australian National University Press, Canberra and the University of Papua New Guinea Press, Port Moresby, 1971, p. 503.

17   Murray, J. K., 'In Retrospect, 1945–1952: Papua New Guinea and Territory of Papua New Guinea', *The History of Melanesia: Second Waigani Seminar*, ed. K. S. Inglis, Australian National University Press, Canberra and the University of Papua New Guinea Press, Port Moresby, 1971, p. 187.

18   Downs, I., *The Australian Trusteeship: Papua New Guinea 1945–75*, Australian Government Publishing Service, Canberra, 1980, p. 39.

19   Cited in Powell, K., The First Papua New Guinea Playwrights and Their Plays, M.A. thesis University of Papua New Guinea, Port Moresby, n.d. p. 18.

[20] Matane, P., 'Recording: Use and Abuse', *Papua New Guinea Writing* No. 16, December 1974, p. 19.

[21] Smith, P. and Guthrie, G., 'Children, Education and Society in *The Education of Papua New Guinea Child*' ed. S. Weeks, University of Papua New Guinea, 1980. p. 8.

[22] Cited in Delpit, L. and Kemelfield, G., 'Building on Melanesian Foundations: viles tok ples skuls in the North Solomons' in King, P., Lee, W., Warakai, V., eds, *From Rhetoric to Reality: Papers from the Fifteenth Waigani Seminar*, University of Papua New Guinea Press, Port Moresby 1985, p. 422.

[23] *Territory of New Guinea, Annual Report*, Vol. 50, 1949, p. 43–46.

[24] Downs, p. 101.

[25] Willis, I., p. 193.

[26] Waiko, cited in Powell, p. 133.

[27] Tawali, K., *Signs in the Sky*, Papua Pocket Poets Series, Port Moresby, 1970, n.p.

[28] Connolly and Anderson, p. 278.

[29] Ibid.

[30] Ibid.

[31] Valentine, C. A., personal communication, 6 August 1978.

Chapter 6

[1] Downs, p. 253.

[2] *International Bank of Reconstruction and Development Report*, Canberra, 1964, p. 32.

[3] Ibid., p. 33–34.

[4] Downs, p. 385.

[5] Ibid., p. 253.

[6] Currie, G., *Commission on Higher Education Report*, 1964.

[7] Gris, G., *Committee of Inquiry into University Education*, 1974.

[8] Weeden, W. J., et al., *Advisory Committee on Education in Papua New Guinea Report*, Department of External Territories, 1969.

[9] Wolfers, E., p. 178.

[10] Powell, p. iv.

[11] Ibid.

[12] Ibid.

[13] Kasaipwalova, J., '*Reluctant Flame*', Papua Pocket Poets Series, Vol. 29, Port Moresby, 1971, n.p.

[14] Ibid.

[15] Downs, p. 250.

[16] Johnson, L. W., *Colonial Sunset: Australia and Papua New Guinea 1970–74*, University of Queensland Press, Brisbane, 1983, p. 3.

[17] Ibid., p. 110.

18 *Papua New Guinea House of Assembly Debates*, Vol. 3, No. 2, p. 587.
19 *Papua New Guinea House of Assembly Debates*, Vol. 4, No. 2, p. 297.
20 Johnson, p. 152.
21 Ibid., p. 252.
22 Ibid.

Chapter 7

1 Denoon, D., 'Papua New Guinea Political Chronicle: January to June 1976', *The Australian Journal of Politics and History*, Vol. 22, No. 3, 1976, p. 436.
2 Jackson, R. D., *Report of the Committee to Review the Australian Aid Program*, Australian Government Publishing Service, Canberra 1984.
3 Amarshi, A., Good, K., Mortimer, R., *Development and Dependency: the Political Economy of Papua New Guinea*, Oxford University Press, Melbourne, 1979, p. xiv.
4 Hegarty, D. W., 'Papua New Guinea Political Chronicle' *The Australian Journal of Politics and History*, Vol. 23, 1977, p. 453–461.
5 Dove, J., Miriung, T., Togolo, M., 'Mining Bitterness' Sack, P. G., *Problem of Choice: Land in Papua New Guinea's Future*, Australian National University Press, 1974, p. 182.
6 Ibid.
7 Hess, M., 'Doing Something for the Workers . . .?': the establishment of Port Moresby's Central District Waterside Workers' Union, *Labour History*, Vol. 54, 1988, p. 83–98.
8 Warakai, V., 'Dancing Yet to the Dim Dim's Beat' *Ondobondo*, No. 4, 1984, cover.
9 Fishman, J. A., *Language and Nationalism: Two Integrative Essays*, Newbury House Publishers, Massachusetts, 1972, p. 73.
10 Narokobi, B. M., 'Transformation in Art and Society', in Simons, S. C. and Stevenson, H., *Luk Luk Gen! Look Again: Contemporary Art from Papua New Guinea*, Perc Tucker Regional Gallery, Townsville, 1990, p. 17.
11 Anon., *The Australian Journal of Politics and History*, Vol. 23, No. 3, p. 454.
12 National Parliamentary Debates, 3 March 1978, *Papua New Guinea Government Gazette*, 5 April 1978, p. 6, p. 14.
13 Ibid.
14 Hegarty, D. W., 'Papua New Guinea: Political Chronicle', *The Australian Journal of Politics and History*, Vol. 25, No. 1, 1979, p. 108.
15 *Ombudsman Commission of Papua New Guinea, Fifth Report*, Government Printer, 1980, p. 5.
16 Peasah, J., 'Provincial Initiatives in Establishing Forms of Local-level Government in Papua New Guinea, *Discussion Paper No. 63*, National

Research Institute, Boroko, 1991, p. 21.

17 North Solomons Province 'Explanatory Note: Community Government Act 1978', unpublished mimeograph, 1978, p. 3.

18 Togolo, M., *Provincial Government in Papua New Guinea: the North Solomons Experience*, Arawa, 1986, p. 12.

19 Peasah, p. 21.

Chapter 8

1 Donigi, P., 'The State and the Property Rights in Papua New Guinea' unpublished paper, p. 3.

2 *National Parliamentary Debates*, 6 November 1976, p. 212.

3 Dorney, S., *Papua New Guinea: People, Politics and History Since 1975*, Random House, Milsons Point, 1990, p. 221–234.

4 Cited in Smalley, S. F., *Contemporary Art of Papua New Guinea*, Anderson Gallery, Bridgewater State College, New York, November 1989, n.p.

Bibliography

Only those sources which have been cited in notes and references or which gave relevant background information appear in this bibliography. For a more comprehensive list of published sources see, for example, *Papua New Guinea National Bibliography* which has been published each year since 1982 by the National Library, Port Moresby, Papua New Guinea.

Allen, B. J., Information Flow and Innovation Diffusion in the East Sepik District, Papua New Guinea (PhD thesis, Australian National University, Canberra, 1976).

Amarshi, A., Good, K., Mortimer, R., *Development and Dependency: the Political Economy of Papua New Guinea* (Oxford University Press, Melbourne 1979).

Annual Report, Territory of New Guinea, 1949.

Anon., *The Australian Journal of Politics and History*, Vol. 23, No. 3.

Ballard, J. A., ed., *Policy Making in a New State: Papua New Guinea 1972–77* (University of Queensland Press, Brisbane, 1981).

Barrett, D., 'The Pacific Islands Regiment', in *The History of Melanesia: Second Waigani Seminar*, ed. K. S. Inglis (Australian National University Press, Canberra and the University of Papua New Guinea Press, Port Moresby, 1971).

Chalk, A. J., The King's Reward: the Australian army's execution of Papua New Guinean 'natives' 1942–1945 (BA Honours thesis, University of New South Wales, 1986).

Cleland, R., *Papua New Guinea: Pathways to Independence* (Artlook Books, Perth, 1983).

Connolly, B. and Anderson, R., *First Contact: New Guinea Highlanders Encounter the Outside World* (Penguin Books, New York, 1987).

Currie, Sir George, Report of the Commission on Higher Education in Papua and New Guinea (Canberra, 1964).

Delbo, G., *The Mastard Seed: From French Mission to Papuan Church 1885–1985* (Institute of Papua New Guinea Studies, Port Moresby, 1985).

Delpit, L. and Kemelfield, G. 'Building on Melanesian Foundations: viles tok ples skuls in the North Solomons' in King, P., Lee, W., Warakai, V., eds, *From Rhetoric to Reality: Papers From the Fifteenth Waigani Seminar* (University of Papua New Guinea Press, Port Moresby, 1985).

Denoon, D., 'Papua New Guinea Political Chronicle: January to June 1976', *The Australian Journal of Politics and History* Vol. 22, No. 2 (1976) pp. 435–43.

Denoon, D., 'Changes in Rural Settlement and Marketing Co-operatives' in *Papua New Guinea Atlas: A Nation in Transition* (Robert Brown and Associates Pty Ltd in association with the University of Papua New Guinea, 1982).

Denoon, D. and Lacey, R. J., eds, *Oral Tradition in Melanesia* (University of Papua New Guinea Press, Port Moresby, 1978).

Denoon, D. and Snowden, C., eds, *A Time to Plant and Time to Uproot: a History of Agriculture in Papua New Guinea* (University of Papua New Guinea Press, Port Moresby, 1981).

Donigi, P., The State and Property Rights in Papua New Guinea, unpublished paper.

Dorney, S., *Papua New Guinea: People, Politics and History since 1975* (Random House, Sydney, 1990).

Dove, J., Miriung, T. and Togolo, M., 'Mining Bitterness' in *Problem of Choice: Land in Papua New Guinea's Future*, ed. P. G. Sack (Australian National University Press, Canberra, 1974).

Downs, I., *The Australian Trusteeship: Papua New Guinea 1945–75* (Australian Government Publishing Service, Canberra, 1980).

Encyclopaedia of Papua New Guinea, Vols. I and II (Melbourne University Press in Association with the University of Papua and New Guinea, 1972).

Eri, V., *The Crocodile* (Jacaranda Press, Brisbane, 1970).

Firth, S., *New Guinea Under the Germans*, (Republished by WEB Books, Port Moresby, 1986).

Fishman, J. A., *Language and Nationalism: Two Integrative Essays*, Newbury House Publishers, Massachusetts, 1972.

Gammage, B., 'The Rabaul Strike, 1929', *Journal of Pacific History*, Vol. 10, Nos 3–4 (1975).

Gash, N. and Whittaker, J., *A Pictorial History of New Guinea* (Jacaranda Press, Brisbane, 1975).

Gitlow, A. L., *Economics of the Mount Hagen Tribes, New Guinea* (University of Washington Press, Seattle, 1947).

Griffin, J., 'Papua New Guinea: Political Chronicle' *The Australian Journal of Politics and History* Vol. 21, No. 1 (1975) pp. 123–31.

Griffin, J., Nelson, H. and Firth, S., *Papua New Guinea: a Political History* (Heinemann Educational Australia, 1979).

Gris, G. B., Papua New Guinea Committee of Inquiry into University Development Report, (1974).

Hannett, L. et al., *Five New Guinea Plays* (Jacaranda Press, Brisbane, 1970).

Hegarty, D. W., 'Papua New Guinea: Political Chronicle' *The Australian Journal of Politics and History* Vol. 23, No. 1 (1977) pp. 453–61.

—— 'Papua New Guinea: Political Chronicle' *The Australian Journal of*

Politics and History Vol. 25, No. 1 (1979) pp. 401–08.

—— 'Papua New Guinea: Political Chronicle' *The Australian Journal of Politics and History* Vol. 28, No. 3 (1982) pp. 401–08.

Hess, M., 'Unionism and Economic Development: a Papua New Guinea Case Study' (PhD thesis, University of New South Wales, Sydney, 1986).

—— 'In the long run . . .: Australian Colonial Labour Policy in the Territory of Papua and New Guinea' *Journal of Industralian Relations* Vol. 25, No. 1 (1983).

—— 'Doing Something for the Workers . . . ? the establishment of Port Moresby's Central District Waterside Workers' Union' *Labour History* Vol. 54, (1988).

Hogbin, H. I., *Transformation Scene: the Changing Culture of a New Guinea Village* (Routledge & Kegan Paul, London, 1951).

Hughes, I. 'Good Money and Bad: Inflation and Devaluation in Colonial Process', *Mankind* Vol. 11 (1976).

Inglis, K. S., ed., *The History of Melanesia: Second Waigani Seminar* (Australian National University Press, Canberra and the University of Papua New Guinea Press, Port Moresby, 1971).

Inglis, K. S., 'War, Race and Loyalty in New Guinea 1939–1945' in *The History of Melanesia: Second Waigani Seminar*, ed. K. S. Inglis (Australian National University Press, Canberra and the University of Papua New Guinea Press, Port Moresby, 1971) pp. 503–30.

International Bank of Reconstruction and Development Report (Canberra, 1964).

Jackson, C. F., *Native Labour Law and Practice in Papua* (Law Book Company, Sydney, 1924).

Jackson, R. D., *Report of the Committee to Review the Australian Aid Program* (Australian Government Publishing Service, Canberra, 1984).

Javodimbari, A., *Return to My Land* (Papuan Pocket Poet Series, Port Moresby, 1974).

Jinks, B., Biskup, P. and Nelson, H., eds, *Readings in New Guinea History* (Angus and Robertson, Sydney, 1973).

Johnson, L. W., *Colonial Sunset: Australia and Papua New Guinea 1970–74* (University of Queensland Press, Brisbane, 1983).

Joyce, R. B., *Sir William MacGregor* (Melbourne University Press, 1971).

Kasaipwalova, J., *Reluctant Flame* (Papua Pocket Poet Series, Vol. 29, Port Moresby, 1971).

Kiki, A. M., *Ten Thousand Years in a Lifetime: A New Guinea Autobiography* (Cheshire, Melbourne, 1968).

King, D. and Ranck, S., eds, *Papua New Guinea Atlas: a Nation in Transition* (Robert Browne Associates, Pty Ltd [Australia] in association with the University of Papua New Guinea, 1982).

King, P., 'Papua New Guinea: Political Chronicle *The Australian Journal of Politics and History* Vol. 28, No. 1 (1982) pp. 461–74), Vol. 29, No. 1 (1983) pp. 530–3, Vol. 30, No. 1 (1984) pp. 279–82.

King, P., Lee, W. and Warakai, V., eds, *From Rhetoric to Reality: Papers From the Fifteenth Waigani Seminar* (University of Papua New Guinea Press, Port Moresby, 1985).

Laracy, H., *Marists and Melanesians: A History of Catholic Missions in the North Solomons* (Australian National University Press, Canberra, 1976).

Lapi, T., The First Contact in My Village (unpublished, 1987).

Latukefu, S., ed., *Papua New Guinea: a Century of Colonial Impact 1884–1984* (The National Research Institute and the University of Papua New Guinea, Port Moresby, 1989).

Legge, J. D., *Australian Colonial Policy* (Angus & Robertson, Sydney, 1956).

Matane, P., 'Recording: Use and Abuse', *Papua New Guinea Writing*, No. 16 (December 1974).

Monckton, C. A. W., *Some Experiences of a New Guinea Resident Magistrate* (Lane & Co., London, 1920).

—— *Last Days in New Guinea, Being Further Experiences of a New Guinea Magistrate* (Lane & Co., London, 1922).

—— *New Guinea Recollections* (Lane & Co., London, 1934).

Moore, C. R. and Griffin, J. T., eds, *Colonial Intrusion* (University of Papua New Guinea Press, Port Moresby, 1984).

Murray, J. K., 'In Retrospect, 1945–1952: Papua New Guinea and Territory of Papua New Guinea' in *The History of Melanesia: Second Waigani Seminar*, ed. K. S. Inglis (Australian National University Press, Canberra and the University of Papua New Guinea Press, Port Moresby, 1971) pp. 177–208.

Narokobi, B. M., 'Transformation in Art and Society', in Simons, S. C. and Stevenson, H., *Luk Luk Gen! Look Again: Contemporary Art from Papua New Guinea* (Perc Tucker Regional Gallery, Townsville, 1990, p. 17).

National Parliamentary Debates (6 November 1976).

National Parliamentary Debates (3 March 1978).

Native Crown Ordinance, Supplement to the British New Guinea Government Gazette, Vol. X, No. 8 (1897).

Native Regulation 1/1897, *Supplement to the British New Guinea Government Gazette*, Vol. X, No. 8 (1897).

Nelson, H. N., *Papua New Guinea: Black Chaos or Black Unity* (Melbourne University Press, 1972).

—— *Black, White and Gold* (Australian National University Press, Canberra, 1976).

Nelson, N. N. and Bowden, T., Australian Broadcasting Commission. *Taim Bilong Masta: the Australian Involvement in Papua New Guinea* (Australian Broadcasting Commission, Sydney, 1982).

Neumann, K., Not the Way It Really Was: Constructing the Tolai Past (PhD thesis, Australian National University, Canberra, 1988).

North Solomons Province 'Explanatory Note: Community Government Act 1978', unpublished mimeograph, 1978.

Ombudsman Commission of Papua New Guinea: Fifth Report, (Government Printer, 1980).

Pacific Island Monthly Vol. 6, No. 3 (1935).

Papua Annual Reports 1900–1901.

Papua New Guinea Department of the Administrator, *Report of the Committee of Enquiry into Local Government Finance and Borrowing* (1972).

Papua New Guinea Government Gazette (April 1978).

Papua New Guinea House of Assembly Debates, Vol. 3, No. 2.

Papua New Guinea House of Assembly Debates Vol. 4, No. 2 (1971).

Papua New Guinea Post Courier (22 August 1978).

Papua New Guinea Writing (No. 6, December 1974).

Parliamentary Debates (22 March 1985).

Peasah, J., 'Provincial Initiatives in Establishing Forms of Local-level Government in Papua New Guinea, *Discussion Paper No. 63*, (National Research Institute, Boroko, 1991).

Pokawin, S., 'Papua New Guinea Political Chronicle: January to December 1979' *The Australian Journal of Politics and History* Vol. 25, No. 1 (1979) pp. 406–11.

Powell, K., The First Papua New Guinea Playwrights and their Plays (MA thesis, University of Papua New Guinea, Port Moresby, n.d.).

Rabaul Times, (5 November 1939).

Reed, S. W., *The Making of Modern New Guinea* (American Philosophical Society, Philadelphia, 1943).

Report of the Royal Commission on Papua 1907.

Rowley, C. D., *The Australians in German New Guinea 1914–21* (Melbourne University Press, 1958).

Ryan, P., 'The Australian New Guinea Administrative Unit (ANGAU)' in *The History of Melanesia: Second Waigani Seminar* ed. K. S. Inglis (Australian National University Press, Canberra and the University of Papua New Guinea Press, Port Moresby, 1971).

Saffu, Y., 'Papua New Guinea: Political Chronicle: January–June 1985' *The Australian Journal of Politics and History* Vol. 31, No. 1 (1985) pp. 531–4, Vol. 32, No. 1 (1985) pp. 94–500.

Shaw, B., 'Yokio Shibata: a Man of Inspiration' in *Remembering the Pacific War* ed. G. White (University of Hawaii Press, Honolulu, 1991).

Silata, W. P. B., The Oral History and Historical Archeology of the Pacific War on Huon Peninsula, Morobe Province (BA Honours thesis, University of Papua New Guinea, Port Moresby, 1986).

Simons, S. C. and Stevenson, H., *Luk Luk Gen! Look Again: Contemporary Art From Papua New Guinea* (Perc Tucker Regional Gallery, Townsville, 1990).

Sinclair, J., *Kiap: Australia's Patrol Officers in Papua New Guinea* (Pacific Publication, Sydney, 1981).

Smalley, S. F., *Contemporary Art of Papua New Guinea* (Anderson Gallery, Bridgewater State College, New York, November 1989).

Smith, P., *Education and Colonial Control in Papua New Guinea: A Documentary History* (Longman Cheshire, Melbourne, 1987).

Smith, P. and Guthrie, G., 'Children, Education and Society' in Weeks, S. ed. *The Education of Papua New Guinea Child* (University of Papua New Guinea Press, Port Moresby, 1980).

Somare, M. T., *Sana* (Port Moresby, 1975).

Stephen, M., Continuity and Change in Mekeo Society, 1890–1971 (PhD thesis, Australian National University, Canberra, 1974).

Tawali, K., *Signs in the Sky* (Papua Pocket Poets Series Port Moresby, 1970).

Territory of New Guinea, Annual Report, Vol. 50 pp. 43–6.

Togolo, M., *Provincial Government in Papua New Guinea: the North Solomons Experience* (Arawa, 1986).

—— Land, Mining and Redistribution: Panguna and Ok Tedi, (MA thesis, East West Centre, Hawaii, 1989).

Waiko, J. D., Be Jijimo: A History According to the Tradition of the Binandere People of Papua New Guinea (PhD thesis, Australian National University, Canberra, 1982).

—— 'Binandere Songs,' *Bikmaus: A Journal of Papua New Guinea Affairs, Ideas and the Arts*, Vol. 5, No. 3 (1984).

——'Binandere Oral Traditions: Problems of Method in a Melanesian Society' *Journal of Pacific History* Vol. xxi, No. 1 (1986).

—— 'The damp soil my bed, rotten log my pillow' *Journal of Solomon Island Studies* No. 4 (1988).

——'Australian Administration under Binandere Thumb' in *Papua New Guinea: A Century of Colonial Impact 1884–1984* ed. S. Latukefu (The National Research Institute and the University of Papua New Guinea, Port Moresby, 1989), pp. 75–108.

——'Oral History and World War Two in Papua New Guinea' in *Remembering the Pacific War* ed. G. White (University of Hawaii Press, Honolulu, 1991) pp. 4–15.

—— 'Oral History and the War', in White, G. ed. *Remembering the Pacific*

War, Occasional Paper Series, (University of Hawaii, Honolulu, 1991).

Warakai, V., 'Dancing Yet to the Dim Dim's Beat' *Ondobondo* No. 4 (1984).

Weeden, W. J. et al., *Advisory Committee on Education in Papua New Guinea Report* (Department of External Territories, 1969).

Whittaker, J. L., Gash, N. G., Hookey, J. F. and Lacey, R. J., eds., *Documents and Readings in New Guinea: Prehistory to 1889* (Queensland University Press, Milton, 1971).

Williams, F. E., *Orokaiva Society* (Clarendon Press, Oxford reprint 1969).

Willis, I., *Lae: Village and City* (Melbourne University Press, 1974).

Winslow, J., ed. *The Melanesian Environment: Papers Presented at the Ninth Waigani Seminar* (Australian National University Press, Canberra, 1977).

Wolfers, E., *Race Relations and Colonial Rule in Papua New Guinea* (Angus and Robertson, Sydney, 1975).

Worsley, P., *The Trumpet Shall Sound* (Second edition, London 1970).

Index